TOP
10
OF
FOOTBALL

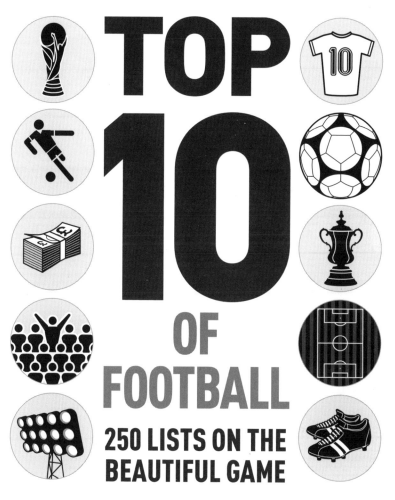

TOP 10 OF FOOTBALL

250 LISTS ON THE BEAUTIFUL GAME

RUSSELL ASH
& IAN MORRISON

hamlyn

An Hachette UK Company
www.hachette.co.uk

First published in Great Britain in 2010 by
Hamlyn, a division of Octopus Publishing Group Ltd
Endeavour House
189 Shaftesbury Avenue
London
WC2H 8JY
www.octopusbooks.co.uk

ISBN 978-0-600-62067-9

A CIP catalogue record for this book is available from the British Library

Printed and bound in China

10 9 8 7 6 5 4 3 2 1

Executive Editor: Trevor Davies
Editor: Ruth Wiseall
Creative Director: Tracy Killick
Designer: Geoff Fennell
Illustrator: Sudden Impact Media
Page Make-up: Dorchester Typesetting Group Ltd
Senior Production Controller: Carolin Stransky

CONTENTS

INTERNATIONAL CLUB TOURNAMENTS

Europe

South America

LEAGUE AND CUP FOOTBALL

Scottish Records

Welsh Records

Northern Irish Records

Republic of Ireland Records

General Records

PREMIER LEAGUE

Premier League Records

LEAGUE AND CUP FOOTBALL WORLDWIDE

European Records

South American Records

North American Records

Worldwide

MISCELLANEOUS

Awards

Crowds and Grounds

Money

Women's football

INTRODUCTION

The birth of the 'beautiful game'

Football, in some form or another, has been played since the days of the Ancient Greeks and Romans. Association Football – or soccer, as Americans prefer to call it – has been played since the mid-19th century. Such is the historical depth of the game that many of our Top 10 lists can draw on 150 years of statistics: the Sheffield Club, founded in 1857, which currently plays in the UniBond Division One South League, is the oldest continuous Association Football club in the world. Following the formation of the English Football Association in 1863, the rules of the game were standardized and have changed very little since. Some essential improvements, such as the crossbar and goal nets have been added, and the offside rule introduced, but the pitch and the principles of the game have not changed significantly since those early years.

A world game

In the development of any sport, there has to be some form of challenge or competition. Football now stages many high-profile competitions for clubs and countries alike, with the world's oldest competition, the FA Cup, starting in 1871 (see 10 FA Cup facts on page 138). This was followed by the world's first league competition, the Football League, in 1888. Both have prompted a number of lists in this book but because the British spread the football word around Europe and South America, league and cup competitions evolved across the world. (As in many sports, from cricket to tennis, England paved the way for other countries to follow suit and they often became better at it than the founders.) We have accordingly followed this in presenting a range of global Top 10 lists.

European neighbours

With the advent of accessible air travel in the 1950s it became possible to stage European football club events. In the same era, as increasing numbers of homes had a television, football fans could revel in the wizardry of players such as Ferenc Puskás and Alfredo di Stéfano. The Hungarian national side and Spanish club side Real Madrid introduced British fans, previously fed on a staple diet of two fullbacks, three halfbacks and five forwards, to a new and breathtaking style of flowing football. The advent of global television coverage has meant that fans can watch the world's greatest players from Italy, Spain and South America on a regular basis, many having moved to England to ply their trade, with winning the Champions League the ultimate aspiration of every football manager. Take a look at the Top 10 clubs in European competitions list on page 91 to get a definitive overview of the most successful clubs in Europe. Because of the popularity of the European game globally, we have devoted a major section of the book to European club football.

Back home

An entire section of the book is deservedly devoted to the Premier League, now the most popular league in the world. Because of the vast amount of money injected into it from television rights, clubs can afford to buy the best players in the world, many of whom have become national heroes. As their fans have come to expect to see the finest footballers, so every four years, as the World Cup comes around, there is a rush to buy players who have made their name on the world stage, provided their club is sufficiently fortunate or wealthy to secure such a star. The presence of these overseas players continues to mean that the Premier League is regarded as the best league in the world.

Something for everyone

Football offers so much to so many: you can watch a Sunday morning game in a local park, see Accrington Stanley play in the Football League, visit the 'Theatre of Dreams' to watch Manchester United or attend a cup final at Wembley. We have tried to make the range of Top 10 lists as diverse as the sport itself and hope there is something for everyone, not just the fans of the big clubs, but also the smaller ones on whom the game relies so much. Do you know which club has the smallest ground in Britain? Take a look at the list on page 233 and you will find out. As well as many surprising statistics and little-known facts, this book contains a wide selection of definitive lists and also a collection of more subjective lists about which you may argue – after all, who is to say who are the 10 greatest players of all time? See page 286 for our opinion.

This book will help to answer pub quiz questions and may be used as a source for questions in the future. So, if you are ever asked 'Which club has the longest name in Welsh League football?', you know where to look...

About the authors

Russell Ash was born on precisely the same day as Fabio Capello and is the godson of Everton and Welsh international T. G. 'Tommy' Jones (1917–2004) – although his attendance at a strictly rugby-playing school proved a hindrance to the development of his footballing interests. He has been compiling *Top 10 of Everything*, which contains numerous football lists, annually since 1989, as well as many related books, including *Top 10 of Sport*, his previous collaboration with Ian Morrison.

Ian Morrison had a trial with Stoke City in the summer of 1964, but failed because the trainer would not allow him to play in his glasses. A sports statistics fanatic, he has been compiling records since receiving the aptly named Maurice Golesworthy's *Encyclopaedia of Association Football* as a Christmas present in 1956. He has written or co-written over 80 books on sports ranging from boxing to American football, snooker to motor racing, as well as *The Hamlyn Encyclopedia of Soccer*.

TOP 10 WORLD CUP COUNTRIES

	Country	Tournaments	Pl	W	D	L	F	A	Pts*
1	**Brazil**	18	92	64	14	14	201	84	**206**
2	**Germany/ West Germany**	16	92	55	19	18	190	112	**184**
3	**Italy**	16	77	44	19	14	122	69	**151**
4	**Argentina**	14	65	33	13	19	113	74	**112**
5	**England**	12	55	25	17	13	74	47	**92**
6	**France**	12	51	25	10	16	95	64	**85**
7	**Spain**	12	49	22	12	15	80	57	**78**
8	**Sweden**	11	46	16	13	17	74	69	**61**
9	**Netherlands**	8	36	16	10	10	59	38	**58**
10	**Russia/USSR**	9	37	17	6	14	64	44	**57**

Up to and including the 2006 World Cup

* Based on three points for a win and one point for a draw. Matches resolved on penalties are classed as a draw for the purpose of this table

Brazil are the only country to have played in every World Cup, winning the tournament a record five times (1958, 1962, 1970, 1994 and 2002). Italy have won it four times (1934, 1938, 1982 and 2006). Other winners are Germany/West Germany with three, Argentina and Uruguay with two each and England and France with one win each.

TOP 10 WORLD CUP GOALSCORERS

	Player/country	Year(s)	Goals
1	**Ronaldo** Brazil	1998/2002/06	**15**
2	**Gerd Müller** West Germany	1970/74	**14**
3	**Just Fontaine** France	1958	**13**
4	**Pelé** Brazil	1958/62/66/70	**12**
5 =	**Sándor Kocsis** Hungary	1954	**11**
=	**Jürgen Klinsmann** Germany	1990/94/98	**11**
7 =	**Helmut Rahn** West Germany	1954/58	**10**
=	**Teófilo Cubillas** Peru	1970/78	**10**
=	**Grzegorz Lato** Poland	1974/78/82	**10**
=	**Gary Lineker** England	1986/90	**10**
=	**Gabriel Batistuta** Argentina	1994/98/2002	**10**
=	**Miroslav Klose** Germany	2002/06	**10**

1930–2006

Fontaine's 13 goals in the 1958 finals is a record for one tournament.

BEHIND THE RECORD
– RONALDO'S RECORD HAUL

Ronaldo made his debut for Brazil in a friendly against Argentina in 1994 and shortly afterwards was drafted into the Brazilian squad for the 1994 World Cup, although he never played. He went on to play for Brazil on 97 occasions, scoring 62 goals – 15 of them in the World Cup. His record-breaking World Cup goals were scored as follows:

1998 World Cup – France

Date	Stage	Opponents	Venue	Result	Goals
16 Jun	Group	**Morocco**	Nantes	won 3–0	**1**
27 Jun	Last 16	**Chile**	Paris	won 4–1	**2***
07 Jul	Semi-final	**Holland**	Marseille	drew 1–1†	**1**

2002 World Cup – South Korea and Japan

Date	Stage	Opponents	Venue	Result	Goals
03 Jun	Group	**Turkey**	Ulsan	won 2–1	**1**
08 Jun	Group	**China**	Seogwipo	won 4–0	**1**
13 Jun	Group	**Costa Rica**	Suwon	won 5–2	**2**
17 Jun	Last 16	**Belgium**	Kobe	won 2–0	**1**
26 Jun	Semi-final	**Turkey**	Saitama	won 1–0	**1**
30 Jun	Final	**Germany**	Yokohama	won 2–0	**2**

2006 World Cup – Germany

Date	Stage	Opponents	Venue	Result	Goals
22 Jun	Group	**Japan**	Dortmund	won 4–1	**2**
27 Jun	Last 16	**Ghana**	Dortmund	won 3–0	**1**

* Including one penalty

† Won on penalties, Ronaldo scored

TOP 10 PLAYERS WITH THE MOST APPEARANCES IN THE WORLD CUP

	Player/country	Years	Appearances
1	**Lothar Matthäus** West Germany/Germany	1982/86/90/94/98	25
2	**Paolo Maldini** Italy	1990/94/98/2002	23
3 =	**Uwe Seeler** West Germany	1958/62/66/70	21
=	**Wladislaw Zmuda** Poland	1974/78/82/86	21
=	**Diego Maradona** Argentina	1982/86/90/94	21
6 =	**Grzegorz Lato** Poland	1974/78/82	20
=	**Cafu** Brazil	1994/98/2002/06	20
8 =	**Wolfgang Overath** West Germany	1966/70/74	19
=	**Berti Vogts** West Germany	1970/74/78	19
=	**Karl-Heinz Rummenigge** West Germany	1978/82/86	19
=	**Ronaldo** Brazil	1998/2002/06	19

Up to and including the 2006 World Cup

Cafu is the only player to have played in three World Cup final matches: in 1994, 1998 and 2002.

TOP 10 WORLD CUP MATCH ATTENDANCES

	Match	Venue	Year	Attendance
1	**Brazil vs. Uruguay**	Rio de Janeiro	1950	**199,854***
2	**Brazil vs. Spain**	Rio de Janeiro	1950	**152,772**
3	**Brazil vs. Yugoslavia**	Rio de Janeiro	1950	**142,409**
4	**Brazil vs. Sweden**	Rio de Janeiro	1950	**138,886**
5	**Mexico vs. Paraguay**	Mexico City	1986	**114,600**
6	**Argentina vs. West Germany** (final)	Mexico City	1986	**114,590**
7 =	**Argentina vs. England**	Mexico City	1986	**114,580**
=	**Mexico vs. Bulgaria**	Mexico City	1986	**114,580**
9	**Argentina vs. Belgium**	Mexico City	1986	**110,420**
10	**Mexico vs. Belgium**	Mexico City	1986	**110,000**

Up to and including the 2006 World Cup

* The number of people inside the Maracanã Stadium – although the number of paying spectators is given as 172,772

The attendance for the Brazil versus Uruguay match in 1950 is the highest of all time for a soccer match. At this tournament there was no official final, the tournament winner was decided by a round-robin competition. This match was one of the last two matches to be played and was the decisive tie.

The biggest crowd outside Mexico or Brazil was that of 98,270 at Wembley Stadium at the 1966 World Cup for England's game against France.

TOP 10 GOALSCORERS IN A SINGLE WORLD CUP

	Player	Country	Year	Goals
1	**Just Fontaine**	France	1958	**13**
2	**Sándor Kocsis**	Hungary	1954	**11**
3	**Gerd Müller**	West Germany	1970	**10**
4 =	**Ademir***	Brazil	1950	**9**
=	**Eusébio**	Portugal	1966	**9**
6 =	**Guillermo Stábile**	Argentina	1930	**8**
=	**Ronaldo**	Brazil	2002	**8**
8 =	**Leonidas da Silva†**	Brazil	1938	**7**
=	**Jairzhino**	Brazil	1970	**7**
=	**Grzegorz Lato**	Poland	1974	**7**

Up to and including the 2006 World Cup

* Some sources quote Ademir as scoring only eight goals as one of his goals against Spain was dubious, some believing it was an own goal by Parra; but FIFA, who previously credited it as an own goal, now credit it to Ademir

† Leonidas was originally credited with four goals in the 6–5 win over Poland, but FIFA have now officially awarded one of them to Perácio

TOP 10 HIGHEST WORLD CUP SCORES*

	Winners/losers	Date	Score
1	**Australia vs. American Samoa**	11 Apr 2001	**31–0**
2	**Australia† vs. Tonga‡**	09 Apr 2001	**22–0**
3	**Iran vs. Guam**	24 Nov 2000	**19–0**
4	**Iran† vs. Maldives**	02 Jun 1997	**17–0**
5 =	**Tajikistan vs. Guam**	26 Nov 2000	**16–0**
=	**Fiji vs. Tuvalu**	25 Aug 2007	**16–0**
7	**Vanuatu† vs. American Samoa**	29 Aug 2007	**15–0**
8 =	**New Zealand vs. Fiji**	16 Aug 1981	**13–0**
=	**Australia vs. Solomon Islands**	11 Jun 1997	**13–0**
=	**Fiji vs. American Samoa**	07 Apr 2001	**13–0**
=	**Bermuda vs. Montserrat**	29 Feb 2004	**13–0**

Up to and including qualification for the 2010 World Cup

* All in qualifying matches

† Away team

‡ Away fixture but played on Australian soil

Australia again beat American Samoa five days after their record win in 2001 but on this occasion by *only* 11–0. In three matches within just seven days Australia scored a staggering 64 goals without conceding any. Archie Thompson scored a World Cup qualifications and finals record 13 goals in the 31–0 win over American Samoa. The highest score in the World Cup finals was in 1982 when Hungary beat El Salvador 10–1.

10 GREAT WORLD CUP MATCHES

1 **Brazil 6 Poland 5** 1938, Strasbourg, France
This first-round match saw Brazil lead 3–1 at half-time. They were 4–3 ahead with just two minutes remaining before Willimowski completed his hat-trick. Brazil raced to a 6–4 lead in extra time thanks to a fourth goal from Leonidas* and one from Romeo. Willimowski then also netted his fourth goal, but it was too late as Brazil ran out winners.

2 **West Germany 3 Hungary 2** 1954, Bern, Switzerland
Hungary led 2–0 within just eight minutes gone but with just 20 minutes on the clock the scores were level thanks to goals from Morlock and Rahn. It stayed like that until the 84th minute when Rahn picked up a loose ball and raced goal-wards before shooting past goalkeeper Grosics from the edge of the penalty area.

3 **England 4 West Germany 2** 1966, London, England
The Germans opened the scoring on 12 minutes in the final when Haller beat Banks. England equalized six minutes later when Geoff Hurst opened his account. With just 12 minutes to go, Peters scored the goal many thought had won the cup for England but, in the dying seconds of time, Weber stabbed home a clumsy goal. Extra time witnessed one of the World Cup's most controversial moments when Hurst's shot hit the crossbar and came back out but the referee, after consultation with his linesman, awarded the goal to make it England 3 West Germany 2. Hurst added a fourth and completed his hat-trick in the closing minutes.

4 **Italy 4 West Germany 3** 1970, Mexico City, Mexico
Five of the seven goals in this semi-final came in extra time. Italy scored from Boninsegna on the 7th minute and defended that lead until two minutes into injury time when Schnellinger struck for the Germans. Five minutes into extra time Müller put Germany in the lead for the first time. That was the start of a remarkable 16 minutes. Burgnich equalized and then Riva put the Italians back in front. With ten minutes to go, Müller equalized but virtually from the restart Rivera restored Italy's lead at 4–3 and that is how it stayed.

5 **Brazil 4 Italy 1** 1970, Mexico City, Mexico
This is widely regarded as the greatest World Cup final, with Pelé playing in his second World Cup final and giving another majestic performance. Pelé opened the scoring. Boninsegna brought the teams level just before the interval. Gérson put Brazil back in front in the 65th minute. Jairzinho scored 20 minutes from time to become the first man to score in every round of the World Cup. Alberto scored Brazil's fourth.

6 **Italy 3 Brazil 2** 1982, Barcelona, Spain
In this final match of Group C Rossi scored his first goal of the tournament after just five minutes. Socrates equalized on 12 minutes but Rossi restored Italy's lead in the 25th minute. Falcão brought the scores level with 22 minutes to go before

Rossi completed his hat-trick after 85 minutes. In the dying minutes, Zoff brought off a great save but the Brazilians claimed the ball was over the line. The referee said it wasn't and it was Italy who progressed to the semis.

7   West Germany 3 France 3 (Germany won on penalties) 1982, Seville, Spain
This was the best match of the 1982 World Cup. A goalkeeping error allowed Littbarski to put Germany ahead in the 18th minute but Platini equalized from the penalty spot nine minutes later. That was the last goal in normal time. Trésor volleyed the French in front after two minutes of extra time and that lead was extended to 3–1 in the 98th minute thanks to Giresse. Rummenigge pulled one back after 102 minutes before Fischer made it 3–3 two minutes from the end and so it was down to penalties. At 4–4 in the shoot-out Schumacher saved from Bossis and it was Hrubesch who scored the winner for the Germans.

8   Belgium 4 USSR 3 1986, León, Mexico
This last 16 match came to life in the 27th minute when Belanov put the Soviets ahead. Belgium equalized in the second half through Scifo before a second strike from Belanov put the USSR back in front. Six minutes later Ceulemans brought the scores level at 2–2. After ten minutes of extra time Belgium led for the first time through Demool and in the second half of the extra period they extended their lead through Claesen. A minute later Belanov converted a penalty but it wasn't enough.

9   France 1 Brazil 1 (France won on penalties) 1986, Guadalajara, Mexico
France had the better of the early play in this quarter-final but it was Careca who gave Brazil the lead in the 18th minute. In the 41st minute Platini became the first man to score past Brazil goalkeeper Carlos in 401 minutes of play. In the 70th minute the legendary Zico was brought on and four minutes later he had a chance to put Brazil in front from the penalty spot but his kick was saved by Bats. Extra time was played but it came to penalties. Socrates missed the first kick for Brazil and after France converted they were always in front.

10   Romania 3 Argentina 2 1994, Pasadena, USA
This second-round meeting was the best game of the tournament. Dumitrescu and Hagi were the inspiration behind the Romanian team and it was the former who put the Europeans ahead in the 11th minute. Batistuta brought the sides level from the penalty spot five minutes later. But Dumitrescu scored his second on 18 minutes. Romania extended their lead in the 58th minute when Hagi found the net. Balbo pulled one back for the Argentinians in the 75th minute but it wasn't enough and Romania hung on for a memorable win.

* FIFA later took one of Leonidas's goals away from him, crediting him with three instead of four goals. They credited his second goal, scored in the 44th minute, to Perácio

10 GREAT WORLD CUP GOALS

1 Pelé
Brazil vs. Sweden, 29 Jun 1958, Stockholm, Sweden
Aged only 17, this was Pelé's first World Cup. He scored his first goal in the quarter-finals against Wales, followed it with a hat-trick in the semi-final win over France and now, in the final against the hosts, he was to net two more goals. The first was an act of sheer brilliance when he collected the ball on his chest, controlled it, rounded his man and volleyed home from close range.

2 Carlos Alberto
Brazil vs. Italy, 21 Jun 1970, Mexico City, Mexico
Brazil had already wrapped up the 1970 final by the time Carlos Alberto scored his memorable goal. Leading 3–1 with just four minutes to go, thanks to goals from Pelé, Gérson and Jairzinho, the move leading to the goal started with some close passing down the left before the ball was pushed to Pelé in the middle of the park. Spotting Carlos Alberto coming up on the right, Pelé slid the ball into his path for him to smash the ball into the goal. It was Carlos Alberto's only World Cup goal.

3 Archie Gemmill
Scotland vs. Holland, 11 Jun 1978, Mendoza, Argentina
To qualify for the next phase Scotland had to beat Holland by three clear goals in the final group game and as one Scottish fan put it: 'Where are we going to find three Dutchmen prepared to score own goals?' Holland scored first from the penalty spot before Kenny Dalglish and Archie Gemmill, also from the penalty spot, made it 2–1 to the Scots before Gemmill brilliantly beat three defenders and then fooled the goalkeeper with a swerving shot into the corner of the net. However, that three-goal advantage never came as Holland scored a second with 19 minutes to go.

4 Arie Haan
Holland vs. Italy, 21 Jun 1978, Buenos Aires, Argentina
Holland went into this match knowing a win would put them into their second successive World Cup final. But an own goal in the 19th minute of a bad-tempered match saw Italy lead at half-time. Holland were level early in the second half and that final place was secured in the 75th minute when Haan finished off a move he had started in his own half, blasting the ball past the experienced Dino Zoff for the match winner.

5 Manuel Negrete
Mexico vs. Bulgaria, 15 Jun 1986, Mexico City
Playing in front of 114,000 fans on home soil was inspiration enough for Mexico to progress from this second-round clash and Manuel Negrete certainly played to the crowd with a dramatic opening goal in a 2–0 win. Playing a neat one-two with Aguirre, Negrete finished off the move with a spectacular acrobatic overhead kick from outside the penalty area that flew into the net.

6 **Diego Maradona**
Argentina vs. England, 22 Jun 1986, Mexico City

Having disgraced himself with one of the most controversial goals in World Cup history early in the second half of this quarter-final match when he punched the ball into the net in the famous 'hand of God' goal, Maradona went on to score what many regard as the greatest ever World Cup goal just four minutes later. He picked up the ball near the halfway line and made a great solo run towards goal, beating a total of five England players before putting the ball past the England goalkeeper, Peter Shilton.

7 **Diego Maradona**
Argentina vs. Belgium, 25 Jun 1986, Mexico City

Three days after his wonder goal against England, Diego Maradona was at it again in the semi-final against Belgium. Having scored Argentina's opening goal in a 2–0 win, his second was reminiscent of the goal against England. He picked up the ball inside the Belgian half and waltzed through the defenders to slot it home for another wonderful individual goal.

8 **Roberto Baggio**
Italy vs. Czechoslovakia, 19 Jun 1990, Rome, Italy

In scoring Italy's second goal in a 2–0 group match win over Czechoslovakia, Roberto Baggio suddenly became Italy's new 'favourite son'. Carrying a £7.7 million price tag on his head, he showed just why he was so highly valued when he gathered the ball on the halfway line and worked a one-two with Giannini before striding through the defence for a great individual goal.

9 **Saed Al-Owairan**
Saudi Arabia vs. Belgium, 29 Jun 1994, Washington, USA

A goal similar to Maradona's second against England. Al-Owairan picked up the ball deep in his own half after just five minutes and went on a great solo run, beating five Belgium players before eventually netting past goalkeeper Michel Preud'homme. It was the only goal of the game and it sent Saudi Arabia through to the second round.

10 **Dennis Bergkamp**
Holland vs. Argentina, 04 Jul 1998, Marseille, France

Going into this quarter-final clash, Argentina had conceded only four goals in their previous ten games. However, Holland soon made it five when they opened the scoring in the 12th minute. Six minutes later Argentina were level and that is how it stayed until the 90th minute, when Bergkamp came up with a wonder goal. He collected the ball from a long pass from Frank de Boer, controlled it and then volleyed it into the net.

TOP 10 MOST-WATCHED WORLD CUPS

	Host country	Year	Average attendance
1	**USA**	1994	**68,991**
2	**Brazil**	1950	**60,773**
3	**Germany**	2006	**52,384**
4	**Mexico**	1970	**52,311**
5	**England**	1966	**50,458**
6	**Italy**	1990	**48,411**
7	**West Germany**	1974	**46,684**
8	**Mexico**	1986	**46,297**
9	**France**	1998	**43,517**
10	**Argentina**	1978	**42,374**

Up to and including the 2006 World Cup

Since its launch in 1930, a total of 31,120,885 spectators have watched the 708 matches in the World Cup final stages, an average of 43,956 per game. The worst-attended finals were in Italy in 1934, when the 17 matches were watched by 395,000 – an average of 23,235 per game.

THE 10 LATEST FATHERS AND SONS TO PLAY IN THE WORLD CUP

	Father	Year(s)	Son	Year(s)	Country
1 =	**Roy Andersson**	1978	**Daniel Andersson**	2002/06	Sweden
=	**Miguel Reina**	1966	**Pepe Reina**	2006	Spain
=	**Anders Linderoth**	1978	**Tobias Linderoth**	2002/06	Sweden
=	**Miguel Ángel Alonso**	1982	**Xabi Alonso**	2006	Spain
=	**Wlodzimierz Smolarek**	1982/86	**Euzebiusz Smolarek**	2006	Poland
6 =	**Cesare Maldini**	1962	**Paolo Maldini**	1990/94/98/2002	Italy
=	**Jean Djorkaeff**	1966	**Youri Djorkaeff**	1998/2002	France
=	**Pablo Forlan**	1966/74	**Diego Forlan**	2002	Uruguay
=	**Jan Verheyen**	1970	**Gert Verheyen**	1998/2002	Belgium
=	**Julio Montero Castillo**	1970/74	**Paolo Montero**	2002	Uruguay
=	**Roy Andersson**	1978	**Patrick Andersson**	1994/2002	Sweden
=	**Cha Bum-Kun**	1986	**Cha Du-Ri**	2002	South Korea

Up to and including the 2006 World Cup

Mario Pérez played for Mexico in the 1970 finals; his grandfather Luis played in the first finals in 1930.

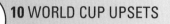

1 **Cuba 2 Romania 1** 1938, Toulouse, France
Cuba held Romania to a 3–3 draw after extra time in the first game and sensationally dropped their star goalkeeper Carvajeles for this replay but his replacement Ayra did equally well. Despite trailing 1–0 at half-time, second-half goals from Socorro and Maquina secured the win. This was Cuba's first World Cup and they qualified only because Mexico withdrew from their qualifying group.

2 **USA 1 England 0** 1950, Belo Horizonte, Brazil
When the result of this match was wired around the world there were many who thought that a '1' had been omitted and England, with players of the calibre of Billy Wright, Tom Finney, Stan Mortensen and Wilf Mannion, had won 10–1 but it was the American part-timers who created the greatest World Cup upset of them all thanks to a goal from 'Larry' Gaetjens in the 37th minute.

3 **North Korea 1 Italy 0** 1966, Middlesbrough, England
North Korea were making their World Cup debut in 1966 and anything less than a win against Italy in their final group game would have meant their going home. But the impossible happened and it was the Italians who flew home in disgrace and to much abuse from their own fans. The Korean win was secured following a goal from Pak Doo-ik in the 41st minute. In the quarter-finals the Koreans nearly caused a bigger upset when after 22 minutes against Portugal they led 3–0, before succumbing to the magic of Eusébio, eventually losing 5–3.

4 **East Germany 1 West Germany 0** 1974, Hamburg, West Germany
This was the first ever meeting between East and West Germany and the West Germans, as reigning European champions, were clear favourites to win this battle until a goal from Sparwasser ten minutes from time won it for the East Germans. Both teams qualified for the next phase, with West Germany going on to lift the trophy.

5 **Algeria 2 West Germany 1** 1982, Gijón, Spain
Under new manager Jupp Derwall, West Germany had won the 1980 European Championship and they went into the 1982 World Cup as 3-1 favourites. Algeria, playing in their debut World Cup match, were 1000-1 outsiders. At the El Molinón Stadium in Gijón, Spain, Algeria took the lead after 54 minutes before Karl-Heinz Rummenigge equalized on 68 minutes. The surprise was rounded off a minute later when Belloumi scored the winning goal.

6 **Northern Ireland 1 Spain 0** 1982, Valencia, Spain

Northern Ireland had to win to guarantee qualification to the second group stage and their opponents and hosts could afford the luxury of a defeat but by no more than a single goal. The Spaniards had been nervous throughout the tournament and when Gerry Armstrong scored the goal of his career one minute into the second half the Irish had to defend their lead, which they succeeded in doing despite playing with ten men for the last 30 minutes after Mal Donaghy was sent off.

7 **Spain 5 Denmark 1** 1986, Querétaro, Mexico

Denmark were one of the favourites for the tournament after winning all three of their first-round group matches, including a 6–1 win over Uruguay and 2–0 defeat of West Germany. Spain had been hit by injury and illness and few gave them a chance in this second-round game, particularly after Denmark opened the scoring after 33 minutes. Spain equalized two minutes before half-time through Butragueño. In the second half Spain scored four more, three of them from Butragueño.

8 **Cameroon 1 Argentina 0** 1990, Milan, Italy

The opening game of the 1990 tournament saw defending champions Argentina play Cameroon, who were playing in only their second World Cup. The Africans were reduced to ten men in the 60th minute when Kana Biyik was sent off but five minutes later his brother Omam Biyik rose to head home the match winner after a goalkeeping blunder. Cameroon ended the match with just nine men.

9 **Bulgaria 2 Germany 1** 1994, East Rutherford, USA

Germany looked odds-on to reach their fourth consecutive World Cup final in 1994 when they were drawn against Bulgaria in the last eight. When Lothar Matthäus gave them the lead just after half-time a semi-final place was looming but then two goals in three minutes from Stoitchkov and Letchkov gave the Bulgarians a surprise win.

10 **Senegal 1 France 0** 2002, Seoul, South Korea

The 2002 World Cup produced several shock results but none bigger than this opening match between the defending champions, France, and Senegal, making their World Cup debut. The only goal of the game was scored after 30 minutes by Papa Bouba Diop, who played for Portsmouth in the 2008 FA Cup final. France were eliminated after finishing bottom of their group.

10 WORLD CUP HEROES

1 Alan Ball
The England squad for the 1966 World Cup was full of household names including Gordon Banks, Bobby Moore, the Charlton brothers and Jimmy Greaves. But the man who turned out to be England's hero, particularly in the final against West Germany, was the right-winger Alan Ball. He played brilliantly for 120 minutes and won the hearts of the nation. The youngest member of the England squad at 21 with just ten caps to his name at the start of the tournament, he instantly established himself as one of the real heroes of 1966.

2 Antonio Carbajal
At the age of 37 Mexican goalkeeper Antonio Carbajal bowed out of World Cup football after a 0–0 draw with Uruguay at Wembley Stadium in 1966. It was only his 11th World Cup game, but those appearances had stretched over five tournaments going back to 1950. In that time he conceded a then record 25 goals and was only once on the winning side. He has since been joined in the record books by Germany's Lothar Matthäus who has also played in five World Cups.

3 Just Fontaine
Although known for his 13 goals in the 1958 tournament not many people realize just how prolific he was. In 21 matches in total for the French national side Moroccan-born Fontaine scored 30 goals. The 13 that he scored in the 1958 World Cup is a record for a single tournament. His World Cup haul included a hat-trick against Paraguay and four against the defending champions West Germany in the third-place play-off match.

4 Joseph Gaetjens
For more than half an hour of their Pool Two match in 1950, the USA had to endure one England attack after another from the likes of Stan Mortensen, Tom Finney and Wilf Mannion. But they withstood the pressure and then, after 37 minutes, Haitian-born 'Larry' Gaetjens glanced in a cross from Walter Bahr to give the USA a lead that they held on to in one of the biggest World Cup upsets of all time.

5 Lucien Laurent
Twenty-three-year-old Lucien Laurent is not a household name in world football but on 13 July 1930 he claimed his own piece of World Cup immortality when, 19 minutes after the start of France's game against Mexico in Montevideo, a powerful shot from the French inside-left beat goalkeeper Bonfiglio to make him the first person to score a goal in the World Cup.

6 Roger Milla
In their first World Cup in 1982 Cameroon were eliminated after drawing their three group games but the Africans left an impression on the tournament. One of the stars of the Cameroon side was Roger Milla, who was 30 when he made his World Cup debut. When Cameroon next qualified, in 1990, Milla was aged 38 and his four

goals helped Cameroon to the quarter-finals, each of his goals celebrated with the now-popular dance around the corner flag. Four years later in the USA he played his last World Cup game at the age of 42 years and 39 days to became the oldest ever World Cup footballer and also the oldest World Cup goalscorer.

7 Pak Doo-Ik

As World Cup shocks go, North Korea's 1–0 win over Italy at Middlesbrough in 1966 ranks among the biggest of all. On paper, the Italians should have trounced the tiny Koreans but they never banked on the spirit and determination of their opponents and 34 minutes into the game Pak Doo-Ik wrote his name into World Cup folklore as the man who scored the goal that beat the Italians. A corporal in the North Korean army at the time, he was promoted to sergeant after the championship.

8 Pelé

Pelé is probably the best-known name in world football but that was not the case at the 1958 World Cup when the 17-year-old was seen on the world stage for the first time. He opened his World Cup account with the only goal of the game that defeated Wales in the quarter-finals. He then gave a dazzling display and scored three against France in the semis and added two more, including a wonder goal in the final against Sweden. That was the last time Pelé was an unsung hero. After that he was simply a hero.

9 Pickles

Had it not been for a mongrel called Pickles the victorious England team of 1966 may not have collected the Jules Rimet Trophy. Prior to the World Cup the trophy was on display at the Westminster Central Hall in London but it was stolen on Sunday 20 March 1966. Pickles came to the rescue by finding it a week later in the garden of a house at Beulah Hill, Norwood, South London. Pickles, now a national hero, and his owner, Thames lighterman David Corbell, received a reward of £6,000.

10 Paolo Rossi

Prior to the 1982 World Cup Paolo Rossi had been banned from football for three years (later reduced to two) following a betting scandal. He returned just before the World Cup but his lacklustre performances in the group games left many Italians questioning his inclusion in the squad. Little did they know what was to come. In the quarter-final round-robin matches Italy were grouped with Argentina and Brazil. Italy beat Argentina and then Rossi burst into life against Brazil, scoring a hat-trick in a 3–2 win. He then scored both the goals in a 2–0 win over Poland in the semi-final and the first goal in Italy's 3–1 win over West Germany in the final. Rossi's World Cup exploits won him the European Footballer of the Year and World Player of the Year awards for 1982.

10 FACTS ABOUT THE SIR THOMAS LIPTON TROPHY – THE 'FIRST WORLD CUP'

1 The Lipton Trophy is often regarded as the 'First World Cup' and was contested on just two occasions, both in Turin, Italy, in 1909 and 1911.

2 The trophy was donated by Sir Thomas Lipton, a Scot who became a self-made millionaire and founder of the Lipton Tea Company.

3 Thomas Lipton always wanted a British representative in his tournament but the English FA declined to nominate a team. It is believed that an employee of Lipton's used to be a referee in the Northern League and he was responsible for finding West Auckland as the British representative.

4 Only four teams competed in each tournament, and West Auckland Town and the hosts, FC Turin, are the only teams to have played in both tournaments.

5 West Auckland won both tournaments, beating FC Winterthur of Switzerland 2–0 in the 1909 final and Juventus of Italy 6–1 in the 1911 final.

6 After winning the trophy for a second time West Auckland were allowed to retain the trophy and in 1974, while being held at the West Auckland Workingmen's Club, it was stolen and never recovered. An exact replica was made.

7 The West Auckland players had to raise the money themselves to finance the trip to Turin for the first Lipton Cup, many pawning possessions in order to do so.

8 After returning from the 1911 tournament, the West Auckland team was in debt because of the cost of getting to Italy and needed to raise £40 quickly. They received a loan from Mrs Lancaster, the landlady of the Wheatsheaf Hotel, the team's headquarters. She kept the trophy as collateral and it was not until 1960 that the club bought it back from her for £100, when it went on display at the Eden Arms.

9 The story of the 'First World Cup' was told by Tyne Tees Television in 1981 in a film called *A Captain's Tale* starring Dennis Waterman and Tim Healy.

10 Lipton also donated another football trophy, the Copa Lipton, which was contested by Argentina and Uruguay 29 times between 1905 and 1992.

SIR THOMAS LIPTON

Sir Thomas Lipton (1850–1931) hailed from Glasgow and went on to become one of the most famous tea merchants the world has known.

After a succession of jobs he saved enough money for his own passage to New York when he was still only 15 years of age. He returned four years later after learning about the grocery trade. He worked in his parents' shop before eventually opening his first shop on his 21st birthday. He was a master of promotion, which included such stunts as releasing giant pigs into the streets of Glasgow emblazoned with the slogan 'I'm going to Lipton's, the best shop in town for Irish bacon'.

His business grew to four shops in the Glasgow area and by 1882 he had spread further afield to Dundee, Edinburgh, Paisley and into England, at Leeds. After further expansion, he ventured into the tea market, which is where he enlarged his fortune into vast wealth.

Lipton was noted for his philanthropy, often handing out cheques to help feed the poor of Glasgow and following the Ibrox Park disaster in 1902, he sent financial support to the families of the victims.

He had an association with many sports, and Lipton Trophies were presented for sailing, horse racing, cricket and association football. He had a passion for yachting, and regularly sailed with the Prince of Wales (later Edward VII) and challenged five times for the America's Cup between 1899 and 1930. All his boats were called Shamrock.

Football's Lipton Cup was inaugurated after Sir Thomas Lipton was made a Knight Commander of the Grand Order of the Crown of Italy. In gratitude for the award, he proposed presenting a trophy to be contested by teams from four nations playing the rapidly growing game of association football. Teams from the host country, Italy, along with teams from Great Britain, Switzerland and Germany, competed for the trophy. West Auckland, an amateur colliery team from County Durham, were chosen as Britain's representatives and after beating Stuttgart of Germany 2–0 in their opening match they beat FC Winterthur of Switzerland, also 2–0, in the final on 12 April 1909.

Sir Thomas Lipton stipulated that any team winning the trophy in consecutive tournaments should keep permanent possession of it. West Auckland did so in 1911 and thus claimed their place in football history as the first outright winners of the Football World Cup.

Following the theft of the trophy in 1974, a replica was made by Sheffield silversmith Jack Spencer, working from photographs and videos of the original trophy.

10 WORLD CUP STORIES

1 The Football War

The Football War of 1969 between Honduras and El Salvador was not, as has been widely believed, a war started by a football match. Tensions between the countries were high because of land reforms involving the Central American neighbours and immigration issues. On 26 June 1969 El Salvador cut off all ties with Honduras. The following day the two countries met in the third qualifying match for the 1970 World Cup after the first two games had ended in a victory for each side. El Salvador won the deciding match 3–2 after extra time. The political tension worsened and war was declared on 14 July 1969. Despite being two weeks after the World Cup qualifying decider it was still labelled The Football War. Four thousand people lost their lives in a four-day war and thousands more were left homeless.

2 Fastest goal

In the third-place play-off in 2002, Turkey's Hakan Sukur scored the fastest goal in World Cup history when he netted after just 11 seconds against South Korea.

3 Clean sheet knockout

Prior to the 2006 World Cup, Switzerland had played 22 games without a clean sheet. That ended in Germany when they topped their group with two wins and a draw. They scored four goals without conceding any. They were knocked out in the next round on penalties by Ukraine after a goalless draw and Switzerland established their place in World Cup history by becoming the first team to leave the tournament without conceding a goal.

4 Shortest World Cup careers

Tunisia's Khemais Labidi and Argentina's Marcelo Trobbiani hold the records for the shortest World Cup careers, just two minutes. Labidi played just 120 seconds against Mexico in 1978 and Trobbiani played in the last two minutes of Argentina's win over West Germany in the 1986 final.

5 Shown the red card

A total of 142 players have been sent off in World Cup history, the first being Peru's Mario de Las Casas against Romania in 1930. Rigobert Song of Cameroon and Zinedine Zidane of France are the only players to have been sent off twice. Song was sent off against Brazil in 1994 and Chile in 1998 while Zidane got his marching orders against Saudi Arabia in 1998 and in the final against Italy in 2006. Pedro Monzon of Argentina in 1990 was the first man sent off in a World Cup final.

6 First ever penalty shoot-out

In 1982 in the semi-finals West Germany beat France 5–4 in the first ever penalty shoot-out in the World Cup after the teams finished 3–3 at the end of extra time. West Germany have the best shoot-out record in the World Cup, winning all four they have been involved in, against France, England, Argentina and Mexico. England have lost all three in which they have been involved, losing to Germany, Argentina and Portugal.

7 A–Z

When France's Daniel Xuereb came on as a substitute for Bruno Bellone against West Germany in 1986 it meant that players' surnames beginning with every letter of the alphabet have appeared in the World Cup since its inception in 1930.

8 Fastest sending off

The fastest dismissal in World Cup history was in the Uruguay versus Scotland match in 1986 when Uruguay's José Batista was sent off after just 56 seconds for a bad foul on Gordon Strachan. However, the South Americans held out for a goalless draw to progress to the next round.

9 First to four

The first player to score four goals in any World Cup game was Paddy Moore for the Irish Free State (now the Republic of Ireland) in their 4–4 draw with Belgium in a qualifier for the 1934 World Cup in Dublin.

10 First British scorer

The first British player to score a goal in any World Cup game was Henry Morris of East Fife who scored for Scotland in their qualifier for the 1950 World Cup against Northern Ireland at Belfast in October 1949. Morris went on to complete a hat-trick in less than four minutes. Remarkably, it was his only game for Scotland in a full international.

THE 10 WORLD CUP COUNTRIES WITH THE WORST RECORDS

	Country	Pl	W	D	L	F	A	Pts*
1	**El Salvador**	6	0	0	6	1	22	**0**
2	**Zaire†**	3	0	0	3	0	14	**0**
3	**Haiti**	3	0	0	3	2	14	**0**
4	**Greece**	3	0	0	3	0	10	**0**
5	**New Zealand**	3	0	0	3	2	12	**0**
6	**China**	3	0	0	3	0	9	**0**
7	**United Arab Emirates**	3	0	0	3	2	11	**0**
8	**Canada**	3	0	0	3	0	5	**0**
9	**Togo**	3	0	0	3	1	6	**0**
10	**Slovenia**	3	0	0	3	2	7	**0**

1930–2006

* Based on three points for a win and one for a draw. Where goal difference is identical, the team scoring more goals is deemed to have the better record

† Now Democratic Republic of the Congo

Source: FIFA

The Dutch East Indies (now part of Indonesia) played just one game in the 1938 World Cup, losing 6–0 to Hungary. However, as they played only one game, FIFA rank them higher than those teams that have played three games without a point. Apart from El Salvador, the only other country to have played six matches without a win is Bolivia, who have played six, drawn one and lost five.

TOP 10 COUNTRIES IN THE EUROPEAN CHAMPIONSHIP

	Country	Tournaments	Pl	W	D	L	F	A	Pts*
1	**West Germany/ Germany**	10	38	19	10	9	55	39	**67**
2	**Netherlands**	8	32	17	8	7	55	32	**59**
3	**France**	7	28	14	7	7	46	34	**49**
4	**Spain**	8	30	13	9	8	38	31	**48**
5	**Italy**	7	27	11	12	4	27	18	**45**
6	**Portugal**	5	23	12	4	7	34	22	**40**
7 =	**Czechoslovakia/ Czech Republic**	7	25	11	5	9	36	32	**38**
=	**USSR/CIS/Russia**	9	27	11	5	11	31	36	**38**
9	**England**	7	23	7	7	9	31	28	**28**
10	**Denmark**	7	24	6	6	12	26	38	**24**

Up to and including the 2008 European Championship

* Based on three points for a win and one for a draw. If a team won on penalties, it is considered a draw for the purpose of this list

Germany/West Germany have won the championship a record three times (1972, 1980 and 1996) and appeared in the most finals, six. France and Spain have each won it twice.

Inaugurated in 1960 as the European Nations Cup, the tournament is played every four years. Between 1960 and 1976 the finals featured only four teams. In 1980 this was increased to eight teams and in the latest tournament in 2008 a total of 16 teams took part in the final stages. The winning country receives the Henri Delaunay Trophy, named after the first general secretary of UEFA. The Soviet Union beat Yugoslavia 2–1 after extra time in the first final in 1960.

TOP 10 GOALSCORERS IN THE EUROPEAN CHAMPIONSHIP

	Player/country	Year(s)	Goals
1	**Michel Platini** France	1984	9
2	**Alan Shearer** England	1996/2000	7
3 =	**Patrick Kluivert** Netherlands	1996/2000	6
=	**Nuno Gomes** Portugal	2000/08	6
=	**Thierry Henry** France	2000/08	6
=	**Ruud van Nistelrooy** Netherlands	2004/08	6
7 =	**Marco van Basten** Netherlands	1988	5
=	**Jürgen Klinsmann** West Germany/Germany	1988/92/96	5
=	**Savo Milošević** Yugoslavia	2000	5
=	**Zinedine Zidane** France	2000/04	5
=	**Milan Baros** Czech Republic	2004	5

Up to and including the 2008 European Championship

Platini's nine goals in 1984 is a record for a single European Championship and with hat-tricks against Belgium and Yugoslavia, he is the only man to score two hat-tricks in the tournament.

TOP 10 HIGHEST-SCORING COUNTRIES IN THE EUROPEAN CHAMPIONSHIP

	Country	Tournaments	Matches	Goals
1 =	**West Germany/Germany**	10	38	**55**
=	**Netherlands**	8	32	**55**
3	**France**	7	28	**46**
4	**Spain**	8	30	**38**
5	**Czechoslovakia/Czech Republic**	7	25	**36**
6	**Portugal**	5	23	**34**
7 =	**England**	7	23	**31**
=	**USSR/CIS/Russia**	9	27	**31**
9	**Italy**	7	27	**27**
10	**Denmark**	7	24	**26**

Up to and including the 2008 European Championship

TOP 10 GOALSCORERS IN A SINGLE EUROPEAN CHAMPIONSHIP

	Player/country	Year	Goals
1	**Michel Platini** France	1984	9
2 =	**Marco van Basten** Netherlands	1988	5
=	**Alan Shearer** England	1996	5
=	**Patrick Kluivert** Netherlands	2000	5
=	**Savo Milošević** Yugoslavia	2000	5
=	**Milan Baros** Czech Republic	2004	5
7 =	**Gerd Müller** West Germany	1972	4
=	**Dieter Müller** West Germany	1976	4
=	**David Villa** Spain	2008	4
10 =	**Klaus Allofs** West Germany	1980	3
=	**Henrik Larsen** Denmark	1992	3
=	**Karl-Heinz Riedle** Germany	1992	3
=	**Dennis Bergkamp** Netherlands	1992	3
=	**Tomas Brolin** Sweden	1992	3

Up to and including the 2008 European Championship

TOP 10 COUNTRIES IN THE COPA AMERICA

	Country	Pl	W	D	L	F	A	Pts*
1	**Argentina**	173	111	31	31	422	166	**364**
2	**Uruguay**	184	103	30	51	384	208	**339**
3	**Brazil**	167	95	30	42	387	191	**315**
4	**Paraguay**	153	61	31	61	242	269	**214**
5	**Chile**	161	53	27	81	247	291	**186**
6	**Peru**	132	45	32	55	193	220	**167**
7	**Colombia**	99	36	20	43	121	174	**128**
8	**Bolivia**	102	19	25	58	97	257	**82**
9 =	**Ecuador**	108	14	19	75	113	297	**61**
=	**Mexico**	38	17	10	11	55	44	**61**

1916–2007

* Based on three points for a win and one for a draw

From 1916 to 1967 the competition was known as the South America Championship and the champions were decided after a series of round-robin matches. Since 1975, when the tournament was revived after an eight-year lay-off when it became the Copa America, the champions are decided after a series of knockout matches following group games. Uruguay and Argentina have each won the trophy a record 14 times while Brazil have won it eight times. The reigning champions are Brazil with the next tournament scheduled to be played in Argentina in 2011.

The tournament is open to countries that are members of the South American Football Confederation (CONMEBOL) and it is played every four years.

TOP 10 GOALSCORERS IN THE COPA AMERICA

	Player/country	Years*	Goals
1 =	**Norberto Méndez** Argentina	1945–47	17
=	**Zizinho** Brazil	1942–57	17
3 =	**Severino Varela** Uruguay	1937–42	15
=	**Teodoro Fernández** Peru	1935–47	15
5 =	**Héctor Scarone** Uruguay	1917–29	13
=	**José Manuel Moreno** Argentina	1941–47	13
=	**Jair** Brazil	1945–49	13
=	**Ademir** Brazil	1945–53	13
=	**Gabriel Batistuta** Argentina	1991–95	13
10=	**Angel Romano** Uruguay	1916–26	12
=	**Roberto Porta** Uruguay	1939–45	12

Up to and including the 2007 tournament

* Years of first and last goals in the tournament

TOP 10 HIGHEST-SCORING MATCHES IN THE COPA AMERICA

	Teams	Year	Score
1	**Argentina vs. Ecuador**	1942	**12–0**
2 =	**Brazil vs. Ecuador**	1945	**9–2**
=	**Brazil vs. Bolivia**	1949	**10–1**
=	**Argentina vs. Venezuela**	1975	**11–0**
5 =	**Brazil vs. Chile**	1937	**6–4**
=	**Argentina vs. Colombia**	1945	**9–1**
=	**Brazil vs. Ecuador**	1949	**9–1**
=	**Argentina vs. Colombia**	1957	**8–2**
9 =	**Uruguay vs. Bolivia**	1927	**9–0**
=	**Chile vs. Ecuador**	1945	**6–3**
=	**Brazil vs. Bolivia**	1953	**8–1**
=	**Chile vs. Peru**	1955	**5–4**
=	**Brazil vs. Colombia**	1957	**9–0**

Up to and including the 2007 tournament

In their demolition of Ecuador, José Manuel Moreno scored five of Argentina's 12 goals and Herminio Masantonio contributed four. Ecuador were also heavily beaten by Brazil (5–1) and Uruguay (7–0) in 1942.

TOP 10 COUNTRIES IN THE AFRICAN NATIONS CUP

	Country	Year(s)	Tournament wins
1	**Egypt**	1957/59/86/98/2006/08	6
2 =	**Ghana**	1963/65/78/82	4
=	**Cameroon**	1984/88/2000/02	4
4 =	**Zaire***	1968/74	2
=	**Nigeria**	1980/94	2
6 =	**Ethiopia**	1962	1
=	**Sudan**	1970	1
=	**Congo**	1972	1
=	**Morocco**	1976	1
=	**Algeria**	1990	1
=	**Ivory Coast**	1992	1
=	**South Africa**	1996	1
=	**Tunisia**	2004	1

Up to and including the 2008 tournament

* Now Democratic Republic of Congo

The African Nations Cup, or Africa Cup of Nations as it is also known, was first contested in 1957 and is the principal international tournament organized by the Confederation of African Football (CAF). Originally held either every one, two or three years up to 1968, it has, since then, been held every two years.

TOP 10 COUNTRIES IN THE ASIAN CUP

	Country	Pl	W	D	L	F	A	Pts*
1	**Iran**	54	31	17	6	106	40	**110**
2	**South Korea**	50	23	14	13	79	53	**83**
3	**Saudi Arabia**	38	18	13	7	57	32	**67**
4 =	**Japan**	31	17	9	5	58	31	**60**
=	**China**	44	16	12	16	72	50	**60**
6	**Kuwait**	36	15	10	11	45	38	**55**
7	**United Arab Emirates**	29	9	7	13	23	39	**34**
8	**Iraq**	25	9	6	10	27	30	**33**
9	**Israel**	13	9	0	4	28	15	**27**
10	**Qatar**	25	4	11	10	24	34	**23**

In all competitions 1956–2007

* Based on three points for a win and one for a draw

Organized by the Asian Football Confederation (AFC), the Asian Cup was inaugurated in 1956 with Hong Kong the first hosts and South Korea the first champions. It is held every four years with the next tournament in Qatar in 2011. Iraq are the reigning champions, having won the cup for the first time in 2007. Saudi Arabia, Iran and Japan have each won the title three times while Saudi Arabia have appeared in a record six Asian Cup finals.

TOP 10 ENGLAND GOALSCORERS

	Player	Appearances	First goal	Total goals
1	**Bobby Charlton**	106	19 Apr 1958 vs. Scotland	**49**
2	**Gary Lineker**	80	26 Mar 1985 vs. Ireland	**48**
3	**Jimmy Greaves**	57	17 May 1959 vs. Peru	**44**
4	**Michael Owen**	89	27 May 1998 vs. Morocco	**40**
5 =	**Tom Finney**	76	28 Sep 1946 vs. Northern Ireland	**30**
=	**Nat Lofthouse**	33	22 Nov 1950 vs. Yugoslavia	**30**
=	**Alan Shearer**	63	19 Feb 1992 vs. France	**30**
8	**Vivian Woodward**	23	14 Feb 1903 vs. Ireland	**29**
9	**Stephen Bloomer**	24	09 Mar 1895 vs. Ireland	**28**
10	**David Platt**	62	26 Jun 1990 vs. Belgium	**27**

As at 1 November 2009

In addition to his 29 goals for the full England team, Vivian Woodward also scored 44 goals in 29 games for England Amateurs.

BEHIND THE RECORD
– BOBBY CHARLTON'S 49 GOALS

When Bobby Charlton scored against Sweden at Wembley Stadium on 22 May 1968 he broke Jimmy Greaves's all-time England record of 44 goals. His 49th and last goal was in the 4–0 win over Colombia in a pre-World Cup friendly in Bogotá on 20 May 1970. It was the 18th country Charlton had scored against.

His totals against all countries were: Northern Ireland 6, Luxembourg 5, Portugal 5, Scotland 5, Wales 5, Mexico 4, USA 4, Switzerland 3, Soviet Union 2, Sweden 2, Argentina 1, Austria 1, Colombia 1, Czechoslovakia 1, East Germany 1, Italy 1, Spain 1, Yugoslavia 1.

Charlton scored four World cup goals:

vs. Argentina 1962

vs. Mexico 1966

vs. Portugal (2 goals) 1966

Charlton scored four hatricks:

vs. USA 28 May 1959

vs. Luxembourg 19 Oct 1960

vs. Mexico 10 May 1961

vs. Switzerland 05 Jun 1963

In the 37 games in which Charlton scored, England lost only twice: at home to Sweden in October 1959 when they lost 3–2 and at home to Austria in October 1965 when, again, they lost 3–2.

The most goals Charlton scored for England in a calendar year was seven in 1958 and the fewest, just one in 1969.

His best scoring streak was four consecutive games, which he achieved on two occasions: between October 1958 and May 1959, with goals against Northern Ireland, the Soviet Union, Scotland and Italy; and between May and October 1963, when he scored against Czechoslovakia, East Germany, Switzerland and Wales.

TOP 10 MOST CAPPED PLAYERS FOR ENGLAND

	Player	Years	Appearances
1	**Peter Shilton**	1970–90	**125**
2	**David Beckham**	1996–2009	**115**
3	**Bobby Moore**	1962–73	**108**
4	**Bobby Charlton**	1958–70	**106**
5	**Billy Wright**	1946–59	**105**
6	**Bryan Robson**	1980–91	**90**
7	**Michael Owen**	1998–2008	**89**
8	**Kenny Sansom**	1979–88	**86**
9	**Gary Neville**	1995–2007	**85**
10	**Ray Wilkins**	1976–86	**84**

As at 1 November 2009

TOP 10 YOUNGEST ENGLAND INTERNATIONALS

	Player	Debut/opponents	Years	Days
1	**Theo Walcott**	30 May 2006 vs. Hungary	**17**	**75**
2	**Wayne Rooney**	12 Feb 2003 vs. Australia	**17**	**111**
3	**James Prinsep**	05 Apr 1879 vs. Scotland	**17**	**252**
4	**Thurston Rostron**	26 Feb 1881 vs. Wales	**17**	**312**
5	**Clem Mitchell**	15 Mar 1880 vs. Wales	**18**	**23**
6	**Michael Owen**	11 Feb 1998 vs. Chile	**18**	**59**
7	**Micah Richards**	15 Nov 2006 vs. Netherlands	**18**	**143**
8	**Duncan Edwards**	02 Apr 1955 vs. Scotland	**18**	**182**
9	**James Brown**	26 Feb 1881 vs. Wales	**18**	**210**
10	**Arthur S. Brown**	29 Feb 1904 vs. Wales	**18**	**327**

As at 1 November 2009

TOP 10 BIGGEST ENGLAND WINS*

	Opponents	Date	Venue	Score
1	**Ireland**	18 Feb 1882	Belfast	**13–0**
2	**Ireland**	18 Feb 1899	Sunderland	**13–2**
3	**Austria**	08 Jun 1908	Vienna	**11–1**
=	**Portugal**	25 May 1947	Lisbon	**10–0**
=	**USA**	27 May 1964	New York	**10–0**
6 =	**Ireland**	09 Mar 1895	Derby	**9–0**
=	**Luxembourg**	19 Oct 1960	Luxembourg	**9–0**
=	**Luxembourg**	15 Dec 1982	London	**9–0**
9 =	**Ireland**	15 Mar 1890	Belfast	**9–1**
=	**Wales**	16 Mar 1896	Cardiff	**9–1**
=	**Belgium**	11 May 1927	Brussels	**9–1**
=	**Finland**	20 May 1937	Helsinki	**8–0**
=	**Mexico**	10 May 1961	London	**8–0**
=	**Turkey**	14 Nov 1984	Istanbul	**8–0**
=	**Turkey**	14 Oct 1987	London	**8–0**

As at 1 November 2009

* Based on winning margin

THE 10 SHORTEST ENGLAND CAREERS

	Player	Date	Opponents	Career (minutes)
1	**Jim Barrett**	22 Oct 1928	Northern Ireland	**4**
2	**Peter Ward**	31 May 1980	Australia	**5**
3	**Stephen Warnock**	01 Jun 2008	Trinidad & Tobago	**6**
4	**Albert Barrett**	19 Oct 1929	Ireland	**8**
5	**Brian Marwood**	16 Nov 1988	Saudi Arabia	**10**
6 =	**Chris Sutton**	15 Nov 1997	Cameroon	**11**
=	**Joey Barton**	07 Feb 2007	Spain	**11**
=	**David Nugent**	28 Mar 2007	Andorra	**11**
9	**Lee Hendrie**	18 Nov 1998	Czech Republic	**14**
10 =	**Peter Davenport**	26 Mar 1985	Republic of Ireland	**17**
=	**Seth Johnson**	15 Nov 2000	Italy	**17**

As at 1 November 2009
www.englandsstats.com

TOP 10 MOST SUCCESSFUL ENGLAND MANAGERS

	Manager	Pl	W	D	L	Goals	Win %
1	**Alf Ramsey**	113	69	27	17	224	**61.1**

First game: 27 Feb 1963, vs. France, Paris; lost 2–5
Last game: 03 Apr 1974, vs. Portugal, Lisbon; drew 0–0
Biggest win: 27 May 1964, vs. USA, New York; 10–0

	Manager	Pl	W	D	L	Goals	Win %
2	**Glenn Hoddle**	28	17	6	5	42	**60.7**

First game: 01 Sep 1996, vs. Moldova, Chisinau; won 3–0
Last game: 18 Nov 1998, vs. Czech Republic, Wembley Stadium; won 2–0
Biggest win: 10 Sep 1997, vs. Moldova, Wembley Stadium; 4–0

	Manager	Pl	W	D	L	Goals	Win %
3	**Ron Greenwood**	55	33	12	10	93	**60.0**

First game: 17 Sep 1977, vs. Switzerland, Wembley Stadium; drew 0–0
Last game: 05 Jul 1982, vs. Spain, Madrid; drew 0–0
Biggest win: 17 Oct 1979, vs. Northern Ireland, Belfast; won 5–1

	Manager	Pl	W	D	L	Goals	Win %
4	**Sven-Göran Eriksson**	67	40	17	10	127	**59.7**

First game: 28 Feb 2001, vs. Spain, Villa Park; won 3–0
Last game: 01 Jul 2006, vs. Portugal, Gelsenkirchen; drew 0–0 (lost on penalties)
Biggest win: 03 Jun 2006, vs. Jamaica, Old Trafford; won 6–0

	Manager	Pl	W	D	L	Goals	Win %
5	**Walter Winterbottom**	139	78	33	28	380	**56.1**

First game: 28 Sep 1946, vs. Northern Ireland, Belfast; won 7–2
Last game: 21 Nov 1962, vs. Wales, Wembley Stadium; won 4–0
Biggest win: 22 May 1947, vs. Portugal, Lisbon; won 10–0

	Manager	Pl	W	D	L	Goals	Win %
6	**Steve McClaren**	18	9	4	5	32	**50.0**

First game: 16 Aug 2006, vs. Greece, Old Trafford; won 4–0
Last game: 21 Nov 2007, vs. Croatia, Wembley Stadium; lost 2–3
Biggest win: 02 Sep 2006, vs. Andorra, Old Trafford; won 5–0

	Manager	Pl	W	D	L	Goals	Win %
7	**Bobby Robson**	95	47	30	18	154	**49.5**

First game: 22 Sep 1982, vs. Denmark, Copenhagen; drew 2–2
Last game: 07 Jul 1990, vs. Italy, Turin; lost 1–2
Biggest win: 15 Dec 1982, vs. Luxembourg, Wembley Stadium; won 9–0

Manager	Pl	W	D	L	Goals	Win %
8 Don Revie	29	14	8	7	49	**48.3**

8 Don Revie
First game: 30 Oct 1974, vs. Czechoslovakia, Wembley Stadium; won 3–0
Last game: 15 Jun 1977, vs. Uruguay, Montevideo; drew 0–0
Biggest win: 16 Apr 1975, vs. Cyprus, Wembley Stadium; won 5–0 and 30 Mar 1977, vs. Luxembourg, Wembley Stadium; won 5–0

9 Terry Venables   23   11   11   1   35   **47.8**
First game: 09 Mar 1994, vs. Denmark, Wembley Stadium; won 1–0
Last game: 26 Jun 1996, vs. Germany, Wembley Stadium; drew 1–1 (lost on penalties)
Biggest win: 17 May 1994, vs. Greece, Wembley Stadium; 5–0

10 Graham Taylor   38   18   13   7   41   **47.4**
First game: 12 Sep 1990 vs. Hungary, Wembley Stadium; won 1–0
Last game: 17 Nov 1993 vs. San Marino, Bologna, Italy; won 7–1
Biggest win: vs. San Marino, as above

Excluding those managers who took the job in a caretaker capacity, the worst manager, in terms of win percentage ratio, is Kevin Keegan with 38.9%.

Fabio Capello is excluded from the list because his record is constantly changing: he is, however, top of the list at the time of publication.

	Player	Years	Appearances
1	**Peter Shilton**	1970–90	125
2	**David Seaman**	1988–2002	75
3	**Gordon Banks**	1963–72	73
4	**Ray Clemence**	1972–84	61
5	**David James**	1997–2009	49
6	**Chris Woods**	1985–93	43
7	**Paul Robinson**	2003–08	41
8	**Ron Springett**	1959–66	33
9	**Harry Hibbs**	1930–36	25
10	**Bert Williams**	1949–55	24

As at 1 November 2009

THE 10 FIRST BLACK PLAYERS TO BE CAPPED BY ENGLAND

	Player/Club	Opponents	Debut
1	**Viv Anderson** Nottingham Forest	Czechoslovakia	**29 Nov 1978**
2	**Laurie Cunningham** West Bromwich Albion	Wales	**23 May 1979**
3	**Cyrille Regis** West Bromwich Albion	Northern Ireland	**23 Feb 1982**
4	**Ricky Hill** Luton Town	Denmark	**22 Sep 1982**
5	**Luther Blissett** Watford	West Germany	**13 Oct 1982**
6	**Mark Chamberlain** Stoke City	Luxembourg	**15 Dec 1982**
7	**John Barnes** Watford	Northern Ireland	**28 May 1983**
8	**Danny Thomas** Coventry City	Australia	**12 Jun 1983**
9	**Brian Stein** Luton Town	France	**29 Feb 1984**
10	**Danny Wallace** Southampton	Egypt	**29 Jan 1986**

Laurie Cunningham was the first black player to play for England in a competitive match.

England's first black captain was Paul Ince who was made captain on the USA tour in the summer of 1993.

England's most capped black footballer is Ashley Cole with 77 caps between 28 Mar 2001, when he made his debut, and 14 Oct 2009.

As at 1 November 2009

TOP 10 MOST CAPPED PLAYERS FOR ENGLAND UNDER-21s

	Player	Years	Appearances
1	James Milner	2004–09	46
2	Tom Huddlestone	2005–09	33
3 =	Scott Carson	2003–07	29
=	Steven Taylor	2004–09	29
5 =	Jamie Carragher	1996–2000	27
=	Gareth Barry	1998–2002	27
7	David Prutton	2000–03	25
8	Jermaine Pennant	2001–04	24
9 =	Jermain Defoe	2001–04	23
=	Nigel Reo-Coker	2003–07	23

As at 1 November 2009
Source: The Football Association

The leading goalscorers for the England Under-21 team are Alan Shearer and Francis Jeffers with 13 goals each.

TOP 10 MOST CAPPED PLAYERS FOR SCOTLAND

	Player	Years	Appearances
1	Kenny Dalglish	1971–86	102
2	Jim Leighton	1983–99	91
3	Alex McLeish	1980–93	77
4	Paul McStay	1984–97	76
5	Tom Boyd	1991–2001	72
6	Christian Dailly	1997–2009	69
7=	Willie Miller	1975–90	65
=	David Weir	1997–2009	65
9	Danny McGrain	1973–82	62
10=	Richard Gough	1983–93	61
=	Ally McCoist	1986–98	61

As at 1 November 2009
Source: Scottish FA

TOP 10 SCOTLAND GOALSCORERS

	Player	Years	Games	Goals
1 =	**Denis Law**	1958–74	55	**30**
=	**Kenny Dalglish**	1971–86	102	**30**
3	**Hugh Gallacher**	1924–35	20	**23**
4	**Lawrie Reilly**	1948–57	38	**22**
5	**Ally McCoist**	1986–98	61	**19**
6 =	**Robert Hamilton**	1899–1911	11	**15**
=	**James McFadden**	2002–09	44	**15**
8	**Mo Johnston**	1984–91	40	**14**
9 =	**Robert Smyth McColl**	1896–1908	13	**13**
=	**Andrew Wilson**	1920–23	12	**13**

As at 1 November 2009

TOP 10 MOST SUCCESSFUL SCOTLAND MANAGERS

	Manager	Year(s)	Pl	W	D	L	Win %
1	**Alex McLeish**	2007	10	7	0	3	**70.00**
2	**Ian McColl**	1960–65	28	17	3	8	**60.71**
3	**Tommy Docherty**	1971–72	12	7	2	3	**58.33**
4 =	**Matt Busby**	1958	2	1	1	0	**50.00**
=	**Malcolm MacDonald**	1966–67	2	1	1	0	**50.00**
6	**Willie Ormond**	1973–77	38	18	8	12	**47.37**
7	**Craig Brown**	1993–2002	70	32	18	20	**45.71**
8	**Walter Smith**	2005–07	16	7	5	4	**43.75**
9	**Jock Stein**	1965–66 1978–85	68	29	13	26	**42.65**
10	**Ally MacLeod**	1977–78	17	7	5	5	**41.18**

As at 1 November 2009

THE 10 LAST SCOTLAND VS. ENGLAND FULL INTERNATIONALS

1   Euro 2000 qualifier play-off second leg, Wembley Stadium, 17 Nov 1999
Having lost the first leg at Hampden Park four days earlier, Scotland gained some revenge – even though they were eliminated – by winning 1–0 thanks to a Don Hutchison first-half goal.

2   Euro 2000 qualifier play-off first leg, Hampden Park, 13 Nov 1999
A double from Paul Scholes in the 21st and 49th minutes put England firmly in the driving seat to qualify for Euro 2000 with a 2–0 victory.

3   Euro 96 group match Wembley Stadium, 15 Jun 1996
Having each drawn their opening group game, victory in this match would virtually assure progression beyond the group stage to the winners, which were England, thanks to goals from Alan Shearer and a wonder strike from Paul Gascoigne in a 2–0 win.

4   Rous Cup Hampden Park, 27 May 1989
This was the last fixture of the short-lived Rous Cup in which England beat Scotland 2–0 with goals from Chris Waddle and Steve Bull. England went on to win the last playing of the competition.

5   Rous Cup Wembley Stadium, 21 May 1988
A goal from Peter Beardsley was enough to give England a 1–0 victory over Scotland. A draw against Colombia in the next game meant they won the trophy for the second time.

6   Rous Cup Hampden Park, 23 May 1987
The goalless draw between Scotland and England left the door open for Brazil to win the trophy. It was the first year that a South American country had been invited to compete for the trophy alongside England and Scotland.

7   Rous Cup Wembley Stadium, 23 Apr 1986
This was Alex Ferguson's only 'auld enemy' game as Scotland manager and it ended in a 2–1 defeat despite a 57th-minute Graeme Souness penalty that was not enough to pull back two first-half England goals from Terry Butcher and Glenn Hoddle.

8 Rous Cup Hampden Park, 25 May 1985
This was the first Rous Cup between Scotland and England, following the demise of the British Home Championship, with Scotland winning 1–0 thanks to a 68th-minute Richard Gough goal.

9 British Home Championship Hampden Park, 26 May 1984
The last Home International at Hampden Park resulted in a 1–1 draw. Mark McGhee gave Scotland the lead after 13 minutes before Tony Woodcock equalized after 37 minutes in front of over 73,000 fans. The match brought an end to the Home Internationals after 100 years.

10 British Home Championship Wembley Stadium, 01 Jun 1983
England beat Scotland 2–0 on their way to winning their 54th and last British Home Championship. A debut goal from Gordon Cowans and another from Bryan Robson secured the victory.

In Scotland these matches are known as 'auld enemy' games.

The first official international between Scotland and England took place at Hamilton Crescent, Glasgow, the home of the West of Scotland Cricket Club, on 30 November 1872. The game, played in front of 4,000 fans, ended in a goalless draw. The next goalless draw between the two countries was at Glasgow in 1970.

TOP 10 ATTENDANCES FOR SCOTLAND VS. ENGLAND GAMES

	Date	Score	attendance
1	**17 Apr 1937**	3–1	**149,415**
2	**15 Apr 1939**	1–2	**149,269**
3	**25 Apr 1970**	0–0	**137,438**
4	**10 Apr 1948**	0–2	**135,376**
5	**03 Apr 1954**	2–4	**134,544**
6	**05 Apr 1952**	1–2	**134,504**
7	**01 Apr 1933**	2–1	**134,170**
8	**24 Feb 1968**	1–1	**134,000**
9	**15 Apr 1950**	0–1	**133,300**
10	**11 Apr 1964**	1–0	**133,245**

All ten matches were held at Hampden Park, Glasgow, and played in the British Home Championship. Number 5 was also a World Cup qualifier and Number 8 a European Championship qualifier.

TOP 10 MOST CAPPED PLAYERS FOR WALES

	Player	Years	Appearances
1	**Neville Southall**	1982–98	**92**
2	**Gary Speed**	1990–2004	**85**
3	**Dean Saunders**	1986–2001	**75**
4 =	**Peter Nicholas**	1979–92	**73**
=	**Ian Rush**	1980–96	**73**
6 =	**Joey Jones**	1976–86	**72**
=	**Mark Hughes**	1984–99	**72**
8	**Ivor Allchurch**	1950–66	**68**
9	**Bryan Flynn**	1975–84	**66**
10	**Andy Melville**	1989–2004	**65**

As at 1 November 2009

Ryan Giggs is in 11th place with 64 appearances between 1991 and June 2007 when he announced his retirement from international football. Before playing for Wales, Giggs captained the England Schoolboys team.

TOP 10 WALES GOALSCORERS

	Player	Years	Games	Goals
1	Ian Rush	1980–96	73	**28**
2 =	Trevor Ford	1946–57	38	**23**
=	Ivor Allchurch	1950–66	68	**23**
4	Dean Saunders	1986–2001	75	**22**
5	Craig Bellamy	1998–2009	58	**17**
6 =	Cliff Jones	1954–69	59	**16**
=	Mark Hughes	1984–99	72	**16**
8	John Charles	1950–65	38	**15**
9 =	John Hartson	1995–2005	51	**14**
=	Robert Earnshaw	2002–09	46	**14**

As at 1 November 2009

TOP 10 MOST CAPPED PLAYERS FOR NORTHERN IRELAND

	Player	Years	Appearances
1	**Pat Jennings**	1964–86	**119**
2	**Mal Donaghy**	1980–94	**91**
3	**Sammy McIlroy**	1972–87	**88**
4	**Keith Gillespie**	1995–2008	**86**
5	**Maik Taylor**	1999–2009	**80**
6	**David Healy**	2000–09	**77**
7	**Jimmy Nicholl**	1976–86	**73**
8	**Michael Hughes**	1992–2004	**71**
9	**Aaron Hughes**	1998–2009	**69**
10	**David McCreery**	1976–90	**67**

As at 1 November 2009

George Best is Northern Ireland's 47th most capped player with 37 appearances between 1964–77, when he played his final game against the Netherlands in Belfast. One of the greatest players in the world, he is undoubtedly the best player never to have played in the final stages of the World Cup.

TOP 10 NORTHERN IRELAND GOALSCORERS

	Player	Years	Games	Goals
1	David Healy	2000–09	77	35
2 =	Billy Gillespie	1913–30	25	13
=	Colin Clarke	1986–93	38	13
4 =	Joe Bambrick	1928–38	11	12
=	Gerry Armstrong	1977–86	63	12
=	Jimmy Quinn	1985–96	46	12
=	Iain Dowie	1990–2000	59	12
8	Olphie Stanfield	1887–97	30	11
9 =	Billy Bingham	1951–64	56	10
=	Jimmy McIlroy	1952–66	55	10
=	Peter McParland	1954–62	34	10
=	Johnny Crossan	1960–68	24	10

As at 1 November 2009

TOP 10 MOST CAPPED PLAYERS FOR THE REPUBLIC OF IRELAND

	Player	Years	Appearances
1	**Steve Staunton**	1988–2002	**102**
2 =	**Kevin Kilbane**	1997–2009	**100**
=	**Shay Given**	1996–2009	**100**
4	**Robbie Keane**	1998–2009	**94**
5	**Niall Quinn**	1986–2002	**91**
6	**Tony Cascarino**	1985–99	**88**
7	**Paul McGrath**	1985–97	**83**
8	**Packie Bonner**	1981–96	**80**
9	**Damien Duff**	1998–2009	**77**
10	**Ray Houghton**	1986–97	**73**

As at 1 November 2009

Some sources quote Kenny Cunningham as having played 72 matches but the FA of Ireland credit him with only 66.

THE 10 BEST RESULTS FOR THE REPUBLIC OF IRELAND UNDER JACK CHARLTON

1 vs. Bulgaria won 2–0,
1988 European Championship qualifier, Lansdowne Road, 14 Oct 1987
When McGrath and Moran gave the Republic of Ireland a 2–0 win in front of 26,000 fans at Lansdowne Road they were unaware that they had qualified for their first major international tournament. Qualification was assured after Scotland did them the favour of beating Bulgaria a month later.

2 vs. England won 1–0,
1988 European Championship first round, Neckarstadion, Stuttgart, 12 Jun 1988
This was the Republic of Ireland's first ever match in a major tournament and they won thanks to a sixth-minute goal from Ray Houghton.

3 vs. USSR drew 1–1,
1988 European Championship first round, Niedersachsenstadion, Hannover, 15 Jun 1988
A spectacular overhead volley from Ronnie Whelan gave the Republic of Ireland the lead after 38 minutes before the USSR equalized. A draw in the final group game against the Netherlands would have seen them progress and they were eight minutes away from doing so when Kieft scored a killer goal for the Dutch.

4 vs. England drew 1–1,
1990 World Cup first round, Stadio Sant'Elia, Cagliari, 11 Jun 1990
This was the Republic of Ireland's first ever match in the World Cup and they earned a draw thanks to a 73rd-minute goal from Kevin Sheedy who cancelled out Gary Lineker's eighth-minute strike for England.

5 vs. Netherlands drew 1–1,
1990 World Cup first round, Stadio Della Favorita, Palermo, 21 Jun 1990
The Netherlands needed a draw to guarantee their progress to the next round and led with a tenth-minute Ruud Gullit goal. For the second time in the tournament Ireland came from behind, this time with a Niall Quinn equalizer after 70 minutes.

6 vs. Romania drew 0–0, won 5–4 on penalties,
1990 World Cup second round, Stadio Luigi Ferraris, Genoa, 25 Jun 1990
The 120 minutes saw very few openings as neither side wanted to lose in their quest to reach the last eight for the first time. In the penalty shoot-out the score was level at 4–4 when Timofte's kick was saved by Packie Bonner before David O'Leary slotted home the winner for the Irish.

7 vs. England drew 1–1,
1992 European Championship qualifier, Lansdowne Road, 14 Nov 1990
Almost 46,000 fans packed into Lansdowne Road and Mick McCarthy, winning his 50th cap, nearly gave the Republic of Ireland the lead before David Platt put England ahead after 67 minutes. However, substitute Tony Cascarino spoiled England goalkeeper Chris Woods' 30th birthday with an equalizer ten minutes from time.

8   **vs. England** drew 1–1,
1992 European Championship qualifier, Wembley Stadium, 27 Mar 1991
The Republic of Ireland managed to hold England again in the 1992 European Championship qualifying campaign. Niall Quinn equalized an early Lee Dixon goal on the half-hour and that is how it stayed. However, despite not losing any of their six qualifying matches the Republic of Ireland failed to qualify; England went through to the finals.

9   **vs. Italy** won 1–0,
1994 World Cup first round, Giants Stadium, East Rutherford, 18 Jun 1994
Having been eliminated by Italy in 1990 this was their chance for revenge and they did so thanks to an 11th-minute strike from Ray Houghton to gain the Republic of Ireland's first ever win in a World Cup match.

10   **vs. England** won 1–0 (abandoned 27 minutes),
Friendly, Lansdowne Road, 15 Feb 1995
This game is remembered not for the only goal of the game scored by David Kelly after 22 minutes but for the rioting from the England fans that caused the game's abandonment. England and the Republic of Ireland have not met each other since this match.

When Jack Charlton was appointed manager of the Republic of Ireland team in February 1986 he was the first Englishman to manage the national side. His first game, against Wales on 26 March 1986, ended in a 1–0 home defeat but that was soon followed by victory in the Icelandic tournament, Ireland's first ever tournament win. He then guided them to the 1988 European Championship, their first ever major finals. Only a narrow defeat by the Netherlands in their final group match meant elimination but in 1990, in their first World Cup appearance, they went to the quarter-finals, where they were beaten 1–0 by Italy.

Despite not losing a match in their qualifying group for the 1992 European Championship they failed to qualify but did qualify for their second World Cup in 1994 and progressed to the knockout stage before losing again to the Netherlands. The qualifying competition for Euro 96 was to be Jack Charlton's last campaign as manager and defeat by the Netherlands yet again in a play-off match was shortly afterwards to bring an end to a great international managerial career when Charlton quit shortly after Christmas 1996. He was in charge for 94 matches in which the Republic of Ireland won 47 and drew 30.

TOP 10 REPUBLIC OF IRELAND GOALSCORERS

	Player	Years	Games	Goals
1	**Robbie Keane**	1998–2009	94	**40**
2	**Niall Quinn**	1986–2002	91	**21**
3	**Frank Stapleton**	1976–90	71	**20**
4 =	**Don Givens**	1969–81	56	**19**
=	**Tony Cascarino**	1985–99	88	**19**
=	**John Aldridge**	1986–96	69	**19**
7	**Noel Cantwell**	1953–67	36	**14**
8 =	**Jimmy Dunne**	1930–39	15	**13**
=	**Gerry Daly**	1973–86	48	**13**
10	**Ian Harte**	1996–2007	64	**11**

As at 1 November 2009

TOP 10 MOST CAPPED PLAYERS FOR BRAZIL

	Player	Years	Appearances
1	**Cafu**	1990–2006	**142**
2	**Roberto Carlos**	1992–2006	**125**
3	**Cláudio Taffarel**	1987–98	**101**
4	**Djalma dos Santos**	1952–68	**98**
5	**Ronaldo**	1994–2006	**97**
6	**Gilmar**	1953–69	**94**
7 =	**Pelé**	1957–71	**92**
=	**Rivelino**	1965–78	**92**
9 =	**Dida**	1995–2006	**91**
=	**Dunga**	1982–98	**91**

As at 1 November 2009

THE 10 TEAMS THAT BRAZIL HAVE PLAYED MOST OFTEN IN THE WORLD CUP

	Opponent(s)	W	D	L	Pl
1	Sweden	5	2	0	7
2 =	Czechoslovakia	3	2	0	5
=	Italy	2	1	2	5
=	Spain	3	1	1	5
5 =	Argentina	2	1	1	4
=	England	3	1	0	4
=	France	1	1	2	4
=	Poland	3	0	1	4
=	Yugoslavia	1	2	1	4
10 =	Mexico	3	0	0	3
=	Netherlands	1	1	1	3
=	Scotland	2	1	0	3

Up to and including the 2006 World Cup

Brazil have played 44 different countries and have enjoyed at least one win against all of them except three: Norway, Portugal and Hungary, Hungary standing alone as the only country to beat Brazil on two occasions without ever losing.

TOP 10 MOST CAPPED PLAYERS FOR FRANCE

	Player	Years	Appearances
1	**Lilian Thuram**	1994–2008	**142**
2	**Thierry Henry**	1997–2009	**117**
3	**Marcel Desailly**	1993–2004	**116**
4	**Zinedine Zidane**	1994–2006	**108**
5	**Patrick Vieira**	1997–2009	**107**
6	**Didier Deschamps**	1989–2000	**103**
7 =	**Laurent Blanc**	1989–2000	**97**
=	**Bixente Lizarazu**	1992–2004	**97**
9	**Sylvain Wiltord**	1999–2006	**92**
10	**Fabien Barthez**	1994–2006	**87**

As at 1 November 2009

TOP 10 FRANCE GOALSCORERS

	Player	Years	Games	Goals
1	**Thierry Henry**	1997–2009	117	**52**
2	**Michel Platini**	1976–87	72	**41**
3	**David Trezeguet**	1998–2008	71	**34**
4	**Zinedine Zidane**	1994–2006	108	**31**
5 =	**Just Fontaine**	1953–60	21	**30**
=	**Jean-Pierre Papin**	1986–95	54	**30**
7	**Youri Djorkaeff**	1993–2002	82	**28**
8	**Sylvain Wiltord**	1999–2006	92	**26**
9	**Jean Vincent**	1953–61	46	**22**
10	**Jean Nicolas**	1933–38	24	**21**

As at 1 November 2009

TOP 10 GERMANY GOALSCORERS

	Player	Years	Games	Goals
1	**Gerd Müller**	1966–74	62	**68**
2	**Miroslav Klose**	2001–09	93	**48**
3 =	**Rudi Völler**	1982–94	90	**47**
=	**Jürgen Klinsmann**	1987–98	108	**47**
5	**Karl-Heinz Rummenigge**	1976–86	95	**45**
6	**Uwe Seeler**	1954–70	72	**43**
7	**Michael Ballack**	1999–2009	97	**42**
8	**Oliver Bierhoff**	1996–2002	70	**37**
9	**Lukas Podolski**	2004–09	68	**35**
10	**Fritz Walter**	1940–58	61	**33**

As at 1 November 2009

1 Friendly
Germany 3 (Hofmann 20, 49, 60) **England 3** (Bradford 7, 31 Jack 78)
Berlin, 10 May 1930, Attendance: 60,000
This was the first full international between the two countries. Hofmann was the first foreign player to score a hat-trick against England.

2 Friendly
Germany 3 (Gellesch 20, Gauchel 44, Pesser 79) **England 6** (Bastin 12, Robinson 26, 50, Broome 30, Matthews 40, Goulden 83)
Berlin, 14 May 1938, Attendance: 110,000
This is the only time Germany have conceded six goals at home. The match was used for propaganda purposes by Hitler, the England players were compelled to give the Nazi salute before the match.

3 1966 World Cup final
England 4 (Hurst 19, 100, 120, Peters 78) **West Germany 2** (Haller 13, Weber 90)
Wembley Stadium, 30 Jul 1966, Attendance: 96,924
After conceding the first goal, England led with only minutes remaining before a German equalizer was scored. In extra time Geoff Hurst scored a controversial third goal – even today there is still some debate as to whether the ball went over the line.

4 1970 World Cup quarter-final
West Germany 3 (Beckenbauer 67, Seeler 82, Müller 109) **England 2** (Mullery 32, Peters 50)
León, Mexico, 14 Jun 1970, Attendance: 24,000
England went into the match without goalkeeper Gordon Banks who had to pull out of the team on the morning of the match due to an upset stomach. Bobby Charlton made his 106th and final appearance for England.

5 1972 European Championship quarter-final
England 1 (Lee 78) **West Germany 3** (Hoeness 26, Netzer 83 (pen), Müller 85)
Wembley Stadium, 29 Apr 1972, Attendance: 96,800
This was the first leg of a two-legged quarter-final. England were eliminated after a goalless draw in Germany.

6 **1990 World Cup semi-final**
West Germany 0 England 0
Turin, Italy, 04 Jul 1990, Attendance: 62,628
After extra time West Germany won 4–3 on penalties. It was 3–3 after the first six kicks of the shoot-out but first Stuart Pearce and then Chris Waddle missed to give victory to the Germans.

7 **1996 European Championship semi-final**
England 1 (Shearer 2) **Germany 1** (Kuntz 15)
Wembley Stadium, 26 Jun 1996, Attendance: 75,862
After extra time Germany won 6–5 on penalties with Gareth Southgate missing the crucial penalty for England.

8 **2002 World Cup qualifier**
England 0 Germany 1 (Hamann 14)
Wembley Stadium, 07 Oct 2000, Attendance: 76,377
This was the last game at the old Wembley Stadium. It was also the first time England had ever lost the opening game of a World Cup qualifying campaign.

9 **2002 World Cup qualifier**
Germany 1 (Jancker 6) **England 5** (Owen 12, 48, 66, Gerrard 45, Heskey 73)
Munich, 01 Sep 2001, Attendance: 63,000
This was England's biggest ever win over their rivals and all five goals were scored by Liverpool players.

10 **Friendly**
England 1 (Lampard 9) **Germany 2** (Kuranyi 26, Pander 40)
Wembley Stadium, 22 Aug 2007, Attendance: 86,133
Having won the last game at the old Wembley Stadium, Germany became the first team to defeat England at the new stadium.

TOP 10 MOST CAPPED PLAYERS FOR ITALY

	Player	Years	Appearances
1	**Fabio Cannavaro**	1997–2009	**130**
2	**Paolo Maldini**	1988–2002	**126**
3	**Dino Zoff**	1968–83	**112**
4	**Gianluigi Buffon**	1997–2009	**98**
5	**Giacinto Facchetti**	1963–77	**94**
6=	**Alessandro Del Piero**	1995–2008	**91**
=	**Gianluca Zambrotta**	1999–2009	**91**
8 =	**Franco Baresi**	1982–94	**81**
=	**Giuseppe Bergomi**	1982–98	**81**
=	**Marco Tardelli**	1976–85	**81**

As at 1 November 2009

TOP 10 ITALY GOALSCORERS

	Player	Years	Games	Goals
1	**Luigi Riva**	1965–74	42	**35**
2	**Giuseppe Meazza**	1930–39	53	**33**
3	**Silvio Piola**	1935–52	34	**30**
4	**Roberto Baggio**	1988–2004	56	**27**
5	**Alessandro Del Piero**	1995–2008	91	**26**
6 =	**Adolfo Baloncieri**	1920–30	47	**25**
=	**Alessandro Altobelli**	1980–88	61	**25**
=	**Filippo Inzaghi**	1997–2007	57	**25**
9 =	**Christian Vieri**	1997–2005	49	**23**
=	**Francesco Graziani**	1975–83	64	**23**

As at 1 November 2009

TOP 10 MOST CAPPED PLAYERS FOR THE NETHERLANDS

	Player	Years	Appearances
1	**Edwin van der Sar**	1995–2008	**130**
2	**Frank de Boer**	1990–2004	**112**
3	**Phillip Cocu**	1996–2006	**101**
4	**Giovanni van Bronckhorst**	1996–2009	**94**
5	**Clarence Seedorf**	1994–2008	**87**
6	**Marc Overmars**	1993–2004	**86**
7	**Aron Winter**	1987–2000	**84**
8	**Ruud Krol**	1969–83	**83**
9 =	**Dennis Bergkamp**	1990–2000	**79**
=	**Patrick Kluivert**	1994–2004	**79**

As at 1 November 2009

TOP 10 BEST FINISHES BY THE NETHERLANDS IN MAJOR INTERNATIONAL COMPETITIONS*

Tournament	Position
1 **1988 European Championship**	**Winners**
2 = **1974 World Cup**	**Runners-up**
= **1978 World Cup**	**Runners-up**
4 **1976 European Championship**	**Third place**
5 = **1992 European Championship**	**Semi-finals**
= **2000 European Championship**	**Semi-finals**
= **2004 European Championship**	**Semi-finals**
8 **1998 World Cup**	**Fourth place**
9 = **1994 World Cup**	**Quarter-finals**
= **1996 European Championship**	**Quarter-finals**
= **2008 European Championship**	**Quarter-finals**

Up to and including the 2008 European Championship

* World Cup and European Championship

There were no third-place play-off matches in the European Championship when the Netherlands were eliminated in the semi-finals in 1992, 2000 and 2004. They were also the bronze medallists in the Olympic Games on three occasions: 1908, 1912 and 1920.

TOP 10 BIGGEST WINS BY SPAIN

	Opponents	Year	Venue	Tournament*	Score
1	**Bulgaria**	1933	Madrid	Friendly	**13–0**
2	**Malta**	1983	Seville	Euro Champ Q	**12–1**
3 =	**Portugal**	1934	Madrid	World Cup qualifier	**9–0**
=	**Albania**	1990	Seville	Euro Champ Q	**9–0**
=	**Austria**	1999	Valencia	Euro Champ Q	**9–0**
=	**San Marino**	1999	Villareal	Euro Champ Q	**9–0**
7	**Cyprus**	1999	Badajoz	Euro Champ Q	**8–0**
8	**France**	1929	Zaragoza	Friendly	**8–1**
9	**Cyprus**	1971	Granada	Euro Champ Q	**7–0**
10	**Mexico**	1928	Amsterdam	Olympic Games	**7–1**

Based on full international matches 28 August 1920–1 November 2009

* Euro Champ Q = European Championship qualifier

Spain has played Portugal more times than any other country. They have met on 32 occasions with Spain winning 15, drawing 12 and losing just 5. Spain's biggest defeat is 7–1 by Italy in Amsterdam during the 1928 Olympic Games and by England at Highbury in a friendly in 1931.

TOP 10 SPAIN GOALSCORERS

	Player	Years	Games	Goals
1	**Raúl**	1996–2006	102	**44**
2	**David Villa**	2005–09	52	**33**
3	**Fernando Hierro**	1989–2002	89	**29**
4	**Fernando Morientes**	1998–2007	47	**27**
5	**Emilio Butragueño**	1984–92	69	**26**
6 =	**Alfredo di Stéfano**	1957–61	31	**23**
=	**Fernando Torres**	2003–09	71	**23**
8	**Julio Salinas**	1986–96	56	**22**
9	**Míchel**	1985–92	66	**21**
10	**Telmo Zarra**	1945–51	20	**20**

As at 1 November 2009

TOP 10 INTERNATIONAL GOALSCORERS

	Player/country	Years	Matches	Goals
1	**Ali Daei** Iran	1993–2006	149	**109**
2	**Ferenc Puskás** Hungary/Spain	1945–56	89	**84**
3	**Pelé** Brazil	1957–71	92	**77**
4 =	**Bashar Abdullah** Kuwait	1996–2007	134	**75**
=	**Sándor Kocsis** Hungary	1948–56	68	**75**
6 =	**Hossam Hassan** Egypt	1985–2006	169	**69**
=	**Stern John** Trinidad & Tobago	1995–2009	109	**69**
8	**Gerd Müller** West Germany	1966–74	62	**68**
9	**Majed Abdullah** Saudi Arabia	1978–94	139	**67**
10	**Kiatisuk Senamuang** Thailand	1993–2007	130	**65**

As at 1 November 2009

In the period 1903–14, Vivian Woodward scored a total of 73 goals for England (29) and England Amateurs (44).

TOP 10 MOST CAPPED PLAYERS

	Player/country	Years	Appearances
1	**Mohamed Al-Deayea** Saudi Arabia	1990–2006	**181**
2	**Claudio Suárez** Mexico	1992–2006	**178**
3	**Hossam Hassan** Egypt	1985–2006	**169**
4	**Iván Hurtado** Ecuador	1992–2009	**165**
5 =	**Cobi Jones** USA	1992–2004	**164**
=	**Adnan Al-Talyani** United Arab Emirates	1984–97	**164**
7	**Sami Al-Jaber** Saudi Arabia	1992–2006	**163**
8	**Ahmed Hassan** Egypt	1995–2009	**161**
9=	**Martin Reim** Estonia	1992–2009	**157**
=	**Vitalijs Astafjevs** Latvia	1992–2009	**157**

As at 1 November 2009

The only other member of the '150 club' is Lothar Matthäus, who played for West Germany /Germany 150 times between 1980 and 2000.

TOP 10 BIGGEST WINS IN INTERNATIONAL FOOTBALL*

	Winners/losers	Date	Tournament†	Score
1	**Australia vs. American Samoa**	11 Apr 2001	WCQ	**31–0**
2	**Australia vs. Tonga**	09 Apr 2001	WCQ	**22–0**
3 =	**Libya vs. Oman**	06 Apr 1966‡	ANC	**21–0**
=	**North Korea vs. Guam**	11 Mar 2005	F	**21–0**
5	**Kuwait vs. Bhutan**	04 Feb 2000	ACQ	**20–0**
6 =	**China vs. Guam**	26 Jan 2000	ACQ	**19–0**
=	**Iran vs. Guam**	24 Nov 2000	WCQ	**19–0**
8	**Tahiti vs. American Samoa**	08 Jun 2000	OCQ	**18–0**
9 =	**Iran vs. Maldives**	02 Jun 1997	WCQ	**17–0**
=	**Australia vs. Cook Islands**	19 Jun 2000	OCQ	**17–0**

As at 1 November 2009

*Ranked by winning margin

† WCQ = World Cup qualifying

F = Friendly

ANC = Arab Nations Cup

ACQ = Asian Cup qualifying

OCQ = Oceania Football Confederation Nations Cup qualifying

‡ Precise date disputed

The Oman players walked off the pitch ten minutes from the end of their 21–0 defeat by Libya in protest against the awarding of a penalty to Libya. The game was abandoned and Oman withdrew from the tournament.

Tahiti beat the Cook Islands 30–0 in the South Pacific Games in 1971 but the tournament was not made up of officially recognized FIFA members, which explains its omission from this list.

The biggest win in women's international football is 24–0 by North Korea, who beat Singapore in Taipei on 6 December 2001.

TOP 10 COUNTRIES WITH THE MOST PLAYERS WITH 100 CAPS

	Country	No. of players with 100 caps
1	**USA**	**11**
2 =	**South Korea**	**7**
=	**Egypt**	**7**
=	**Mexico**	**7**
5 =	**Estonia**	**6**
=	**France**	**6**
=	**Saudi Arabia**	**6**
8 =	**Costa Rica**	**5**
=	**Denmark**	**5**
=	**England**	**5**
=	**West Germany/Germany**	**5**
=	**Sweden**	**5**
=	**United Arab Emirates**	**5**

As at 1 November 2009

The 11 USA players to win more than 100 caps are: Cobi Jones (164), Jeff Agoos (134), Marcelo Balboa (128), Claudio Reyna (112), Paul Caligiuri (110), Landon Donovan (120), Eric Wynalda (106), Kasey Keller (102), Earnie Stewart (101), Joe-Max Moore (100) and Tony Meola (100).

When he captained England against Scotland at Wembley Stadium on 11 April 1959, Billy Wright became the world's first footballer to win 100 caps.

TOP 10 OLYMPIC FOOTBALL COUNTRIES

	Country	Gold	Silver	Bronze	Total
1 =	**Hungary**	3	1	1	**5**
=	**USSR**	2	0	3	**5**
=	**Yugoslavia**	1	3	1	**5**
4 =	**Argentina**	2	2	0	**4**
=	**Brazil**	0	2	2	**4**
=	**Denmark**	0	3	1	**4**
=	**East Germany**	1	1	2	**4**
8 =	**Great Britain**	3	0	0	**3**
=	**Italy**	1	0	2	**3**
=	**Netherlands**	0	0	3	**3**
=	**Poland**	1	2	0	**3**
=	**Spain**	1	2	0	**3**
=	**Sweden**	1	0	2	**3**

Up to and including the 2008 Games

The leading nation in the women's Olympic competition is the USA with three gold medals and one silver.

TOP 10 CLUBS IN EUROPEAN COMPETITIONS

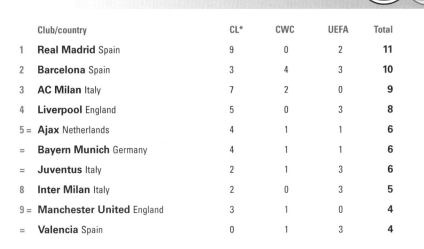

	Club/country	CL*	CWC	UEFA	Total
1	**Real Madrid** Spain	9	0	2	11
2	**Barcelona** Spain	3	4	3	10
3	**AC Milan** Italy	7	2	0	9
4	**Liverpool** England	5	0	3	8
5 =	**Ajax** Netherlands	4	1	1	6
=	**Bayern Munich** Germany	4	1	1	6
=	**Juventus** Italy	2	1	3	6
8	**Inter Milan** Italy	2	0	3	5
9 =	**Manchester United** England	3	1	0	4
=	**Valencia** Spain	0	1	3	4

Up to and including the 2009 Champions League and UEFA Cup finals

* CL = European Champion Clubs' Cup/Champions League

CWC = European Cup Winners' Cup

UEFA = Fairs Cup/UEFA Cup (UEFA Europa League from 2009–10 season)

If European Super Cup titles were to be included, AC Milan's five wins would give them a total of 14, two more than Real Madrid, who have won the Super Cup just once.

TOP 10 COUNTRIES PROVIDING THE MOST WINNERS OF EUROPEAN TROPHIES

	Country	CL	CWC	UEFA	Total
1	**Spain**	12	7	11	**30**
2	**England**	11	8	10	**29**
3	**Italy**	11	7	10	**28**
4	**West Germany/Germany**	6	4	6	**16**
5	**Netherlands**	6	1	4	**11**
6	**Portugal**	4	1	1	**6**
7	**USSR/Russia**	0	3	2	**5**
8	**Belgium**	0	3	1	**4**
9	**Scotland**	1	2	0	**3**
10 =	**France**	1	1	0	**2**
=	**Sweden**	0	0	2	**2**
=	**Yugoslavia**	1	0	1	**2**

Up to and including the 2009 Champions League and UEFA Cup finals

CL = European Champion Clubs' Cup/Champions League

CWC = European Cup Winners' Cup

UEFA = Fairs Cup/UEFA Cup (UEFA Europa League from 2009–10 season)

TOP 10 GOALSCORERS IN EUROPEAN COMPETITIONS

	Player/club(s)	Years†	CL	CWC	UEFA	Total
1	**Gerd Müller** Bayern Munich	1966–77	35	20	11	**66**
2	**Raúl** Real Madrid	1995–2008	64	0	0	**64**
3 =	**Andriy Schevchenko** Dinamo Kiev, AC Milan, Chelsea	1994–2008	56	0	4	**60**
=	**Ruud van Nistelrooy** PSV Eindhoven, Manchester United, Real Madrid	1998–2008	60	0	0	**60**
5 =	**Eusébio** Benfica	1961–75	46	7	4	**57**
=	**Filippo Inzaghi** Parma, Juventus, AC Milan	1995–2008	46	2	9	**57**
7	**Henrik Larsson** Feyenoord, Celtic, Barcelona, Manchester United, Helsingborgs IF	1994–2008	11	8	37	**56**
8	**Thierry Henry** AS Monaco, Arsenal, Barcelona	1996–2009	47	0	8	**55**
9	**Jupp Heynckes** Hannover, Borussia Mönchengladbach	1968–77	14	8	29	**51**
10	**Alfredo di Stefano** Real Madrid‡	1955–64	49	0	0	**49**

Up to and including the 2008–09 season

CL = European Champion Clubs' Cup/Champions League

CWC = European Cup Winners' Cup

UEFA = Fairs Cup/UEFA Cup (UEFA Europa League from 2009–10 season)

† Year of first and last goals scored in Europe

‡ Also played for Español in the Inter-Cities Fairs Cup, but failed to score

TOP 10 CLUBS THAT HAVE PLAYED THE MOST CONSECUTIVE SEASONS IN EUROPEAN COMPETITIONS

	Club/country	From	To	Total
1	**Barcelona** Spain	1955–58*	2008–09	**51**
2	**Anderlecht** Belgium	1964–65	2008–09	**45**
3	**Benfica** Portugal	1960–61	2000–01	**41**
4 =	**Porto** Portugal	1974–75	2008–09	**35**
=	**PSV Eindhoven** Netherlands	1974–75	2008–09	**35**
6	**Sporting Lisbon** Portugal	1977–78	2008–09	**32**
7 =	**Juventus** Italy	1963–64	1990–91	**28**
=	**Rangers** Scotland	1981–82	2008–09	**28**
9	**Sparta Prague** Czech Republic	1983–84	2008–09	**26**
10 =	**Ajax** Netherlands	1966–67	1989–90	**24**
=	**Red Star Belgrade** Serbia	1968–69	1991–92	**24**
=	**Spartak Moscow** Russia	1980–81	2003–04	**24**

Up to and including 2008–09

* Barcelona have competed in Europe every season since the inaugural Fairs Cup, which started in 1955 and was concluded in 1958.

The record for an English club is held by Liverpool; 21 seasons between 1964–65 and 1984–85.

TOP 10 UK CLUBS IN EUROPEAN COMPETITIONS

	Club	CL	CWC	UEFA	Total
1	**Liverpool**	5	0	3	**8**
2	**Manchester United**	3	1	0	**4**
3	**Tottenham Hotspur**	0	1	2	**3**
4 =	**Arsenal**	0	1	1	**2**
=	**Chelsea**	0	2	0	**2**
=	**Leeds United**	0	0	2	**2**
=	**Nottingham Forest**	2	0	0	**2**
8 =	**Aberdeen**	0	1	0	**1**
=	**Aston Villa**	1	0	0	**1**
=	**Celtic**	1	0	0	**1**
=	**Everton**	0	1	0	**1**
=	**Ipswich Town**	0	0	1	**1**
=	**Manchester City**	0	1	0	**1**
=	**Newcastle United**	0	0	1	**1**
=	**Rangers**	0	1	0	**1**
=	**West Ham United**	0	1	0	**1**

Up to and including the 2009 Champions League and UEFA Cup finals

CL = European Champion Clubs' Cup/Champions League

CWC = European Cup Winners' Cup

UEFA = Fairs Cup/UEFA Cup (UEFA Europa League from 2009–10 season)

TOP 10 CLUBS WITH THE MOST CONSECUTIVE CHAMPIONS LEAGUE GAMES WITHOUT DEFEAT*

	Club	First win	Last win	Games
1	**Manchester United**	19 Sep 2007	05 May 2009	**25**
2	**Bayern Munich**	14 Mar 2001	02 Apr 2002	**19**
3	**Ajax**	14 Sep 1994	20 Mar 1996	**18**
4	**Barcelona**	01 May 2002	09 Apr 2003	**16**
5 =	**Liverpool**	08 Dec 2004	06 Dec 2005	**14**
=	**Lyon**	08 Dec 2004	29 Mar 2006	**14**
7 =	**Arsenal**	09 Mar 2005	25 Apr 2006	**13**
=	**Valencia**	17 Apr 2001	18 Feb 2003	**13**
9	**Porto**	22 Oct 2003	14 Sep 2004	**12**
10	**Juventus**	23 May 1996	23 Apr 1997	**11**

Up to and including the 2008–09 Champions League

* Only best unbeaten run per team is included

Manchester United's run of 25 matches without defeat started with a 1–0 win at Sporting Lisbon thanks to a Cristiano Ronaldo goal. The run came to an end when they lost 2–0 to Barcelona in the final on 27 May 2009. If the parameters were extended beyond the best unbeaten run per team, Manchester United would also be joint third having played 18 matches unbeaten between 4 March 1998 and 29 September 1999.

TOP 10 PLAYERS WITH THE MOST APPEARANCES IN THE CHAMPIONS LEAGUE

Player	Club(s)	Years	Appearances
1 **Ryan Giggs**	Manchester United	1993–2009	**129**
2 **Raúl**	Real Madrid	1995–2009	**128**
3 **Roberto Carlos**	Real Madrid, Fenerbahce	1996–2008	**120**
4 **Thierry Henry**	AS Monaco, Juventus, Arsenal, Barcelona	1995–2009	**117**
5 **Paul Scholes**	Manchester United	1994–2009	**116**
6 = **Gary Neville**	Manchester United	1993–2008	**111**
= **David Beckham**	Manchester United, Real Madrid	1994–2007	**111**
8 **Paolo Maldini**	AC Milan	1985–2008	**108**
9 **Oliver Khan**	Bayern Munich	1994–2007	**103**
10 **Clarence Seedorf**	Ajax, Real Madrid, Inter Milan, AC Milan	1994–2008	**101**

Up to and including the 2008–09 Champions League , including qualifying rounds

Ryan Giggs made his Champions League debut on 15 September 1993 in a 3–2 win at Kispest Honvéd. He made his European debut two years earlier, on 6 November 1991, in a European Cup Winners' Cup tie against Atlético Madrid at Old Trafford.

TOP 10 GOALSCORERS IN THE CHAMPIONS LEAGUE

	Player/club(s)	Years	Goals*
1	**Raúl** Real Madrid	1995–2008	**64**
2	**Ruud van Nistelrooy** PSV Eindhoven, Manchester United, Real Madrid	1998–2008	**60**
3	**Andriy Shevchenko** Dynamo Kiev, AC Milan, Chelsea	1994–2007	**56**
4	**Thierry Henry** AS Monaco, Arsenal, Barcelona	1997–2009	**51**
5	**Filippo Inzaghi** Parma, Juventus, AC Milan	1997–2007	**46**
6	**Alessandro Del Piero** Juventus	1995–2009	**43**
7	**Fernando Morientes** Real Madrid, AS Monaco, Liverpool, Valencia	1997–2007	**39**
8 =	**Sergei Rebrov** Dynamo Kiev	1993–2007	**31**
=	**David Trezeguet** AS Monaco, Juventus	1997–2006	**31**
=	**Rivaldo** Barcelona, AC Milan, Olympiakos, AEK Athens	1998–2007	**31**

Up to and including the 2008–09 Champions League

* Totals include goals scored in qualifying matches, league matches and knockout matches

TOP 10 FAIRS CUP/UEFA CUP WINNERS

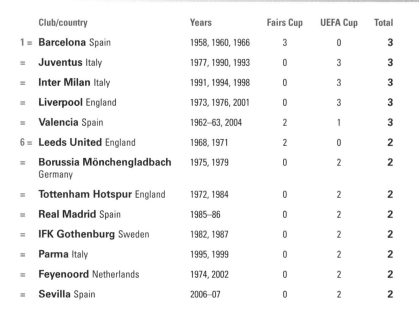

	Club/country	Years	Fairs Cup	UEFA Cup	Total
1 =	**Barcelona** Spain	1958, 1960, 1966	3	0	**3**
=	**Juventus** Italy	1977, 1990, 1993	0	3	**3**
=	**Inter Milan** Italy	1991, 1994, 1998	0	3	**3**
=	**Liverpool** England	1973, 1976, 2001	0	3	**3**
=	**Valencia** Spain	1962–63, 2004	2	1	**3**
6 =	**Leeds United** England	1968, 1971	2	0	**2**
=	**Borussia Mönchengladbach** Germany	1975, 1979	0	2	**2**
=	**Tottenham Hotspur** England	1972, 1984	0	2	**2**
=	**Real Madrid** Spain	1985–86	0	2	**2**
=	**IFK Gothenburg** Sweden	1982, 1987	0	2	**2**
=	**Parma** Italy	1995, 1999	0	2	**2**
=	**Feyenoord** Netherlands	1974, 2002	0	2	**2**
=	**Sevilla** Spain	2006–07	0	2	**2**

Up to and including the 2009 final

The original Fairs Cup was contested by cities that sponsored international trade fairs and was called the International Industries Fairs Inter-Cities Cup, commonly known as the Fairs Cup. The second tournament, held between 1958 and 1960, consisted mainly of club sides and in 1966 was renamed the European Fairs Cup, in 1971 becoming known as the UEFA Cup. Barcelona were the first winners of the Fairs Cup and Leeds United the last. The two met in a special play-off match at the Nou Camp in 1971, which Barcelona won 2–1.

In 2009 the UEFA Cup was rebranded as the UEFA Europa League.

TOP 10 EUROPEAN CUP/CHAMPIONS LEAGUE WINNERS

	Club/country	Years	Wins
1	**Real Madrid** Spain	1956–60, 1966, 1998, 2000, 2002	9
2	**AC Milan** Italy	1963, 1969, 1989–90, 1994, 2003, 2007	7
3	**Liverpool** England	1977–78, 1981, 1984, 2005	5
4 =	**Ajax** Netherlands	1971–73, 1995	4
=	**Bayern Munich** Germany	1974–76, 2001	4
6 =	**Manchester United** England	1968, 1999, 2008	3
=	**Barcelona** Spain	1992, 2006, 2009	3
8 =	**Benfica** Portugal	1961–62	2
=	**Inter Milan** Italy	1964–65	2
=	**Nottingham Forest** England	1979–80	2
=	**Juventus** Italy	1985, 1996	2
=	**Porto** Portugal	1987, 2004	2

Up to and including the 2009 final

The European Cup, or European Champion Club's Cup, was the brainchild of Gabriel Hanot, the football editor of the French daily sports newspaper *L'Equipe*. The first tournament was held in 1955–56, with Real Madrid beating French side Stade de Reims 4–3 in the final. Although originally open only to domestic league champions of nations affiliated to UEFA, there was a major change in 1992–93 when it was rebranded as the UEFA Champions League, and in 1997–98 runners-up in the leading domestic leagues around Europe were allowed to enter. At present, up to the top four teams are eligible to enter the competition. Real Madrid have appeared in a record 12 finals and 21 semi-finals.

BEHIND THE RECORD
– REAL MADRID'S RECORD NINE TITLES

Real Madrid dominated the European Cup in its early days, winning it for the first five years. The first team to eliminate them was fellow Spaniards Barcelona in the first round in 1960–61. Real Madrid regained the title in 1966 and have since won it three more times. These are their nine record-winning finals:

1956 vs. Stade de Reims, Score: 4–3, Venue: Paris, Attendance: 38,239
Team: Alonso; Atienza, Marquitos, Lesmes; Muñoz, Zárraga; Joseito, Marchal, Di Stéfano, Rial, Gento **Scorers:** Marquitos, Stéfano, Rial (2)

1957 vs. Fiorentina, Score: 2–0, Venue: Madrid, Attendance: 124,000
Team: Alonso; Torres, Marquitos, Lesmes; Muñoz, Zárraga; Kopa, Mateos, Di Stéfano, Rial, Gento **Scorers:** Di Stéfano (penalty), Gento

1958 vs. AC Milan, Score: 3–2 (aet), Venue: Brussels, Attendance: 67,000
Team: Alonso; Atienza, Santamaría, Lesmes; Santistebán, Zárraga; Kopa, Joseito, Di Stéfano, Rial, Gento **Scorers:** Di Stéfano, Rial, Gento

1959 vs. Stade de Reims, Score: 2–0, Venue: Stuttgart, Attendance: 80,000
Team: Dominguez; Marquitos, Santamaría, Zárraga; Santistebán, Ruiz; Kopa, Mateos, Di Stéfano, Rial, Gento **Scorers:** Mateos, Di Stéfano

1960 vs. Eintracht Frankfurt, Score: 7–3, Venue: Glasgow, Attendance: 127,621
Team: Dominguez; Marquitos, Santamaría, Pachin; Vidal, Zárraga; Canario, Del Sol, Di Stéfano, Puskás, Gento **Scorers:** Puskás (4, 1 penalty), Di Stéfano (3)

1966 vs. Partizan Belgrade, Score: 2–1, Venue: Brussels, Attendance: 55,000
Team: Araquistain; Pachin, De Felipe, Zoco; Sanchis; Pirri, Velazquez; Serena, Amancio, Grosso, Gento **Scorers:** Amancio, Serena

1998 vs. Juventus, Score: 1–0, Venue: Amsterdam, Attendance: 47,500
Team: Illgner, Hierro, Sanchis, Panucci, Roberto Carlos, Raúl (Amavisca), Karembeu, Seedorf, Redondo, Mijatovic (Suker), Morientes (Jaime) **Scorer:** Mijatovoic

2000 vs. Valencia, Score: 3–0, Venue: Paris, Attendance: 78,759
Team: Casillas; Salgado (Hierro), Roberto Carlos, Karanka, Campo, McManaman, Redondo, Helguera, Raúl, Anelka (Sanchís), Morientes (Sávio) **Scorers:** Morientes, McManaman, Raúl

2002 vs. Bayer Leverkusen, Score: 2–1, Venue: Glasgow, Attendance: 51,456
Team: Cesar (Casillas); Salgado, Roberto Carlos, Makelele (Conceição), Hierro, Helguera, Figo (McManaman), Morientes, Raúl, Zidane, Solari **Scorers:** Raúl, Zidane

'Paco' Gento's six winner's medals are a record for the tournament.

10 GREAT EUROPEAN CUP/ CHAMPIONS LEAGUE FINALS

1 1956 **Real Madrid vs. Stade de Reims**, Score: 4–3,
Venue: Paris, Attendance: 38,239
This was the first European Cup final and also the first of five consecutive victories
for Real Madrid. However, after just ten minutes it looked as if the French were
going to be the inaugural champions as the Spanish club side trailed to goals from
Leblond and Templin. But Madrid were inspired by Di Stéfano who pulled one back.
Rial equalized but then Reims went 3–2 up before a second equalizer from
Marquitos and then a 79th-minute winner from Rial won Madrid their first of a
record nine titles.

2 1960 **Real Madrid vs. Eintracht Frankfurt**, Score: 7–3,
Venue: Glasgow, Attendance: 127,621
The great Real Madrid side were in their fifth consecutive final. Trailing after only
18 minutes, Madrid turned that deficit into a 6–1 lead in little over 50 minutes,
before going on to seal it with a 7–3 win with a display of flowing football. Ferenc
Puskás scored four goals, assisted by the majestic Alfredo di Stéfano who scored
a hat-trick.

3 1962 **Benfica vs. Real Madrid**, Score: 5–3,
Venue: Amsterdam, Attendance: 65,000
In 1961 Benfica replaced Real Madrid as European champions; now, a year later,
the two teams met in the final. Puskás put Madrid two goals up after just 23
minutes as a sixth trophy beckoned the Spanish team. But Aguas and Cavém
brought the score level with just 35 minutes gone before Puskás completed his
hat-trick just before half-time. Coluna equalized after 51 minutes before two goals
within three minutes from the new star of Portuguese football, Eusébio, gave
Benfica their second successive victory.

4 1967 **Celtic vs. Inter Milan**, Score: 2-1, Venue: Lisbon, Attendance: 54,000
On paper, the star-studded Inter Milan side were clear favourites to win the trophy.
Despite going down to a Mazzola penalty in the seventh minute, Celtic fought back
and secured victory thanks to goals from Tommy Gemmell and Stevie Chalmers'
85th-minute winner. Dubbed 'The Lisbon Lions', Celtic became the first British
winners of the European Cup.

5 1968 **Manchester United vs. Benfica**, Score: 4–1 (aet),
Venue: London, Attendance: 100,000
Ten years after the Munich air crash Matt Busby fulfilled his European dream by
guiding United to become the first English side to lift the trophy. Bobby Charlton,
one of the survivors of the Munich crash, put United ahead in the 53rd minute with
a rare headed goal before Graça took it to extra time with a 75th-minute equalizer.
But then United ran riot with two goals in two minutes from George Best and Brian
Kidd, before Bobby Charlton wrapped it up.

6 1977 **Liverpool vs. Borussia Mönchengladbach**, Score: 3–1,
Venue: Rome, Attendance: 52,000
A year after winning the UEFA Cup, Liverpool were chasing their first European Cup. They opened the scoring thanks to Terry McDermott. The Germans drew level early in the second half through Allan Simonsen before Tommy Smith put Liverpool back in front in the 64th minute. A Phil Neal penalty eight minutes from time meant Liverpool and Bob Paisley lifted the European Cup for the first time.

7 1989 **AC Milan vs. Steaua Bucharest**, Score: 4–0,
Venue: Barcelona, Attendance: 97,000
Within two minutes of the start of the second half, this final was all over as Milan scored their fourth goal and saw off their Romanian opponents. But it was more than just the score that secured Milan's third title as the crowd was treated to a dazzling display of football from Milan's Dutch trio of Ruud Gullit, Frank Rijkaard and Marco van Basten, with Gullit and van Basten each scoring two goals.

8 1994 **AC Milan vs. Barcelona**, Score: 4–0,
Venue: Athens, Attendance: 75,000
Milan were without two central defenders, Franco Baresi and Alessandro Costacurta, but the Milan defence coped admirably with the attacking threat of Stoichkov and Romário, and it was a first-half brace from Massaro that gave Milan a 2–0 half-time lead. A superb lob from Savićević in the 47th minute put the game beyond Barcelona and it was all over ten minutes later when Marcel Desailly completed the scoring. He became the first man to win the trophy with different clubs in consecutive seasons, having won it with Marseille in 1993.

9 1999 **Manchester United vs. Bayern Munich**, Score: 2–1,
Venue: Barcelona, Attendance: 90,000
A Mario Basler free kick in the sixth minute put Bayern Munich ahead. But the game came to life as Teddy Sheringham scored from close range one minute into the three minutes of added time. As extra time loomed, Ole Gunnar Solskjaer stuck out a foot to meet a Sheringham header and it went high into the Bayern net for not only a remarkable victory but a match that completed the treble of Premier League, FA Cup and Champions League for Manchester United.

10 2005 **Liverpool vs. AC Milan**, Score: 3–3 (aet),
Venue: Istanbul, Attendance: 60,000
This final provided one of the greatest comebacks in the history of this tournament. Liverpool fell behind to a first-minute goal from Paolo Maldini followed by two more from Hernán Crespo before the interval. Within 15 minutes of the restart Liverpool were level as Steve Gerrard, Vladimir Smicer and Xabi Alonso scored within a six-minute period. The next hour produced no more goals and the match went to penalties. Liverpool led 3–2 as Andriy Shevchenko stepped up to keep Milan in the final but Dudek saved and Liverpool won their fifth title in remarkable fashion.

THE 10 LEAST SUCCESSFUL ENGLISH CLUBS IN THE EUROPEAN CUP/CHAMPIONS LEAGUE

	Club	Seasons	Games played	Games won	Win %
1	**Manchester City**	1	2	0	**00.00**
2	**Blackburn Rovers**	1	6	1	**16.67**
3	**Everton**	3	10	2	**20.00**
4	**Wolverhampton Wanderers**	2	8	2	**25.00**
5	**Newcastle United**	3	24	11	**45.83**
6	**Arsenal**	13	127	60	**47.24**
7	**Chelsea**	7	87	43	**49.43**
8 =	**Burnley**	1	4	2	**50.00**
=	**Derby County**	2	12	6	**50.00**
=	**Tottenham Hotspur**	1	8	4	**50.00**

Up to and including the 2008–09 tournament

Ipswich Town have the best record of the 16 English teams that have played in the European Cup/Champions League, with a win percentage of 75.00 from three wins from four games played. In those four matches they scored 16 goals.

Avenir Beggen of Luxembourg have the all-time worst record with no wins from 12 matches in six campaigns, in which they have scored one goal and conceded 56.

10 CHAMPIONS LEAGUE FIRSTS

1   The first team to progress beyond the group stage after losing their first three matches was Newcastle United in 2002–03.

2   The first derby between teams from the same city was in the 2003 semi-final when Inter Milan and AC Milan met each other.

3   The first team to win all its group matches was AC Milan in 1992–93, who won all six of their games with an 11–1 goal difference.

4   The first team to draw all six of their group games was AEK Athens in 2002–03.

5   The first man to win the Champions League playing for three different teams was Clarence Seedorf in 2003. He won his medals with Ajax, Real Madrid and AC Milan. He won a fourth medal with Milan in 2007.

6   The first player to be sent off in a Champions League final was Jens Lehmann of Arsenal, for a professional foul in the 2006 final against Barcelona.

7   The first winners of the Champions League not to have won their domestic title or Champions League the previous year was Manchester United in 1999.

8   The first player to score a hat-trick in the Champions League was Juul Ellerman for PSV Eindhoven in their first-round first-leg match against Zalgiris Vilnius of Lithuania on 16 September 1992.

9   The first player from a British club to score a goal in the Champions League was Mark Hateley for Rangers against Lyngby of Denmark in the first round first leg, also on 16 September 1992.

10 The first team to progress following a penalty shoot-out was Skonto FC of Latvia who beat Olimpija Ljubljana of Slovenia 11–10 on penalties after the teams ended 1–1 on aggregate in the preliminary round on 1 September 1993.

TOP 10 CLUBS IN THE EUROPEAN CUP/ CHAMPIONS LEAGUE

	Club/country *	Tournaments played	Matches played	W	D	L	Pts
1	**Real Madrid** Spain	39	315	180	54	81	**594**
2	**Bayern Munich** Germany	25	226	121	58	47	**421**
3	**Manchester United** England	20	206	114	51	41	**393**
4	**AC Milan** Italy	23	205	112	48	45	**384**
5	**Barcelona** Spain	19	196	111	46	39	**379**
6	**Juventus** Italy	25	195	98	47	50	**341**
7	**Liverpool** England	19	169	97	38	34	**329**
8	**Benfica** Portugal	29	179	85	41	53	**296**
9	**Dinamo Kiev** Ukraine	27	190	85	39	66	**294**
10	**Ajax** Netherlands	26	157	77	37	43	**268**

Up to and including 2008–09

* Total points based on three points for a win and one for a draw

TOP 10 COUNTRIES APPEARING IN THE MOST CUP WINNERS' CUP FINALS

	Country	Winners	Runners-up	Appearances
1	**Spain**	7	7	**14**
2	**England**	8	5	**13**
3	**Italy**	7	4	**11**
4	**West Germany/Germany**	4	4	**8**
5	**Belgium**	3	4	**7**
6 =	**Scotland**	2	2	**4**
=	**USSR**	3	1	**4**
8 =	**Austria**	0	3	**3**
=	**East Germany**	1	2	**3**
=	**France**	1	2	**3**

First held in 1960–61, the competition was open to domestic cup winners of UEFA affiliated countries. The first final was played over two legs with Fiorentina of Italy beating Glasgow Rangers 4–1 on aggregate. All subsequent finals were a single game and the last Cup Winners' Cup final was held in 1999, when Italy's Lazio beat Real Mallorca of Spain 2–1 at Villa Park, Birmingham.

10 GREAT EUROPEAN COMEBACKS

1   **1961–62 Cup Winners' Cup** first round
First leg: FC La Chaux-de-Fonds (Switzerland) 6 Leixões (Portugal) 2
Second leg: Leixões 5 FC La Chaux-de-Fonds 0
Result: Leixões won 7–6 on aggregate.

2   **1970 Fairs Cup** final
First leg: Anderlecht (Belgium) 3 Arsenal (England) 1
Second leg: Arsenal 3 Anderlecht 0
Result: Arsenal won 4–3 on aggregate.

3   **1984–85 Cup Winners' Cup** first round
First leg: FC Metz (France) 2 Barcelona (Spain) 4
Second leg: Barcelona 1 FC Metz 4
Result: FC Metz won 6–5 on aggregate.

4   **1984–85 UEFA Cup** second round
First leg: Queens Park Rangers (England) 6 Partizan Belgrade (Yugoslavia) 2
Second leg: Partizan Belgrade 4 Queens Park Rangers 0
Result: 6–6 on aggregate, Partizan Belgrade won on away goals.

5   **1985–86 UEFA Cup** third round
First leg: Borussia Mönchengladbach (West Germany) 5 Real Madrid (Spain) 1
Second leg: Real Madrid 4 Borussia Mönchengladbach 0
Result: 5–5 on aggregate, Real Madrid won on away goals.

6   **1985–86 Cup Winners' Cup** quarter-final
First leg: Dynamo Dresden (East Germany) 2 Bayer Uerdingen (West Germany) 0
Second leg: Bayer Uerdingen 7 Dynamo Dresden 3
Result: In the second leg Dresden were 3–1 up at half-time and were leading 5–1 on aggregate. Uerdingen eventually won 7–5 on aggregate.

7   **1987–88 UEFA Cup** final
First leg: Español (Spain) 3 Bayer Leverkusen (West Germany) 0
Second leg: Bayer Leverkusen 3 Español 0 (aet)
Result: 3–3 on aggregate, Bayer Leverkusen won on penalties.

8 **1989–90 UEFA Cup** first round
First leg: Levski Spartak (Bulgaria) 0 Antwerp (Belgium) 0
Second leg: Antwerp 4 Levski Spartak 3
Result: In the second leg, with three minutes to go Antwerp were trailing 3–1.
Antwerp won 4–3 on aggregate.

9 **2003–04 Champions League** quarter-final
First leg: AC Milan (Italy) 4 Deportivo (Spain) 1
Second leg: Deportivo 4 AC Milan 0
Result: Deportivo won 5–4 on aggregate.

10 **2004–05 Champions League** final
Liverpool (England) 3 AC Milan (Italy) 3
Liverpool were trailing 3–0 at half-time but within 15 minutes of the restart they
were level. It ended 3–3 and Liverpool went on to win on penalties.

The star of the penalty shoot-out between Liverpool and AC Milan in 2005 was the
Liverpool goalkeeper Jerzy Dudek. He distracted Serginho who put Milan's first spot
kick over the bar. Dietmar Hamann scored to give Liverpool the lead and then Dudek
saved from Andrea Pirlo. By the time the fifth Milan penalty came around they were
trailing Liverpool 3–2. It was down to Andriy Shevchenko to keep the Italians in the
competition. Dudek went the wrong way but managed to get his hand to the ball to
make the save that gave Liverpool their fifth trophy.

TOP 10 BIGGEST WINS IN EUROPE*

	Winners/losers	Year/competition	Score
1	**Sporting Lisbon vs. APOEL Nicosia**	1963–64 Cup Winners' Cup	**16–1**
2	**Ajax vs. Red Boys Differdange**	1984–85 UEFA Cup	**14–0**
3 =	**Cologne vs. US Luxembourg**	1965–66 Fairs Cup	**13–0**
=	**Chelsea vs. Jeunesse Hautcharage**	1971–72 Cup Winners' Cup	**13–0**
5 =	**Feyenoord vs. US Rumelange**	1972–73 UEFA Cup	**12–0**
=	**Derby County vs. Finn Harps**	1976–77 UEFA Cup	**12–0**
=	**Swansea City vs. Sliema Wanderers**	1982–83 Cup Winners' Cup	**12–0**
8 =	**Feyenoord vs. KR Reykjavic**	1969–70 European Cup	**12–2**
=	**Levski-Spartak vs. Reipas**	1976–77 Cup Winners' Cup	**12–2**
10 =	**Dynamo Bucharest vs. Crusaders**	1973–74 European Cup	**11–0**
=	**Malmö vs. Pezoporikos**	1973–74 Cup Winners' Cup	**11–0**
=	**Liverpool vs. Strømsgodset**	1974–75 Cup Winners' Cup	**11–0**
=	**Viking Stavanger vs. CE Principat**	1999–2000 UEFA Cup	**11–0**

Up to and including the 2008–09 Champions League and UEFA Cup

* European Cup/Champions League; European Cup Winners' Cup; Fairs Cup/UEFA Cup. Based on winning margin

Liverpool are the only team to have scored ten or more goals in a game on three occasions: 10–0 vs. Dundalk, 1969–70 Fairs Cup; 11–0 vs. Strømsgodset, 1974–75 Cup Winners' Cup; 10–1 vs. OPS Oula, 1980–81 European Cup. APOEL Nicosia are the only team to have conceded ten goals in a game three times.

Prior to beating Jeunesse Hautcharage 13–0 at Stamford Bridge in the 1971–72 Cup Winners' Cup, Chelsea had beaten the Luxembourg team 8–0 in the first leg. Their 21–0 aggregate win is a European record, which was equalled the following season in the 1972–73 UEFA Cup when Feyenoord beat US Rumelange 9–0 and 12–0.

	Club/country	Years	Wins
1	**Independiente** Argentina	1964–65, 19727–5, 1984	7
2	**Boca Juniors** Argentina	1977–78, 2000–01, 2003, 2007	6
3	**Peñarol** Uruguay	1960–61, 1966, 1982, 1987	5
4	**Estudiantes** Argentina	1968–70, 2009	4
5 =	**Nacional** Uruguay	1971, 1980, 1988	3
=	**Olimpia** Paraguay	1979, 1990, 2002	3
=	**São Paulo** Brazil	1992–93, 2005	3
8 =	**Santos** Brazil	1962–63	2
=	**Grêmio** Brazil	1983, 1995	2
=	**River Plate** Argentina	1986, 1996	2
=	**Cruzeiro** Brazil	1976, 1997	2

Up to and including 2009

Following the success of the European Cup, the Copa Libertadores, now the most prestigious club event in South American football, was launched in 1960. There was an earlier tournament, the Copa de Campeones, which was held just once in 1948 when it was won by Vasco da Gama of Brazil.

TOP 10 SOUTH AMERICAN CUP WINNERS*

	Club/country	CL	S	CC	R	CSA	Total
1	**Boca Juniors** Argentina	6	1	0	4	2	**13**
2	**Independiente** Argentina	7	2	0	1	0	**10**
3	**São Paulo** Brazil	3	1	1	2	0	**7**
4	**Olimpia** Paraguay	3	1	0	2	0	**6**
5 =	**Cruzeiro** Brazil	2	2	0	1	0	**5**
=	**Peñarol** Uruguay	5	0	0	0	0	**5**
7 =	**Estudiantes** Argentina	4	0	0	0	0	**4**
=	**Nacional** Uruguay	3	0	0	1	0	**4**
9 =	**Gremio** Brazil	2	0	0	1	0	**3**
=	**Santos** Brazil	2	0	1	0	0	**3**
=	**River Plate** Argentina	2	1	0	0	0	**3**
=	**Vélez Sarsfield** Argentina	1	1	0	1	0	**3**

Up to and including 2009

* Based on wins in the major tournaments for club sides organized by CONMEBOL (South American Football Confederation)

CL = Copa Libertadores

S = Supercopa

CC = Copa Conmebol

R = Recopa Sudamericana

CSA = Copa Sudamericana

TOP 10 COUNTRIES WITH THE MOST FINALISTS IN THE AFC CHAMPIONS LEAGUE

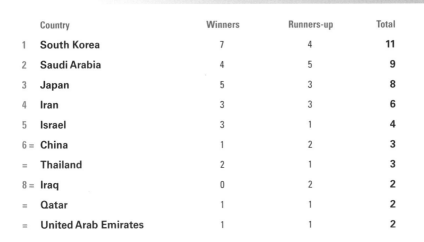

	Country	Winners	Runners-up	Total
1	**South Korea**	7	4	**11**
2	**Saudi Arabia**	4	5	**9**
3	**Japan**	5	3	**8**
4	**Iran**	3	3	**6**
5	**Israel**	3	1	**4**
6 =	**China**	1	2	**3**
=	**Thailand**	2	1	**3**
8 =	**Iraq**	0	2	**2**
=	**Qatar**	1	1	**2**
=	**United Arab Emirates**	1	1	**2**

Up to and including 2008

The leading club tournament in Asia organized by the Asian Football Confederation (AFC), the AFC Champions Cup was first held in 1967, when it was known as the Asian Champion Club Tournament. The first winners were Hapoel Tel Aviv of Israel who beat Selangor of Malaysia 2–1 in the inaugural final. It was known as the Asian Club Championship from 1985–2002 after which its name was changed to the AFC Champions League following a merger with the Asian Cup Winners' Cup.

TOP 10 COUNTRIES WITH THE MOST WINNERS OF THE AFRICAN CHAMPIONS CUP/CAF CHAMPIONS LEAGUE

	Country	Years	Wins
1	**UAR/Egypt**	1969, 1982, 1984, 1986–87, 1993, 1996, 2001–2, 2005–06, 2008	**12**
2 =	**Cameroon**	1964, 1971, 1978–80	5
=	**Morocco**	1985, 1989, 1992, 1997, 1999	5
4	**Algeria**	1976, 1981, 1988, 1990	4
5 =	**Ghana**	1970, 1983, 2000	3
=	**Guinea**	1972, 1975, 1977	3
=	**Tunisia**	1991, 1994, 2007	3
=	**Zaire/DR Congo**	1967–68, 1973	3
9 =	**Ivory Coast**	1966, 1998	2
=	**Nigeria**	2003–04	2

Up to and including 2008

An annual tournament similar to the UEFA Champions League, the competition is organized by the Confederation of African Football (CAF) and was first held in 1964 when Oryx Douala of Cameroon beat Stade Malien of Mali 2–1 in the final. It was originally called the African Champions Cup but it was renamed the CAF Champions League in 1997. The only other countries to have provided winners of the tournament are Congo in 1974 and South Africa in 1995. The most successful club has been Egypt's Al-Ahly, with six wins between 1982 and 2008.

TOP 10 PLAYERS WITH THE MOST ENGLISH LEAGUE APPEARANCES

	Player	Appearances
1	**Peter Shilton** 1966–97 Clubs: Leicester City, Stoke City, Nottingham Forest, Southampton, Derby County, Plymouth Argyle, Bolton Wanderers, Leyton Orient	**1,005**
2	**Tony Ford** 1975–2002 Clubs: Grimsby Town, Sunderland, Stoke City, West Bromwich Albion, Bradford City, Scunthorpe United, Mansfield Town, Rochdale	**931**
3	**Terry Paine** 1957–77 Clubs: Southampton, Hereford United	**824**
4	**Tommy Hutchison** 1968–91 Clubs: Blackpool, Coventry City, Manchester City, Burnley, Swansea City	**795**
5	**Neil Redfearn** 1982–2004 Clubs: Bolton Wanderers, Lincoln City, Doncaster Rovers, Crystal Palace, Watford, Oldham Athletic, Barnsley, Charlton Athletic, Bradford City, Wigan Athletic, Halifax Town, Boston United, Rochdale	**790**
6	**Robbie James** 1973–93 Clubs: Swansea City, Stoke City, Queens Park Rangers, Leicester City, Bradford City, Cardiff City	**782**
7	**Alan Oakes** 1959–83 Clubs: Manchester City, Chester, Port Vale	**776**
8	**Dave Beasant** 1980–2003 Clubs: Wimbledon, Newcastle United, Chelsea, Grimsby Town, Wolverhampton Wanderers, Southampton, Nottingham Forest, Portsmouth, Brighton & Hove Albion	**774**
9	**John Trollope** 1960–80 Club: Swindon Town	**770**
10	**Jimmy Dickinson** 1946–65 Club: Portsmouth	**764**

Up to and including the 2008–09 season

Source: The Football League

Peter Shilton made his debut for Leicester City as a 16-year-old against Everton in May 1966 and played his 1,005th and last League game in front of 3,014 fans playing for Leyton Orient against Wigan Athletic on 21 January 1997, at the age of 47.

TOP 10 PLAYERS WITH THE MOST ENGLISH LEAGUE GOALS IN A CAREER

	Player	Goals
1	**Arthur Rowley** 1946–65 Clubs: West Bromwich Albion, Fulham, Leicester City, Shrewsbury Town	434 *
2	**Dixie Dean** 1923–39 Clubs: Tranmere Rovers, Everton, Notts County	379
3	**Jimmy Greaves** 1957–71 Clubs: Chelsea, Tottenham Hotspur, West Ham United	357
4	**Steve Bloomer** 1892–1914 Clubs: Derby County, Middlesbrough	352
5	**George Camsell†** 1924–39 Clubs: Durham City, Middlesbrough	345
6	**John Aldridge** 1978–98 Clubs: Newport County, Oxford United, Liverpool, Tranmere Rovers	329
7 =	**Joe Smith** 1908–29 Clubs: Bolton Wanderers, Stockport County	315
=	**John Atyeo** 1951–66 Clubs: Bristol City	315
9	**Vic Watson** 1920–36 Clubs: West Ham United, Southampton	312
10	**Harry Bedford** 1919–34 Clubs: Nottingham Forest, Blackpool, Derby County, Newcastle United, Sunderland, Bradford Park Avenue, Chesterfield	308

Up to and including the 2008–09 season

* Some sources give Rowley's total as 433

† Most authorities quote George Camsell as playing only for Middlesbrough but he scored 20 goals playing for Durham City, then of Third Division North, in 1924–25

Dixie Dean scored 349 goals for Everton, the most for a single club. Dean also holds the record for the most League hat-tricks, 34.

All of Jimmy Greaves's 357 goals were in the top level of English football.
The most goals in a single game is ten by Joe Payne for Luton Town in their 12–0 win over Bristol Rovers on 13 April 1936.

TOP 10 PLAYERS WITH THE MOST GOALS IN AN ENGLISH LEAGUE SEASON

	Player/club	Division	Season	Goals
1	**Dixie Dean** Everton	First	1927–28	60
2	**George Camsell** Middlesbrough	Second	1926–27	59
3 =	**Ted Harston** Mansfield Town	Third North	1936–37	55
=	**Joe Payne** Luton Town	Third South	1936–37	55
5	**Terry Bly** Peterborough United	Fourth	1960–61	52
6 =	**Pongo Waring** Aston Villa	First	1930–31	49
=	**Clarrie Bourton** Coventry City	Third South	1931–32	49
8	**Harry Morris** Swindon Town	Third South	1926–27	47
9 =	**Peter Simpson** Crystal Palace	Third South	1930–31	46
=	**Alf Lythgoe** Stockport County	Third North	1933–34	46
=	**Derek Dooley** Sheffield Wednesday	Second	1951–52	46

Up to and including 2008–09

The most goals in a Premier League season is 34, held jointly by Andy Cole (Newcastle United) in 1993–94 and Alan Shearer (Blackburn Rovers) in 1994–95.

The last player to score over 40 goals in a season was Guy Whittingham who scored 42 for First Division Portsmouth in the 1992–93 season.

TOP 10 CLUBS WITH THE MOST TOP-FLIGHT ENGLISH LEAGUE TITLES

	Club	Football League	Premier League	Total
1=	**Liverpool**	18	0	**18**
=	**Manchester United**	7	11	**18**
3	**Arsenal**	10	3	**13**
4	**Everton**	9	0	**9**
5	**Aston Villa**	7	0	**7**
6	**Sunderland**	6	0	**6**
7 =	**Newcastle United**	4	0	**4**
=	**Sheffield Wednesday**	4	0	**4**
9 =	**Huddersfield Town**	3	0	**3**
=	**Wolverhampton Wanderers**	3	0	**3**
=	**Leeds United**	3	0	**3**
=	**Blackburn Rovers**	2	1	**3**
=	**Chelsea**	1	2	**3**

1888–89 to 2008–09

TOP 10 CLUBS THAT HAVE PLAYED THE MOST MATCHES IN ENGLISH LEAGUE FOOTBALL *

	Club	Seasons	Matches played
1	**Notts County**	110	**4,526**
2	**Preston North End**	110	**4,500**
3	**Burnley**	110	**4,484**
4	**Wolverhampton Wanderers**	110	**4,464**
5	**West Bromwich Albion**	110	**4,430**
6	**Grimsby Town**	105	**4,412**
7	**Bolton Wanderers**	110	**4,408**
8	**Derby County**	110	**4,394**
9	**Bury**	104	**4,392**
10	**Blackburn Rovers**	110	**4,374**

* In all divisions from 1888–89 to 2008–09

All teams except Grimsby Town and Bury were founder members of the Football League.

TOP 10 HIGHEST-SCORING ENGLISH LEAGUE GAMES

	Winners/losers	Division	Date	Score	Goals
1	**Tranmere Rovers vs. Oldham Athletic**	Third North	26 Dec 1935	13–4	**17**
2 =	**Aston Villa vs. Accrington**	First	12 Mar 1892	12–2	**14**
=	**Manchester City vs. Lincoln City**	Second	23 Mar 1895	11–3	**14**
=	**Tottenham Hotspur vs. Everton**	First	11 Oct 1958	10–4	**14**
5 =	**Stockport County vs. Halifax Town**	Third North	06 Jan 1934	13–0	**13**
=	**Newcastle United vs. Newport County**	Second	05 Oct 1946	13–0	**13**
=	**Barrow vs. Gateshead**	Third North	05 May 1934	12–1	**13**
=	**Sheffield United vs. Cardiff City**	First	01 Jan 1926	11–2	**13**
=	**Oldham Athletic vs. Chester**	Third North	19 Jan 1952	11–2	**13**
=	**Hull City vs. Wolverhampton Wanderers**	Second	27 Dec 1919	10–3	**13**
=	**Middlesbrough vs. Sheffield United**	First	18 Nov 1933	10–3	**13**
=	**Stoke City vs. West Bromwich Albion**	First	04 Feb 1937	10–3	**13**
=	**Bristol City vs. Gillingham**	Third South	15 Jan 1927	9–4	**13**
=	**Gillingham vs. Exeter City**	Third South	17 Jan 1951	9–4	**13**
=	**Derby County vs. Blackburn Rovers**	First	06 Sep 1890	8–5	**13**
=	**Burton Swifts vs. Walsall Town Swifts**	Second	24 Feb 1894	8–5	**13**
=	**Stockport County vs. Chester**	Third North	06 May 1933	8–5	**13**
=	**Charlton Athletic vs. Huddersfield Town**	Second	21 Dec 1957	7–6	**13**

Up to and including the 2008–09 season

The highest-scoring Premier League game is Portsmouth 7 Reading 4, which was played on 29 September 2007.

BOXING DAY 1963 –
A GOALSCORING BONANZA

Maybe too much festive food was to blame but Boxing Day 1963 saw a staggering 157 goals scored in 39 League games, with a remarkable 66 being scored in just ten First Division games – an average of 6.6 per game. These are the results from that amazing day in the top flight:

Blackpool (0) **1**		**5** (4)	**Chelsea** (4) 5
Durie			Bridges (2), Murray, Houseman, Venables
Burnley (2) **6**		**1** (1)	**Manchester United**
Lochhead (4), Morgan (2)			Herd
Fulham (5) **10**		**1** (1)	**Ipswich Town**
Leggatt (4), Howfield (3), Cook, Mullery, Robson			Baker
Leicester City (1) **2**		**0** (0)	**Everton** (0) 0
Keyworth (2)			
Liverpool (1) **6**		**1** (1)	**Stoke City**
Hunt (4), St. John, Arrowsmith			Ritchie
Nottingham Forest (3) **3**		**3** (0)	**Sheffield United**
Wignall, Vowden, Moore			Jones (2), Allchurch (pen)
Sheffield Wednesday (2) **3**		**0** (0)	**Bolton Wanderers**
Dobson (2), Pearson			
West Bromwich Albion (2) **4**		**3** (4)	**Tottenham Hotspur**
Kaye, Clark, Fudge, Howe			Greaves (2), Smith, Jones
West Ham United (1) **2**		**4** (8)	**Blackburn Rovers**
Byrne (2)			Pickering (3), McEvoy (3), Douglas, Ferguson
Wolverhampton Wanderers (0) **3**		**3** (0)	**Aston Villa**
Crawford (2), Wharton			Pountney, Crowe, Hateley

Figures in brackets indicate half-time scores

In their reverse fixtures two days later Blackburn Rovers, after winning 8–2 at West Ham United, lost 3–1 at home; Manchester United turned a 6–1 defeat into a 5–1 win and Ipswich Town avenged their 10–1 drubbing by Fulham to beat the Londoners 4–2.

The highest score in the other divisions on that same Boxing Day was Manchester City's 8–1 win over Scunthorpe United in the Second Division.

TOP 10 CLUBS WITH THE MOST WINS IN ENGLISH LEAGUE FOOTBALL IN ONE SEASON

	Club	Season	Division	Games played	Games won
1	**Doncaster Rovers**	1946–47	Third North	42	**33**
2 =	**Tottenham Hotspur**	1919–20	Second	42	**32**
=	**Aston Villa**	1971–72	Third	46	**32**
=	**Lincoln City**	1975–76	Fourth	46	**32**
=	**Swindon Town**	1985–86	Fourth	46	**32**
6 =	**Rotherham United**	1950–51	Third North	46	**31**
=	**Grimsby Town**	1955–56	Third North	46	**31**
=	**Tottenham Hotspur***	1960–61	First	42	**31**
=	**Hull City**	1965–66	Third	46	**31**
=	**York City**	1983–84	Fourth	46	**31**
=	**Sunderland**	1998–99	First	46	**31**
=	**Fulham**	1998–99	Second	46	**31**
=	**Manchester City**	2001–02	First	46	**31**
=	**Plymouth Argyle**	2001–02	Third	46	**31**
=	**Reading**	2005–06	Championship	46	**31**

Up to and including 2008–09

* A record for the top flight of English League football

The Premier League record is 29, set on two occasions by Chelsea, in 2004–05 and 2005–06.

TOP 10 CLUBS THAT HAVE SPENT THE MOST SEASONS IN THE TOP FLIGHT OF ENGLISH FOOTBALL

	Club	Seasons
1	**Everton**	**107**
2	**Aston Villa**	**99**
3	**Liverpool**	**95**
4	**Arsenal**	**93**
5	**Manchester United**	**85**
6	**Manchester City**	**81**
7 =	**Newcastle United**	**79**
=	**Sunderland**	**79**
9 =	**Chelsea**	**75**
=	**Tottenham Hotspur**	**75**

1888–89 to 2009–10

There are six teams that have played in the top flight of the English Football League for just one season: Northampton Town, Carlisle United, Barnsley, Swindon Town, Leyton Orient and Glossop North End. Glossop played only 34 matches, the fewest of all teams who have played at the top level.

TOP 10 ENGLISH CLUBS WITH THE MOST SEASONS IN THE TOP FLIGHT WITHOUT WINNING THE TITLE

	Club	Seasons
1	Bolton Wanderers	70
2	Middlesbrough	60
3	Birmingham City	55
4	Stoke City	53
5	West Ham United	52
6	Leicester City	46
7	Southampton	35
8	Coventry City	34
9	Notts County	30
10	Blackpool	27

1888–89 to 2008–09

THE 10 LAST CLUBS TO SCORE DOUBLE FIGURES IN ONE ENGLISH LEAGUE GAME

	Winners/losers	Score	Division	Date
1	**Manchester City vs. Huddersfield Town**	10–1	Second	**07 Nov 1987**
2	**Gillingham vs. Chesterfield**	10–0	Third	**05 Sep 1987**
3	**Doncaster Rovers vs. Darlington**	10–0	Fourth	**25 Jan 1964**
4	**Fulham vs. Ipswich Town**	10–1	First	**26 Dec 1963**
5	**Oldham Athletic vs. Southport**	11–0	Fourth	**26 Dec 1962**
6	**Wrexham vs. Hartlepools United**	10–1	Fourth	**03 Mar 1962**
7	**Aston Villa vs. Charlton Athletic**	11–1	Second	**14 Nov 1959**
8	**Hartlepools United vs. Barrow**	10–1	Fourth	**04 Apr 1959**
9	**Tottenham Hotspur vs. Everton**	10–4	First	**11 Oct 1958**
10	**Oldham Athletic vs. Chester**	11–2	Third North	**19 Jan 1952**

Up to and including the 2008–09 season

Manchester City were the last team to score ten goals in an English League game, and in beating Huddersfield Town 10–1 they also equalled a piece of Football League history as only the fifth team to have three players score hat-tricks in one game. Neil McNab opened the scoring for City, after Huddersfield had dominated the opening minutes of the game, but then the floodgates opened as Paul Stewart, Tony Adcock and David White each scored three goals. Huddersfield's consolation goal, in what was their heaviest ever defeat, was a penalty from the former Manchester City player Andy May. The Huddersfield manager at the time was the former Newcastle United, Arsenal and England centre forward Malcolm Macdonald.

THE 10 CLUBS THAT HAVE SCORED THE FEWEST GOALS IN ONE ENGLISH LEAGUE SEASON

	Club	Season	Division	Games played	Goals scored
1	**Loughborough**	1899–1900	Second	34	**18**
2	**Derby County***	2007–08	Premier League	38	**20**
3	**Sunderland**	2002–03	Premier League	38	**21**
4	**Darwen**	1898–99	Second	34	**22**
5	**Doncaster Rovers**	1904–05	Second	34	**23**
6 =	**Loughborough**	1897–98	Second	30	**24**
=	**Watford**	1971–72	Second	42	**24**
=	**Stoke City**	1984–85	First	42	**24**
9 =	**Stoke City**	1888–89	Football League	22	**26**
=	**Crewe Alexandra**	1894–95	Second	30	**26**
=	**Woolwich Arsenal**	1912–13	First	38	**26**
=	**Leicester City**	1977–78	First	42	**26**
=	**Sunderland**	2005–06	Premier League	38	**26**

Up to and including the 2008–09 season

* Top-flight record

TOP 10 CLUBS WITH THE HIGHEST PERCENTAGE OF ENGLISH LEAGUE WINS*

	Club	Seasons	Matches	Wins	Percentage
1	Liverpool	105	4,182	1,981	**47.37**
2	Manchester United	106	4,214	1,990	**47.22**
3	New Brighton Tower	3	102	48	**47.06**
4	Burton Wanderers	3	90	42	**46.67**
5	Arsenal	105	4,182	1,889	**45.17**
6	Stalybridge Celtic	2	76	33	**43.42**
7	Aston Villa	110	4,318	1,804	**41.78**
8	Leeds United	82	3,434	1,430	**41.64**
9	Tottenham Hotspur	90	3,682	1,512	**41.06**
10	Everton	110	4,306	1,765	**40.99**

* All games played in the Football League/Premier League 1888–89 to 2008–09

TOP 10 CLUBS THAT HAVE SCORED THE MOST GOALS IN AN ENGLISH LEAGUE SEASON

	Club	Season	Division	Games played	Goals scored
1	**Peterborough United**	1960–61	Fourth	46	**134**
2 =	**Bradford City**	1928–29	Third North	42	**128**
=	**Aston Villa***	1930–31	First	42	**128**
4 =	**Millwall**	1927–28	Third South	42	**127**
=	**Arsenal**	1930–31	First	42	**127**
6	**Doncaster Rovers**	1946–47	Third North	42	**123**
7	**Middlesbrough**	1926–27	Second	42	**122**
8 =	**Everton**	1930–31	Second	42	**121**
=	**Lincoln City**	1951–52	Third North	46	**121**
10	**Chester**	1964–65	Fourth	46	**119**

Up to and including 2008–09

* Top-flight record

The record for the Premier League is 97 by Manchester United in 1999–2000.

The last team to score over 100 goals in a season was Manchester City, who scored 108 goals in the First Division in 2001–02. Reading came close in 2005–06, when they scored 99 goals in the Championship.

TOP 10 CLUBS WITH THE LONGEST UNBEATEN RUNS IN ENGLISH LEAGUE FOOTBALL*

	Club	From	To	Division	Matches unbeaten
1	**Arsenal**	07 May 2003	16 Oct 2004	Premier League	**49**
2	**Nottingham Forest**	26 Nov 1977	25 Nov 1978	First	**42**
3	**Chelsea**	23 Oct 2004	29 Oct 2005	Premier League	**40**
4	**Leeds United**	26 Oct 1968	26 Aug 1969	First	**34**
5	**Reading**	09 Aug 2005	14 Feb 2006	Championship	**33**
6	**Bristol Rovers**	07 Apr 1973	27 Jan 1974	Third	**32**
7	**Liverpool**	04 May 1987	16 Mar 1988	First	**31**
8 =	**Liverpool**	02 Sep 1893	03 Sep 1894	Second	**30**
=	**Burnley**	06 Sep 1920	25 Mar 1921	First	**30**
=	**Leeds United**	09 May 1973	09 Feb 1974	First	**30**
=	**Arsenal**	23 Dec 2001	06 Oct 2002	Premier League	**30**

Up to and including the 2008–09 season

* Including the Premier League

The world record is 108 games undefeated by ASEC Mimosas (Abidjan) in the Ivory Coast League between 1989 and 1994. Between February 1957 and March 1965, Real Madrid went 122 home league games without defeat. The British record is 62 games by Celtic between November 1915 and April 1917. Arsenal went through the entire season 2003–04 without losing any of their 38 games.

10 LITTLE-KNOWN FACTS ABOUT ENGLISH LEAGUE FOOTBALL

1   The first penalty kick to be awarded in a Football League game was to Wolverhampton Wanderers against Accrington Stanley on 14 September 1891. It was converted by John Heath in a 5–0 victory for Wolves. This first penalty came a season after the spot kick was introduced by the Irish Football Association.

2   Reuben Noble-Lazarus became the Football League's youngest ever player when he came off the bench for Barnsley against Ipswich Town on 30 September 2008. He was just 15 years and 45 days old at the time, beating the 79-year-old record of 15 years and 158 days set by Albert Geldard in 1929. This record was equalled by Ken Roberts of Wrexham in 1951, who made his debut, also at 15 years and 158 days, in a 5–0 defeat at Bradford Park Avenue.

3   The oldest player to appear in a Football League game is Neil McBain at the age of 51 years and 120 days. The manager of New Brighton at the time, his team was hit by injuries for the match against Hartlepools United on 15 March 1947 and McBain, a former outfield player, helped out by playing in goal, conceding three goals in a 3–0 defeat. A former Scottish international, McBain is also one of the few players to have played for both Everton and Liverpool. He was involved with management in England, Scotland and Argentina for more than 33 years.

4   When goalkeeper Peter Shilton played for Leyton Orient against Brighton & Hove Albion on 22 December 1996, he became the first man to play in a 1,000 League games in English football.

5   On 6 November 1968 Tommy Docherty quit as Rotherham United manager. He was appointed as Doug Ellis's first manager at Aston Villa on 18 December 1968, but in between he was manager of Queens Park Rangers for just 29 days, which meant he managed three League clubs within the space of 42 days. Docherty does not hold the record for the shortest period in charge of an English club. That 'honour' belongs to Leroy Rosenior, who was in charge of Torquay United for just ten minutes on 17 May 2007. Immediately after his appointment another press conference was called to say a consortium was taking over the club and bringing in its own manager!

6 In the 1986–87 season goalkeeper Eric Nixon became the first man to play in all four divisions of the Football League in the same season. He was on First Division Manchester City's books but was loaned out to Southampton (also First Division), Bradford City (Second Division), Carlisle United (Third Division) and Wolverhampton Wanderers (Fourth Division). Tony McNamara in 1957–58 and 1958–59 was the first man to play in all four divisions within 12 months when he played for Everton (First Division), Liverpool (Second Division), Crewe Alexandra (Fourth Division) and Bury (Third Division).

7 The only three clubs to be both founder members of the Football League in 1888 and the Premier League in 1992 were Aston Villa, Blackburn Rovers and Everton. Only Everton have never been outside the top two divisions of English Football since the League's inauguration.

8 Goalkeeper John Burridge holds the record for playing for the most Football League clubs – 15. He played for Workington, Blackpool, Aston Villa, Southend United, Crystal Palace, Queens Park Rangers, Wolverhampton Wanderers, Derby County, Sheffield United, Southampton, Newcastle United, Scarborough, Lincoln City, Manchester City and Darlington. He also made League appearances for five Scottish clubs: Hibernian, Aberdeen, Falkirk, Dumbarton and Queen of the South. Despite a career of more than 26 years, he won just two domestic honours in England: the League Cup with Aston Villa in 1977 and the Anglo-Italian Cup with Blackpool in 1971. He also won the Skol Cup (League Cup) in Scotland with Hibernian in 1991.

9 In the days of the two regional Third Divisions – South and North – only one team was promoted to the Second Division at the end of the season. Plymouth Argyle finished second in the Third Division South in six consecutive seasons – 1921–22 to 1926–27. They eventually won promotion in 1929–30.

10 Many teams have now met each other on 100 occasions or more in the Football League but the first time this happened was on 1 January 1953 when Sunderland and Aston Villa played each other for the hundredth time, at Roker Park. The match ended in a 2–2 draw.

Up to and including the 2008–09 season

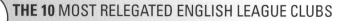
	Club	Times relegated
1	**Notts County**	**15**
2	**Birmingham City/Small Heath**	**13**
3 =	**Bolton Wanderers**	**12**
=	**Grimsby Town**	**12**
=	**Leicester City/Leicester Fosse**	**12**
6 =	**Cardiff City**	**11**
=	**Manchester City**	**11**
=	**Preston North End**	**11**
=	**Sheffield Wednesday**	**11**
10 =	**Bradford City**	**10**
=	**Bristol City**	**10**
=	**Bury**	**10**
=	**Derby County**	**10**
=	**Luton Town**	**10**
=	**Middlesbrough**	**10**
=	**Sheffield United**	**10**
=	**West Bromwich Albion**	**10**

Up to and including 2008–09

In the days before automatic relegation out of the Football League, the bottom four clubs had to apply for re-election to the League. Hartlepools United successfully applied for re-election a record 14 times.

TOP 10 CLUBS WITH THE MOST FA CUP FINAL WINS

	Club	First win	Last win	Total
1	**Manchester United**	1909	2004	**11**
2	**Arsenal**	1930	2005	**10**
3	**Tottenham Hotspur**	1901	1991	**8**
4 =	**Aston Villa**	1887	1957	**7**
=	**Liverpool**	1965	2006	**7**
6 =	**Blackburn Rovers**	1884	1928	**6**
=	**Newcastle United**	1910	1955	**6**
8 =	**Wanderers**	1872	1878	**5**
=	**West Bromwich Albion**	1888	1968	**5**
=	**Everton**	1906	1995	**5**
=	**Chelsea**	1970	2009	**5**

Up to and including the 2008–09 season

Wanderers won the first ever FA Cup final when they beat the Royal Engineers 1–0 at Kennington Oval on 16 March 1872 in front of just 2,000 spectators. The only goal was scored by Morton Betts, who played under the pseudonym A. H. Chequer as he was a former member of the Harrow chequers team.

TOP 10 CLUBS THAT HAVE APPEARED IN THE MOST FA CUP FINALS

	Club	First final	Last final	Total
1	**Manchester United**	1909	2007	**18**
2	**Arsenal**	1927	2005	**17**
3 =	**Everton**	1893	2009	**13**
=	**Newcastle United**	1905	1999	**13**
=	**Liverpool**	1914	2006	**13**
6 =	**West Bromwich Albion**	1886	1968	**10**
=	**Aston Villa**	1887	2000	**10**
8 =	**Tottenham Hotspur**	1901	1991	**9**
=	**Chelsea**	1915	2009	**9**
10 =	**Blackburn Rovers**	1882	1960	**8**
=	**Wolverhampton Wanderers**	1889	1960	**8**
=	**Manchester City**	1904	1981	**8**

Up to and including the 2008–09 season

Blackburn Rovers were the first present-day League team to appear in an FA Cup final, losing 1–0 to Old Etonians in 1892. Arsenal and Manchester United have each appeared in a record 26 semi-finals.

THE 10 LAST NON-TOP-FLIGHT CLUBS TO REACH THE FA CUP FINAL

	Club	Opponents	Result	Year
1	**Cardiff City**	Portsmouth	lost 0–1	**2008**
2	**Millwall**	Manchester United	lost 0–3	**2004**
3	**Sunderland**	Liverpool	lost 0–2	**1993**
4	**Queens Park Rangers**	Tottenham Hotspur	lost 0–1	**1982***
5	**West Ham United**	Arsenal	won 1–0	**1980**
6	**Southampton**	Manchester United	won 1–0	**1975**
7	**Fulham**	West Ham United	lost 0–2	**1975**
8	**Sunderland**	Leeds United	won 1–0	**1973**
9	**Preston North End**	West Ham United	lost 2–3	**1964**
10	**Leicester City**	Wolverhampton Wanderers	lost 1–3	**1949**

Up to and including the 2008–09 season

* Lost after a replay

All of the teams from outside the top flight were from the second level of English League football. The only other non-top-flight team to reach the final since the end of the Second World War is Burnley, who lost 1–0 to Charlton Athletic in 1947.

1 **Walsall** (Third)* 2 vs. Arsenal (First) 0, third round, 1933
Arsenal were the leading team in the 1930s and were on their way to the first of three consecutive League titles when they were drawn against Walsall in the Cup. Without three star players, Arsenal were no match for the Midlanders who won thanks to goals from Gilbert Alsop and Bill Sheppard.

2 **Yeovil Town** (NL) 2 vs. Sunderland (First) 1, fourth round, 1949
Yeovil have had a long tradition of beating League sides in the Cup and in the third round in 1949 they knocked out Second Division Bury before meeting the mighty Sunderland and pulling off one of the biggest FA Cup shocks of all time, winning partly thanks to an Alec Stock goal on the sloping Huish Ground pitch. In the next round Yeovil lost 8–0 to Manchester United.

3 **Mansfield Town** (Third) 3 vs. West Ham United (First) 0, fifth round, 1969
Lying sixth in Division One, West Ham, who had World Cup heroes Bobby Moore, Martin Peters and Geoff Hurst in their side, were strong favourites. But how different it was on a Wednesday evening at Field Mill in front of 21,117 fans as The Stags won. In the sixth round they lost 1–0 at home to Leicester City.

4 **Hereford United** (NL) 2 vs. Newcastle United (First) 1, third round, 1972
Having held Newcastle to a 2–2 draw in the first game, Hereford looked to be going out of the Cup in this replay, until Ronnie Radford scored what is considered one of the best FA Cup goals of all time. Playing a one-two with Brian Owen, he plucked the ball out of the mud and blasted it past the Newcastle goalkeeper Willie McFaul from 27.5 metres (30 yards). The game went to extra time and Ricky George scored the winner as Hereford became the first non-League side to beat top-flight opposition since Yeovil in 1949.

5 Burnley (First) 0 vs. **Wimbledon** (NL) 1, third round, 1975
Had it not been for the exploits of Wimbledon goalkeeper Dickie Guy against Burnley, the Southern Leaguers may well not have written their name into FA Cup giant-killing folklore. Mick Mahon scored the only goal of the game. In the next round a Dave Bassett own goal in the replay against Leeds saw the Dons eliminated. It was hard to imagine that 13 years later Wimbledon would win the FA Cup.

6 Stoke City (Second) 2 vs. **Blyth Spartans** (NL) 3, fourth round, 1978
Stoke beat non-Leaguers Tilbury in the third round and must have been hoping for a good Cup run when they saw the draw for the fourth round, but their north-eastern opponents had other ideas. The Spartans came from 2–1 down to win 3–2 thanks to goals from Terry Johnson (2) and Steve Carney, the winning goal from Johnson coming in the last minute.

7 Birmingham City (First) 1 vs. **Altrincham** (NL) 2, third round, 1986
Second to bottom in the First Division, a Conference side in the third round of the Cup was probably the last thing Birmingham wanted and their fans suspected what might happen because only 6,636 turned up at St Andrews. Birmingham opened the scoring through Robert Hopkins before Ronnie Ellis equalized and then Hopkins scored an own goal past goalkeeper David Seaman.

8 **Sutton United** (NL) 2 vs. Coventry City (First) 1, third round, 1989
Coventry had won the Cup just two seasons earlier, but those statistics counted for nothing in the early rounds of the FA Cup as Coventry lost to non-League opposition. Tony Rains and Matthew Hanlan scored the winning goals for the Isthmian League team.

9 West Bromwich Albion (Second) 2 vs. **Woking** (NL) 4, third round, 1991
Hovering near the bottom of the Second Division, West Brom were always vulnerable. Despite trailing 1–0 at half-time, Woking took advantage of Albion's lacklustre defence that allowed Terry Worsfold and Tim Buzaglo, who scored a hat-trick, to score four goals in a comfortable win. In the next round Woking narrowly lost to Everton 1–0.

10 **Wrexham** (Fourth) 2 vs. Arsenal (First) 1, third round, 1992
Wrexham were the League's last club the previous season while Arsenal were the League's top-flight champions, but 13,342 fans witnessed one of the great FA Cup giant-killing acts as Wrexham came from a goal down at half-time to beat Arsenal with goals from Mickey Thomas and Steve Watkin, eight minutes from time.

** Information in brackets indicates the level in English football the club was playing in at the time.
NL = non-League club*

10 FA CUP FACTS

1   When they won the FA Cup in 1948, Manchester United became the first and, so far, only club to beat top-flight opposition in every round on the way to lifting the trophy. In the third round they beat Aston Villa 6–4, in the fourth round they beat Liverpool 3–0, in the fifth round they beat Charlton Athletic 2–0 and in the sixth round they beat Preston North End 4–1. They beat Derby County 3–1 in the semi-final at Hillsborough and in the final beat Blackpool 4–2 at Wembley Stadium. Not one of their games was played at Old Trafford because their ground was out of commission due to war damage. They played their 'home' ties against Liverpool, Charlton and Preston at Goodison Park, Leeds Road, Huddersfield and Villa Park respectively.

2   Leicester City have played in more finals without winning the Cup than any other team – they have played in four finals and lost all four. Their first final was in 1949 when they lost 3–1 to Wolverhampton Wanderers. They were beaten 2–0 by Tottenham Hotspur when Spurs won the double in 1961. Two years later Leicester were beaten by Manchester United 3–1 when, surprisingly, Leicester started the match as favourites. Their fourth and final appearance was in 1969 when they lost 1–0 to Manchester City.

3   Eric Cantona of Manchester United became the first and, so far, only player to score two penalties in one final in 1994. The first was the opening goal of the game on 60 minutes and the second just six minutes later. Both goals were scored past Chelsea's Russian goalkeeper Dmitri Kharine, who conceded two more goals from Mark Hughes and Brian McClair as United went on to win 4–0.

4   When they won the FA Cup by beating Liverpool in 1988, Wimbledon became the 42nd team to win the FA Cup. They are the last team to have won the trophy for the first time. They were captained by Dave Beasant, the first goalkeeper to captain an FA Cup-winning team and also the first goalkeeper to save a penalty in an FA Cup final in a Wembley Cup Final. Remarkably it was only Wimbledon's 11th season in the Football League.

5   Of the 11 founder members of the Football League still active, Stoke City are the only club never to have won the FA Cup. Remarkably they have appeared in only three semi-finals; in 1899 when they lost to Derby County and in 1971 and 1972 when they lost to Arsenal in a replay on both occasions.

6   Four clubs have reached the FA Cup final and been relegated in the same season: Manchester City (1926), Leicester City (1969), Brighton & Hove Albion (1983) and Middlesbrough (1997).

7   The fastest FA Cup final goal was scored after just 25 seconds by Louis Saha for Everton against Chelsea in 2009. Chelsea went on to win 2–1. The final was played on 30 May, the latest date any FA Cup final has been played. Saha's record beat that of Chelsea's Roberto di Matteo, who netted after just 43 seconds in the 1997 final against Middlesbrough.

8   As a result of bad weather, many third-round FA Cup ties were postponed on 5 January 1963. The Lincoln City vs. Coventry City tie was postponed 15 times and eventually played on 7 March.

9   Seven Scottish clubs have played in the FA Cup: Cowlairs, Heart of Midlothian, Partick Thistle, Queen's Park, Rangers, Renton and Third Lanark. Queen's Park reached two finals, losing to Blackburn Rovers in both 1884 (2–1) and 1885 (2–0), while Rangers reached the semi-final on one occasion, losing to Aston Villa 3–1 at Nantwich Road, Crewe in 1887.

10   The only time the FA Cup has been taken out of England was in 1927 when Cardiff City beat Arsenal 1–0 in the final. They had a chance to win the Cup two years earlier but lost the 1925 final 1–0 to Sheffield United. They had another opportunity to emulate the 1927 winners in 2008 but lost, again to a solitary goal, when beaten by Portsmouth.

Up to and including the 2008–09 season

TOP 10 CLUBS THAT HAVE WON THE MOST TROPHIES IN ENGLISH FOOTBALL*

	Club	First	Second	Third	Fourth	FAC	FLC	Total
1	**Liverpool**	18	4	0	0	7	7	**36**
2	**Manchester United**	18	2	0	0	11	3	**34**
3	**Arsenal**	13	0	0	0	10	2	**25**
4	**Aston Villa**	7	2	1	0	7	5	**22**
5	**Tottenham Hotspur**	2	2	0	0	8	4	**16**
6 =	**Everton**	9	1	0	0	5	0	**15**
=	**Manchester City**	2	7	0	0	4	2	**15**
=	**Wolverhampton Wanderers**	3	3	2	1	4	2	**15**
9 =	**Chelsea**	3	2	0	0	5	4	**14**
=	**Sunderland**	6	5	1	0	2	0	**14**

Up to and including the 2008–09 season

* Major trophies open to all League teams: League titles, FA Cup and League Cup

First = First level of English football: Football League 1888–1892, First Division 1892–1992; Premier League 1992–present

Second = Second level of English football: Second Division 1892–1992, First Division 1992–2004, Championship 2004–present

Third = Third level of English football: Third Division 1920–21, Third Division North and South 1921–58, Third Division 1958–92, Second Division 1992–2004, League 1 2004–present

Fourth = Fourth level of English football: Fourth Division 1958–92, Third Division 1992–2004, League 2 2004–present

FAC = FA Cup 1872–present

FLC = Football League Cup 1961–present

Preston North End and Wolverhampton Wanderers are the only two teams to have won titles at all four levels of the English game, with Wolves standing alone as the only one to have won titles at all four levels and also won the FA Cup and League Cup.

TOP 10 CLUBS WITH THE MOST FOOTBALL LEAGUE CUP WINS*

	Club	First win	Last win	Total
1	**Liverpool**	1981	2003	7
2	**Aston Villa**	1961	1996	5
3 =	**Chelsea**	1965	2007	4
=	**Tottenham Hotspur**	1971	2008	4
=	**Nottingham Forest**	1978	1990	4
6 =	**Leicester City**	1964	2000	3
=	**Manchester United**	1992	2009	3
8 =	**Norwich City**	1962	1985	2
=	**Manchester City**	1970	1976	2
=	**Wolverhampton Wanderers**	1974	1980	2
=	**Arsenal**	1987	1993	2

Up to and including 2009

* Now known as the Carling Cup, but previously known as: the Worthington Cup, Coca-Cola Cup, Rumbelows League Cup, Littlewoods Cup, Milk Cup and, from 1960 to 1981, simply as the Football League Cup or just League Cup

Aston Villa beat Rotherham United 3–2 on aggregate to win the first trophy in 1961. From then until 1966 all finals were over two legs but since 1967 it has been a single-game final. Third Division Queens Park Rangers beat First Division West Bromwich Albion 3–2 in the first final at Wembley Stadium.

THE 10 FIRST TEAMS TO COMPLETE THE LEAGUE AND CUP DOUBLE

1   Preston North End 1888–89

Football League record:	Pl	W	D	L	F	A	Pts
	22	18	4	0	74	15	40

FA Cup final: Preston North End 3 Wolverhampton Wanderers 0
Kennington Oval, Attendance: 22,000

2   Aston Villa 1896–97

Division One record:	Pl	W	D	L	F	A	Pts
	30	21	5	4	73	38	47

FA Cup final: Aston Villa 3 Everton 2
Crystal Palace, Attendance: 65,891

3   Tottenham Hotspur 1960–61

Division One record:	Pl	W	D	L	F	A	Pts
	42	31	4	7	115	55	66

FA Cup final: Tottenham Hotspur 2 Leicester City 0
Wembley Stadium, Attendance: 100,000

4   Arsenal 1970–71

Division One record:	Pl	W	D	L	F	A	Pts
	42	29	7	6	71	29	65

FA Cup final: Arsenal 2 Liverpool 1 (aet)
Wembley Stadium, Attendance: 100,000

5   Liverpool 1985–86

Division One record:	Pl	W	D	L	F	A	Pts
	42	26	10	6	89	37	88

FA Cup final: Liverpool 3 Everton 1
Wembley Stadium, Attendance: 98,000

6   Manchester United 1993–94

Premier League record:	Pl	W	D	L	F	A	Pts
	42	27	11	4	80	38	92

FA Cup final: Manchester United 4 Chelsea 0
Wembley Stadium, Attendance: 79,634

7   Manchester United 1995–96

Premier League record:	Pl	W	D	L	F	A	Pts
	38	25	7	6	73	35	82

FA Cup final: Manchester United 1 Liverpool 0
Wembley Stadium, Attendance: 79,007

8   Arsenal 1997–98

Premier League record:	Pl	W	D	L	F	A	Pts
	38	23	9	6	68	33	78

FA Cup final: Arsenal 2 Newcastle United 0
Wembley Stadium, Attendance: 79,183

9   Manchester United 1998–99

Premier League record:	Pl	W	D	L	F	A	Pts
	38	22	13	3	80	37	79

FA Cup final: Manchester United 2 Newcastle United 0
Wembley Stadium, Attendance: 79,101

10   Arsenal 2001–02

Premier League record:	Pl	W	D	L	F	A	Pts
	38	26	9	3	79	36	87

FA Cup final: Arsenal 2 Chelsea 0
Millennium Stadium, Attendance: 73,963

These are the only teams to have achieved this double as at the end of the 2008–09 season

TOP 10 CLUBS WITH THE MOST FA COMMUNITY SHIELD WINS*

	Club	First win	Last win	Outright wins	Shared wins	Total wins
1	**Manchester United**	1908	2008	13	4	**17**
2	**Liverpool**	1964†	2006	10	5	**15**
3	**Arsenal**	1930	2004	11	1	**12**
4	**Everton**	1928	1995	8	1	**9**
5	**Tottenham Hotspur**	1921	1991†	4	3	**7**
6 =	**Wolverhampton Wanderers**	1949†	1960†	1	3	**4**
=	**Chelsea**	1955	2009	4	0	**4**
8	**Manchester City**	1937	1972	3	0	**3**
9 =	**West Bromwich Albion**	1920	1954†	1	1	**2**
=	**Burnley**	1960†	1973	1	1	**2**
=	**Leeds United**	1969	1992	2	0	**2**

Up to and including 2009

* Including the Charity Shield 1908–2001

† Shared win

The Charity Shield was first contested in 1908 between the winners of the Football League (Manchester United) and the Southern League champions (Queens Park Rangers). United won the first trophy by winning 4–0 in a replay. The first time it was contested by the FA Cup winners and League champions was in 1921 and, with a few exceptions, this has been the case ever since. All finals have been played at Wembley Stadium since 1974, except those years when Wembley was being rebuilt when it was played at the Millennium Stadium in Cardiff. It was renamed the FA Community Shield in 2002.

TOP 10 CLUBS WITH THE MOST SCOTTISH TOP-FLIGHT LEAGUE TITLES*

	Club	First title	Last title	Total
1	**Rangers**	1891†	2009	**52**
2	**Celtic**	1893	2008	**42**
3 =	**Heart of Midlothian**	1895	1960	**4**
=	**Hibernian**	1903	1952	**4**
=	**Aberdeen**	1955	1985	**4**
6	**Dumbarton**	1891†	1892	**2**
7 =	**Third Lanark**	1904	1904	**1**
=	**Motherwell**	1932	1932	**1**
=	**Dundee**	1962	1962	**1**
=	**Kilmarnock**	1965	1965	**1**
=	**Dundee United**	1983	1983	**1**

First Division 1890–91 to 1974–75, Premier Division 1975–76 to 1997–98, Premier League (SPL) 1998–99 to 2008–09

† Rangers and Dumbarton shared the first title in 1891

Dumbarton have uniquely won titles in all four levels of Scottish football.

TOP 10 CLUBS WITH THE MOST SCOTTISH FA CUP WINS

	Club	First win	Last win	Total
1	**Celtic**	1892	2007	**34**
2	**Rangers**	1894	2009	**33**
3	**Queen's Park**	1874	1893	**10**
4 =	**Aberdeen**	1947	1990	**7**
=	**Heart of Midlothian**	1891	2006	**7**
6 =	**Vale of Leven**	1877	1879	**3**
=	**Kilmarnock**	1920	1997	**3**
=	**St Mirren**	1926	1987	**3**
=	**Clyde**	1939	1958	**3**
10 =	**Renton**	1885	1888	**2**
=	**Hibernian**	1887	1902	**2**
=	**Third Lanark**	1889	1905	**2**
=	**Falkirk**	1913	1957	**2**
=	**Dunfermline Athletic**	1961	1968	**2**
=	**Motherwell**	1952	1991	**2**

Up to and including the 2008–09 season

Queen's Park won the first Scottish FA Cup final in 1874 by beating Clydesdale 2–0 at the first Hampden Park in front of a crowd of 3,500. Despite having appeared in 103 finals between them, Celtic and Rangers have met just 15 times in the final.

TOP 10 CLUBS WITH THE MOST SCOTTISH LEAGUE CUP WINS

	Club	First win	Last win	Total
1	**Rangers**	1947	2008	**25**
2	**Celtic**	1957	2009	**14**
3	**Aberdeen**	1956	1996	**5**
4	**Heart of Midlothian**	1955	1963	**4**
5 =	**East Fife**	1948	1954	**3**
=	**Dundee**	1952	1974	**3**
=	**Hibernian**	1973	2007	**3**
8	**Dundee United**	1980	1981	**2**
9 =	**Motherwell**	1951	1951	**1**
=	**Partick Thistle**	1972	1972	**1**
=	**Raith Rovers**	1995	1995	**1**
=	**Livingston**	2004	2004	**1**

Up to and including 2008–09

Rangers beat Aberdeen 4–0 to win the first Scottish League Cup final in 1947. The forerunner of the League Cup was the Scottish Southern League Cup, which was contested during the Second World War. The last winners were Aberdeen, who beat Rangers in the 1946 final.

The trophy was sponsored for the first time in 1979 when it became known as the Bell's League Cup. It has subsequently been known as: the Skol Cup (1984–93), Coca-Cola Cup (1994–98), CIS Insurance Cup (1999–2008) and it is now known as the Co-operative Insurance Cup.

TOP 10 SCOTTISH LEAGUE GOALSCORERS

	Player	Years	Club(s)	Goals
1	**Jimmy McGrory**	1922–38	Celtic, Clydebank	**410**
2	**Bob McPhail**	1923–39	Airdrie, Arthurlie, Rangers	**305**
3 =	**Hugh Ferguson**	1916–30	Motherwell, Dundee	**285**
=	**Ally McCoist**	1978–2001	St Johnstone, Rangers, Kilmarnock	**285**
5	**Willie Reid**	1904–22	Morton, Third Lanark, Motherwell, Rangers, Albion Rovers	**275**
6	**Willie McFadyen**	1921–37	Motherwell, Bo'ness, Clyde	**260**
7	**Jimmy McColl**	1913–32	Celtic, Partick Thistle, Hibernian, Leith	**258**
8	**Bob Ferrier**	1917–37	Motherwell	**255**
9	**David Wilson**	1928–39	Hamilton	**254**
10	**Gordon Wallace**	1963–80	Montrose, Raith Rovers, Dundee, Dundee United	**251**

Up to and including the 2008–09 season

TOP 10 SCOTTISH PREMIER LEAGUE GOALSCORERS

	Player	Years	Club(s)	Goals
1	**Henrik Larsson**	1998–2004	Celtic	**158**
2	**Kris Boyd**	2000–09	Kilmarnock, Rangers	**142**
3	**John Hartson**	2001–06	Celtic	**88**
4	**Scott McDonald**	2004–09	Motherwell, Celtic	**83**
5	**Derek Riordan**	2001–09	Hibernian, Celtic	**71**
6	**Nacho Novo**	2002–09	Dundee, Rangers	**67**
7 =	**Billy Dodds**	1998–2006	Aberdeen, Dundee United, Rangers	**65**
=	**Stephen Crawford**	1998–2008	Hibernian, Dunfermline Athletic, Dundee United, Aberdeen	**65**
=	**Chris Sutton**	2000–06	Celtic	**65**
10	**Steve Lovell**	2002–09	Dundee, Aberdeen, Falkirk	**63**

Since the formation of the SPL in 1998 to 2008–09

Henrik Larsson was the SPL's top scorer in five of the first six years of the league's existence. Larsson's Celtic teammate Mark Viduka was the other.

TOP 10 PLAYERS WITH THE MOST SCOTTISH LEAGUE APPEARANCES

	Player/club	Years	Clubs	Appearances
1	**Graeme Armstrong**	1975–2001	Meadowbank Thistle, Stirling Albion, Berwick Rangers, Stenhousemuir, Alloa Athletic	**910**
2	**Andy Millen**	1986–2008	St Johnstone, Alloa Athletic, Hamilton Academical, Kilmarnock, Hibernian, Raith Rovers, Ayr United, Morton, Clyde, St Mirren	**739**
3	**Keith Knox**	1982–2005	Stranraer, Clyde, Alloa Athletic, Gretna, Stenhousemuir	**717**
4	**Harry Cairney**	1980–2003	Airdrieonians, Stenhousemuir, Brechin City	**710**
5	**John Martin**	1980–2001	Airdrieonians, Albion Rovers, Cowdenbeath	**701**
6	**Gordon Marshall**	1982–2005	East Stirling, East Fife, Falkirk, Celtic, St Mirren, Kilmarnock, Motherwell	**667**
7	**Davie Cooper**	1974–95	Clydebank, Rangers, Motherwell	**663**
8	**Tommy Bryce**	1980–2000	Kilmarnock, Stranraer, Queen of the South, Clydebank, Ayr United, Partick Thistle, Arbroath	**656**
9	**Kenny Thomson**	1970–92	Dunfermline Athletic, Alloa Athletic, St Johnstone, Cowdenbeath	**653**
10	**Jim Gallacher**	1969–92	Arbroath, Clydebank	**649**

Up to and including 2008–09
Source: David Ross

When Andy Millen made his final appearance for St Mirren against Hearts on 15 March 2008, he was 42 years 279 days old, the oldest man to play in the Scottish Premier League.

THE 10 LAST NON-TOP-FLIGHT CLUBS TO REACH THE SCOTTISH FA CUP FINAL

	Club	Opponents	Year	Result
1	**Queen of the South** (Second)*	Rangers	2008	lost **2–3**
2	**Gretna** (Third)	Hearts	2006	drew **1–1** †
3	**Falkirk** (Second)	Kilmarnock	1997	lost **0–1**
4	**Airdrieonians** (Second)	Celtic	1995	lost **0–1**
5	**East Fife** (Second)	Kilmarnock	1938	won **4–2** ‡
6	**East Fife** (Second)	Celtic	1927	lost **1–3**
7	**Queen's Park** (NL)	Celtic	1900	lost **3–4**
8	**Kilmarnock** (Second)	Rangers	1898	lost **0–2**
9	**Dumbarton** (Second)	Rangers	1897	lost **1–5**
10	**Renton** (Second)	Saint Bernard's	1895	lost **1–2**

Up to and including 2009

* Information in brackets indicates level at which they were playing at the time of the final. NL = non-League club

† Lost 4–2 on penalties

‡ Won after a replay

East Fife have uniquely won the Scottish FA Cup and League Cup as a Second Division side, beating Kilmarnock in the Scottish FA Cup (as above) and Falkirk 4–1 in a replay in the 1947–48 League Cup final.

THE 10 CLUBS THAT HAVE CONCEDED THE MOST GOALS IN A SCOTTISH LEAGUE SEASON

	Club	Season	Division	Games played	Goals conceded
1	**Edinburgh City**	1931–32	Second	38	**146**
2	**Brechin City**	1937–38	Second	34	**139**
3	**Forfar Athletic**	1938–39	Second	38	**138**
4	**Leith Athletic**	1931–32	First	38	**137**
5	**Edinburgh City**	1937–38	Second	34	**135**
6	**Edinburgh City**	1934–35	Second	34	**134**
7 =	**Edinburgh City**	1932–33	Second	34	**133**
=	**Montrose**	1955–56	B*	36	**133**
9	**East Stirlingshire**	1938–39	Second	34	**130**
10	**Morton**	1937–38	First	38	**127**

Up to and including 2008–09

*Between 1946 and 1956 the Scottish Second Division became known as the B Division

The last team to concede over 100 goals was Berwick Rangers in 2007–08 when they conceded 101 goals from 36 matches. The SPL record is 83 goals: Aberdeen, from 36 matches in 1999–2000; Gretna in 2007–08 from 38 matches.

10 UNUSUAL NICKNAMES OF SCOTTISH CLUBS

Club

Nickname

1 Aberdeen — **The Dons**
It is believed they were named The Dons because the city has two universities.

2 Arbroath — **The Red Lichties**
'Red lichties' means 'red lights' and refers to the red lights at the entrance to
Arbroath harbour used for guiding fishing boats into port.

3 Ayr United — **The Honest Men**
Their nickname comes from a line in a Robert Burns poem: 'Auld Ayr, where ne'er
a toon surpasses for honest men and bonnie lasses.'

4 Dundee United — **The Terrors**
Thought to have first been credited to the team when, as a Second Division team,
they beat the mighty Celtic 4–3 in the first round of the Scottish Cup in January
1949.

5 Falkirk — **The Bairns**
From the Falkirk motto: 'Better meddle wi the de'il than the bairns of Falkirk.'

6 Montrose — **Gable Enders**
During a period of rebuilding of the town in the 1700s, the town council gave
permission for a row of houses to be demolished. Once completed, property
owners on either side sought permission to extend their houses and the easiest
way of doing so was by building gable ends, a nickname given to the town, as well
as its football team.

7 Peterhead — **Blue Toon**
So named after the distinctive blue clothing the fishermen of Peterhead started
wearing to distinguish themselves from the folk of Fraserburgh.

8 Queen of the South — **The Doonhammers**
People from Dumfries, where Queen of the South are based, are called
Doonhammers, 'doon hame' being the Scots dialect for 'down home'. This is
because of the town's position in the south of Scotland.

9 St Johnstone — **Super Js**
This refers to the fact that they are the only League club in Scotland or England
with a 'J' in their name.

10 St Mirren — **The Buddies**
They are based in Paisley, where locals are known as Paisley Buddies.

TOP 10 BIGGEST WINS IN THE SCOTTISH LEAGUE*

	Winners/losers	Season	Division	Score
1	**Airdrieonians vs. Dundee Wanderers**	1894–95	Second	**15–1**
2	**Aberdeen Reserves vs. Montrose**	1950–51	C†	**13–0**
3	**East Fife vs. Edinburgh City**	1937–38	Second	**13–2**
4 =	**Dundee United vs. East Stirling**	1935–36	Second	**12–1**
=	**Motherwell vs. Dundee United**	1953–54	Second	**12–1**
6	**King's Park vs. Forfar Athletic**	1929–30	Second	**12–2**
7	**Celtic vs. Dundee**	1895–96	First	**11–0**
8 =	**Albion Rovers vs. Dumbarton**	1925–26	Second	**11–1**
=	**Airdrieonians vs. Falkirk**	1950–51	A†	**11–1**
=	**Clyde vs. Cowdenbeath**	1951–52	Second	**11–1**
=	**Hibernian‡ vs. Airdrieonians**	1959–60	First	**11–1**
=	**Hibernian vs. Hamilton Academical**	1965–66	First	**11–1**

Up to and including the 2008–09 season

* Based on score of the winning team

† Between 1946–56 the Scottish First and Second Divisions became known as A and B Divisions. A third division, called C Division, was added in 1946–47 and this consisted largely of reserve teams from A and B Divisions

‡ Away team

Three other teams have scored 11 goals: Dunfermline Athletic 11 Stenhousemuir 2, 1930–31; Dundee United 11 East Stirling 2, 1935–36; Morton 11 Raith Rovers 2, 1935–36.

TOP 10 MOST NORTHERLY SCOTTISH LEAGUE GROUNDS

	Club	Stadium/location
1	**Elgin City**	Borough Briggs, Elgin
2	**Ross County**	Victoria Park, Dingwall
3	**Peterhead**	Balmoor Stadium, Peterhead
4	**Inverness Caledonian Thistle**	Caledonian Stadium, Inverness
5	**Aberdeen**	Pittodrie, Aberdeen
6	**Brechin City**	Glebe Park, Brechin
7	**Montrose**	Links Park, Montrose
8	**Forfar Athletic**	Station Park, Forfar
9	**Arbroath**	Gayfield Park, Arbroath
10	**Dundee**	Dens Park, Dundee

Dens Park, the home of Dundee, and Tannadice, Dundee United's ground, are the two grounds closest to each other in British League football. The most northerly part of Dens Park is at coordinate: 56° 28' 31.7" north while Tannadice is at: 56° 28' 30.51" north, which means Dens Park is further north by about 20 metres (66 feet).

TOP 10 CLUBS WITH THE MOST WELSH CUP WINS

	Club	First win	Last win	Total
1	**Wrexham/Wrexham Town**	1878	1995	**23**
2	**Cardiff City**	1912	1993	**22**
3	**Swansea Town/City**	1913	1991	**10**
4	**Druids**	1880	1904	**8**
5	**Bangor City**	1896	2009	**7**
6 =	**Shrewsbury Town**	1891	1985	**6**
=	**Barry Town**	1955	2003	**6**
8	**Chirk**	1887	1894	**5**
9	**Rhyl**	1952	2006	**4**
10 =	**Wellington Town***	1902	1940	**3**
=	**Chester/Chester City**	1908	1947	**3**
=	**Merthyr Tydfil**	1949	1987	**3**

Up to and including 2009

* Later Telford United

The inaugural Welsh Cup final was contested in 1878 when Wrexham beat Druids 1–0 to win the first trophy. Shrewsbury, Chester and Wellington are three of the nine English clubs to have won the Welsh Cup, the others are: Crewe Alexandra, Oswestry United, Oswestry White Stars, Tranmere Rovers, Bristol City and South Liverpool.

TOP 10 LONGEST CLUB NAMES IN WELSH LEAGUE FOOTBALL*

	Club	Division	Letters
1	**Treharris Athletic Western**	Two	**24**
2	**Cambrian & Clydach Vale BGC†**	One	**23**
3 =	**Ento Aberaman Athletic**	One	**20**
=	**Penrhiwceiber Rangers**	Two	**20**
5 =	**Haverfordwest County**	Premier League	**19**
=	**Briton Ferry Athletic**	Three	**19**
=	**Newport Civil Service**	Three	**19**
8 =	**Bryntirion Athletic**	One	**18**
=	**Cardiff Corinthians**	One	**18**
10	**Airbus UK Broughton**	Premier League	**17**

* In the Welsh Premier League and Welsh Football League Divisions One, Two and Three in the 2008–09 season

† If its full title was adopted then Cambrian & Clydach Vale Boys and Girls Club would be the longest named team in the Welsh League

Sources: The Welsh Football League and the Welsh Premier League

Treharris Athletic Western, based at Treharris near Merthyr Tydfil, were founded in 1889 and are the oldest club in South Wales. They were founder members of the Welsh Football League in 1902–03.

TOP 10 CLUBS WITH THE MOST IRISH LEAGUE TITLES*

	Club	First title	Last title	Total
1	**Linfield**	1891	2008	**48**
2	**Glentoran**	1894	2009	**23**
3	**Belfast Celtic**	1900	1948	**14**
4	**Distillery**	1896	1963	**6†**
5	**Crusaders**	1973	1997	**4**
=	**Portadown**	1990	2002	**4**
7 =	**Cliftonville**	1906	1998	**3**
=	**Glenavon**	1952	1960	**3**
9 =	**Queen's Island**	1924	1924	**1**
=	**Ards**	1958	1958	**1**
=	**Derry City**	1965	1965	**1**
=	**Coleraine**	1974	1974	**1**

Up to and including 2008–09

* Irish Football League 1891–2003, Irish Premier League 2004–08, IFA Premiership 2008–09

† Includes one shared title

TOP 10 CLUBS THAT HAVE SPENT THE MOST SEASONS IN IRISH LEAGUE FOOTBALL*

	Club	Debut season	Seasons
1 =	**Cliftonville**	1890	**109**
=	**Glentoran**	1890	**109**
=	**Linfield**	1890	**109**
=	**Lisburn Distillery/Distillery**	1890	**109**
5	**Glenavon**	1911	**87**
6	**Portadown**	1924	**78**
7 =	**Ards**	1923	**76**
=	**Coleraine**	1927	**76**
9	**Ballymena/Ballymena United**	1928	**75**
10	**Bangor**	1927	**70**

Up to and including 2008–09

* *Irish Football League 1891–2003, Irish Premier League 2004–08, IFA Premiership 2008–09*

Founded in 1890 with eight teams, seven of them from Belfast, the Irish League is the second oldest national football league in the world after the English League. The four founder members no longer in the League are: Ulster, Oldpark, Clarence and Milford (Co. Armagh). The first champions were Linfield.

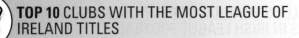
	Club	First title	Last title	Total
1	**Shamrock Rovers**	1923	1994	**15**
2	**Shelbourne**	1926	2006	**13**
3	**Bohemians**	1924	2009	**11**
4	**Dundalk**	1933	1995	**9**
5 =	**Cork United/Cork Athletic**	1941	1951	**7**
=	**St Patrick's Athletic**	1952	1999	**7**
7	**Waterford United**	1966	1973	**6**
8	**Drumcondra**	1948	1965	**5**
9 =	**St James's Gate**	1922	1940	**2**
=	**Sligo Rovers**	1937	1977	**2**
=	**Limerick**	1960	1980	**2**
=	**Athlone Town**	1981	1983	**2**
=	**Derry City**	1989	1997	**2**
=	**Cork City**	1993	2005	**2**

Up to and including the 2008 season

The first League of Ireland champions were St James's Gate in 1921–22. From its inauguration until 2006, the League was run by the clubs, but a merger in 2006 saw the League being run by the FAI (Football Association of Ireland) and renamed the FAI League of Ireland, with a Premier Division and First Division. The season now starts in March and runs to October.

TOP 10 CLUBS WITH THE MOST TOP-FLIGHT LEAGUE TITLES IN THE BRITISH ISLES*

	Club	Country	Titles
1	**Rangers**	Scotland	**52**
2	**Linfield**	Northern Ireland	**48**
3	**Celtic**	Scotland	**42**
4	**Glentoran**	Northern Ireland	**23**
5 =	**Liverpool**	England	**18**
=	**Manchester United**	England	**18**
7	**Shamrock Rovers**	Republic of Ireland	**15**
8	**Belfast Celtic**	Northern Ireland	**14**
9 =	**Arsenal**	England	**13**
=	**Shelbourne**	Republic of Ireland	**13**

Up to and including the 2008–09 season

* Top-flight titles in England, Northern Ireland, Scotland, Wales and the Republic of Ireland

The most titles won by a Welsh team is seven by Barry Town.

TOP 10 LONGEST CLUB NAMES IN ENGLISH AND SCOTTISH LEAGUE FOOTBALL*

	CLUBS	Letters
1	**Inverness Caledonian Thistle**	**26**
2	**Wolverhampton Wanderers**	**22**
3 =	**Brighton & Hove Albion**	**19**
=	**Dunfermline Athletic**	**19**
5 =	**Dagenham & Redbridge**	**18**
=	**Hamilton Academical**	**18**
=	**Peterborough United**	**18**
=	**Sheffield Wednesday**	**18**
=	**West Bromwich Albion**	**18**
10 =	**Accrington Stanley**	**17**
=	**East Stirlingshire**	**17**
=	**Heart of Midlothian**	**17**
=	**Queens Park Rangers**	**17**

* Based on names of teams playing in the English and Scottish Leagues in 2009–10

TOP 10 CLUBS WITH THE MOST POINTS IN A PREMIER LEAGUE SEASON

	Club	Season	Pts
1	**Chelsea**	2004–05	**95**
2	**Manchester United**	1993–94*	**92**
3 =	**Manchester United**	1999–2000	**91**
=	**Chelsea**	2005–06	**91**
5 =	**Arsenal**	2003–04	**90**
=	**Manchester United**	2008–09	**90**
7 =	**Blackburn Rovers**	1994–95*	**89**
=	**Manchester United**	2006–07	**89**
9	**Manchester United†**	1994–95*	**88**
10 =	**Arsenal**	1992–93*	**87**
=	**Manchester United**	2007–08	**87**

Up to and including 2008–09

* Maximum number of points 126; all other seasons had a maximum of 114 points available

† Premier League runners-up

In Chelsea's record-breaking season, they lost only one game, away to Manchester City. They also dropped points in eight drawn games against Tottenham Hotspur, Bolton Wanderers, Manchester City, Birmingham City and Arsenal (at home), Aston Villa, Arsenal and Newcastle United (away).

TOP 10 PREMIER LEAGUE CLUBS

	Club	Pl	W	D	L	F	A	Pts
1	**Manchester United**	658	422	143	93	1,288	562	**1,409**
2	**Arsenal**	658	352	180	126	1,116	584	**1,236**
3	**Chelsea**	658	335	176	147	1,045	630	**1,181**
4	**Liverpool**	658	331	168	159	1,069	634	**1,161**
5	**Aston Villa**	658	247	198	213	836	772	**939**
6	**Newcastle United**	616	247	165	204	883	777	**906**
7	**Tottenham Hotspur**	658	237	174	247	884	892	**885**
8	**Everton**	658	228	179	251	813	845	**863**
9	**Blackburn Rovers**	582	230	156	196	792	715	**846**
10	**West Ham United**	540	187	135	218	633	744	**696**

From 1992–93 to the end of the 2008–09 season

Source: FA Premier League

Manchester United's 422 wins is a Premier League record. The record for most drawn games is 198 by Aston Villa, and the most defeats 251 by Everton. Manchester United also have a record win percentage of 64.13 and a best points average of 2.14 points per game. Their goal difference of 726 is also a Premier League best, while Sunderland's minus 164 is the worst. Middlesbrough are the only Premier League team to have had points deducted: for failing to fulfil a fixture with Blackburn Rovers they had three points taken away in the 1996–97 season, which ultimately cost them their Premier League place as they were relegated at the end of the season.

As at the start of the 2009–10 season, Barnsley and Swindon Town are the only clubs to have played just one season in the Premier League, while Burnley made their debut in 2009–10.

The Premier League was founded on 17 July 1991 when the basic principles for establishing the new league were agreed, including negotiating their own TV rights independently of the Football Association or Football League.

All members of the First Division resigned on 20 February 1992 and in May that year the Premier League was established as a limited company and sold TV rights to Sky TV for £191 million. Now, a four-year deal for broadcasting Premier League matches is almost ten times that amount. The level of income has also brought an influx of top-quality footballers from all over the world. In the inaugural season, there were only 11 non-British or Irish footballers in the league, whereas today there are more than 250.

The League was sponsored for the first time in 1993 when it became known as the FA Carling Premiership. Barclaycard became the new sponsors in 2001 when the league was known as the Barclaycard Premiership. From 2004–07 it was the Barclays Premiership and since 2007, the Barclays Premier League.

There were 22 teams in the Premier League in its first three seasons but since 1995–96 there have been only 20. Burnley, in 2009–10, were the Premier League's 43rd team. Only seven teams have played in each of the league's 17 seasons: Arsenal, Aston Villa, Chelsea, Everton, Liverpool, Manchester United and Tottenham Hotspur. Only four different teams have won the Premier League title: Manchester United (11 titles), Arsenal (3), Chelsea (2) and Blackburn Rovers (1). Manchester United uniquely have never finished lower than third.

The league kicked off over the weekend of 15/16/17 August 1992 with the opening weekend results:

Arsenal	2	4	Norwich City
Chelsea	1	1	Oldham Athletic
Coventry City	2	1	Middlesbrough
Crystal Palace	3	3	Blackburn Rovers
Everton	1	1	Sheffield Wednesday
Ipswich Town	1	1	Aston Villa
Leeds United	2	1	Wimbledon
Manchester City	1	1	Queen's Park Rangers
Nottingham Forest	1	0	Liverpool
Sheffield United	2	1	Manchester United
Southampton	0	0	Tottenham Hotspur

The Nottingham Forest–Liverpool game was the first live Premier League game broadcast on BSkyB.

TOP 10 PREMIER LEAGUE GOALSCORERS

	Player	Club(s)	Appearances	Goals
1	**Alan Shearer**	Blackburn Rovers, Newcastle United	441	**260**
2	**Andy Cole**	Newcastle United, Manchester United, Blackburn Rovers, Fulham, Manchester City, Portsmouth	413	**187**
3	**Thierry Henry**	Arsenal	252	**174**
4	**Robbie Fowler**	Liverpool, Leeds United, Manchester City	377	**163**
5	**Les Ferdinand**	Queens Park Rangers, Newcastle United, Tottenham Hotspur, West Ham United, Leicester City, Bolton Wanderers	351	**149**
6	**Teddy Sheringham**	Nottingham Forest, Tottenham Hotspur, Manchester United, Portsmouth, West Ham United	418	**147**
7	**Michael Owen**	Liverpool, Newcastle United	287	**144**
8	**Jimmy Floyd Hasselbaink**	Leeds United, Chelsea, Middlesbrough, Charlton Athletic	288	**127**
9	**Dwight Yorke**	Aston Villa, Manchester United, Blackburn Rovers, Birmingham City, Sunderland	375	**123**
10	**Robbie Keane**	Coventry City, Leeds United, Tottenham Hotspur, Liverpool	305	**115**

Up to and including the 2008–09 season

Source: FA Premier League

Of the 16 players to have scored 100 or more Premier League goals as at the end of the 2008–09 season, Thierry Henry had the best strike rate of one goal for every 1.45 games.

PREMIER LEAGUE GOALSCORING MILESTONES

Goal	Scorer	For/Against	Date
1	**Brian Deane**	Sheffield United vs. Manchester United	15 Aug 1992
500	**Lawrie Sanchez**	Wimbledon vs. Norwich City	05 Dec 1992
1,000	**Mike Newell**	Blackburn Rovers vs. Nottingham Forest	07 Apr 1993
2,000	**Mick Quinn**	Coventry City vs. Manchester City	19 Feb 1994
3,000	**Klas Ingesson**	Sheffield Wednesday vs. Everton	26 Dec 1994
4,000	**Alan Shearer**	Blackburn Rovers vs. West Ham United	02 Dec 1995
5,000	**Andy Townsend*** **Chris Sutton***	Aston Villa vs. Southampton Blackburn Rovers vs. Leicester City	07 Dec 1996 07 Dec 1996
6,000	**Nathan Blake**	Bolton Wanderers vs. Wimbledon	29 Nov 1997
7,000	**Dennis Bergkamp**	Arsenal vs. Aston Villa	13 Dec 1998
8,000	**Gus Poyet**	Chelsea vs. Sunderland	04 Dec 1999
9,000	**Nicky Butt**	Manchester United vs. Derby County	25 Nov 2000
10,000	**Les Ferdinand**	Tottenham Hotspur vs. Fulham	15 Dec 2001
11,000	**Jay-Jay Okocha**	Bolton Wanderers vs. Blackburn Rovers	07 Dec 2002
12,000	**Alan Shearer**	Newcastle United vs. Tottenham Hotspur	13 Dec 2003
13,000	**Fredi Kanoute**	Tottenham Hotspur vs. Middlesbrough	28 Nov 2004
14,000	**Jermain Defoe**	Tottenham Hotspur vs. Birmingham City	26 Dec 2005
15,000	**Mortiz Volz**	Fulham vs. Chelsea	30 Dec 2006
16,000	**Tomas Rosicky**	Arsenal vs. Fulham	19 Jan 2008
17,000	**Peter Lovenkrands**	Newcastle United vs. West Bromwich Albion	07 Feb 2009

Some sources list Townsend as being the scorer of the 5,000th goal and some list Sutton. As they both scored at around 33 minutes of their respective matches both can justifiably lay claim to being the scorer of that historic goal.

TOP 10 PLAYERS WITH THE MOST APPEARANCES IN THE PREMIER LEAGUE

	Player	Club(s)	Appearances
1	**David James**	Liverpool, Aston Villa, West Ham United, Manchester City, Portsmouth	**547**
2	**Gary Speed**	Leeds United, Everton, Newcastle United, Bolton Wanderers	**535**
3	**Ryan Giggs**	Manchester United	**521**
4	**Sol Campbell**	Tottenham Hotspur, Arsenal, Portsmouth	**483**
5	**Alan Shearer**	Blackburn Rovers, Newcastle United	**441**
6	**Emile Heskey**	Leicester City, Liverpool, Birmingham City, Wigan Athletic, Aston Villa	**437**
7	**Frank Lampard**	West Ham United, Chelsea	**427**
8	**Gareth Southgate**	Crystal Palace, Aston Villa, Middlesbrough	**426**
9	**Teddy Sheringham**	Nottingham Forest, Tottenham Hotspur, Manchester United, Portsmouth, West Ham United	**418**
10	**Andy Cole**	Newcastle United, Manchester United, Blackburn Rovers, Fulham, Manchester City, Portsmouth, Sunderland	**413**

Up to and including the 2008–09 season

Source: FA Premier League

BEHIND THE RECORD –
DAVID JAMES'S CAREER

David James made his Football League debut for Watford in a 2–1 home defeat by Millwall in the Second Division on 25 August 1990. He made his Premier League debut on the opening weekend of the new league for Liverpool at Nottingham Forest. Forest won 1–0 thanks to a Teddy Sheringham goal, in the first live televised Premier League game. To the end of the 2008–09 season, David James had made 661 Football League and Premier League appearances in total.

His 547 Premier League appearances have been for the following clubs:

Liverpool	**214**
Aston Villa	**67**
West Ham United	**64**
Manchester City	**93**
Portsmouth	**109**

During his time as a Premier League player, James has won the FA Cup twice, with Liverpool in 1995 and with Portsmouth in 2008. He has played for England 49 times since making his debut against Mexico in 1997.

THE 10 CLUBS WITH THE FEWEST POINTS IN A PREMIER LEAGUE SEASON

	Club	Season	Pts
1	**Derby County**	2007–08	**11**
2	**Sunderland**	2005–06	**15**
3	**Sunderland**	2002–03	**19**
4	**Watford**	1999–2000	**24**
5 =	**Bradford City**	2000–01	**26**
=	**West Bromwich Albion**	2002–03	**26**
7	**Ipswich Town**	1994–95*	**27**
8 =	**Leicester City**	2001–02	**28**
=	**Watford**	2006–07	**28**
10 =	**Leicester City**	1994–95*	**29**
=	**Bolton Wanderers**	1995–96	**29**

Up to and including 2008–09

* Maximum number of points 126; all other seasons had a maximum of 114 points available

In collecting just 11 points in 2007–08, Derby County lost 29 of their 38 matches.

TOP 10 CLUBS WITH THE MOST CONSECUTIVE WINS IN THE PREMIER LEAGUE*

	Club	From	To	Wins
1	**Arsenal**	10 Feb 2002	18 Aug 2002	**14**
2	**Manchester United**	11 Mar 2000	20 Aug 2000	**12**
3 =	**Liverpool**	29 Oct 2005	31 Dec 2005	**10**
=	**Chelsea**	19 Nov 2005	15 Jan 2006	**10**
5 =	**Sheffield Wednesday**	28 Dec 1992	23 Feb 1993	**7**
=	**Blackburn Rovers**	29 Oct 1994	10 Dec 1994	**7**
=	**Wimbledon**	04 Sep 1996	19 Oct 1996	**7**
=	**Newcastle United**	04 Sep 1996	20 Oct 1996	**7**
=	**Leeds United**	17 Feb 1999	03 Apr 1999	**7**
10 =	**Everton**	19 Oct 2002	23 Nov 2002	**6**
=	**Wigan Athletic**	24 Sep 2005	05 Nov 2005	**6**

Up to and including 2008–09

* Best unbeaten run only for each club

Arsenal's run eventually came to an end on 24 August 2002 when they drew 2–2 at West Ham United.

TOP 10 CLUBS WITH THE MOST CONSECUTIVE GAMES WITHOUT DEFEAT IN THE PREMIER LEAGUE*

	Club	From	To	Games undefeated
1	**Arsenal**	07 May 2003	16 Oct 2004	**49**
2	**Chelsea**	23 Oct 2004	29 Oct 2005	**40**
3	**Manchester United**	26 Dec 1998	25 Sep 1999	**29**
4	**Nottingham Forest**	26 Feb 1995	6 Nov 1995	**25**
5	**Liverpool**	30 Mar 2008	29 Oct 2008	**17**
6 =	**Leeds United**	30 Aug 1993	08 Dec 1993	**14**
=	**Wimbledon**	04 Sep 1996	14 Dec 1996	**14**
=	**Aston Villa**	02 May 1998	14 Nov 1998	**14**
9	**Manchester City**	01 Apr 2005	10 Sep 2005	**13**
10 =	**Blackburn Rovers**	29 Oct 1994	14 Jan 1995	**12**
=	**Sheffield Wednesday**	19 Oct 1996	11 Jan 1997	**12**
=	**Newcastle United**	15 Mar 1997	23 Aug 1997	**12**

Up to and including 2008–09

* Best unbeaten run only for each club

BEHIND THE RECORD –
ARSENAL'S 49-GAME RUN

Arsenal's record-breaking run started with a 6–1 win over Southampton at Highbury on 7 May 2003, thanks to hat-tricks from Robert Pires and Jermaine Pennant. They won their next match, the last one of the 2002–03 season, and then went through the 2003–04 season undefeated in all their 38 games – the first club since Preston North End in 1888–89 to achieve that feat – although Preston played 16 fewer games than Arsenal.

On 25 August 2004 Arsenal broke Nottingham Forest's all-time Football League record of 42 matches without defeat, but while attempting to make it 50 games without loss, Arsenal's amazing run eventually came to an end on 24 October 2004 when they lost 2–0 at Old Trafford to two late goals – a penalty from Van Nistelrooy and a 90th-minute goal from Wayne Rooney, celebrating his 19th birthday.

During their unbeaten run, Arsenal's biggest win was 5–0 against Leeds at Highbury on 16 April 2004 when Thierry Henry netted four times. Henry was Arsenal's top scorer during their record-breaking run with 39 goals. Robert Pires was the next best with 23 goals. During their 49 games, they kept 20 clean sheets, 19 of them credited to Jans Lehmann and the other to David Seaman, in his last League game for the Gunners on the final day of the 2002–03 season.

TOP 10 CLUBS WITH THE MOST CONSECUTIVE HOME WINS IN THE PREMIER LEAGUE

	Club	Run started	Run ended	Ended by	Wins
1	**Newcastle United**	14 May 1995	04 Mar 1996	Manchester United	**14**
2 =	**Blackburn Rovers**	30 Oct 1993	24 Apr 1994	Queens Park Rangers	**13**
=	**Arsenal**	14 Feb 2005	18 Dec 2005	Chelsea	**13**
=	**Chelsea**	23 Apr 2005	22 Jan 2006	Charlton Athletic	**13**
5	**Manchester United**	27 Sep 2008	14 Mar 2009	Liverpool	**12**
6	**Liverpool**	02 Feb 2008	20 Sep 2008	Stoke City	**10**
7	**Manchester City**	15 Aug 2007	27 Dec 2007	Blackburn Rovers	**9**
8 =	**Aston Villa**	12 Dec 1992	10 Mar 1993	Tottenham Hotspur	**7**
=	**West Ham United**	27 Sep 1997	31 Jan 1998	Everton	**7**
=	**Leeds United**	19 Sep 1999	03 Jan 2000	Aston Villa	**7**

Up to and including the 2008–09 season

Newcastle's 14-game run was ended by a 51st-minute Eric Cantona goal as Manchester United won 1–0 at St James' Park. The defeat jolted Newcastle's impetus in their ultimately doomed attempt to win their first Premier League title.

During their eight-game unbeaten run at home in 1997–98, West Ham lost all the away games they played.

THE 10 CLUBS WITH THE MOST CONSECUTIVE
GAMES WITHOUT A WIN IN THE PREMIER LEAGUE*

	Club	From	To	Winless games
1	**Derby County**	22 Sep 2007	11 May 2008	**32**
2	**Sunderland**	21 Dec 2002	17 Sep 2005	**26**
3	**Norwich City**	01 Apr 1995	13 Nov 2004	**21**
4	**Nottingham Forest**	08 Sep 1998	16 Jan 1999	**19**
5 =	**Leicester City**	08 Dec 2001	23 Mar 2002	**16**
=	**West Bromwich Albion**	11 Feb 2006	30 Aug 2008	**16**
7 =	**Swindon Town**	14 Aug 1993	20 Nov 1993	**15**
=	**Manchester City**	29 Apr 1995	28 Oct 1995	**15**
=	**Crystal Palace**	29 Nov 1997	14 Mar 1998	**15**
=	**Ipswich Town**	25 Aug 2001	17 Dec 2001	**15**

Up to and including the 2008–09 season

* Longest winless run only for each club

Derby County won just one game in the Premier League in 2007–08, 1–0 against Newcastle on 17 September. Of their remaining 37 games that season they drew eight and lost 29.

TOP 10 PLAYERS WHO HAVE SCORED THE MOST GOALS IN A PREMIER LEAGUE SEASON

	Player/club	Season	Goals
1 =	**Andy Cole** Newcastle United	1993–94	**34**
=	**Alan Shearer** Blackburn Rovers	1994–95	**34**
3 =	**Alan Shearer** Blackburn Rovers	1993–94	**31**
=	**Alan Shearer** Blackburn Rovers	1995–96	**31**
=	**Cristiano Ronaldo** Manchester United	2007–08	**31**
6 =	**Kevin Phillips** Sunderland	1999–2000	**30**
=	**Thierry Henry** Arsenal	2003–04	**30**
8	**Robbie Fowler** Liverpool	1995–96	**28**
9	**Thierry Henry** Arsenal	2005–06	**27**
10 =	**Matt Le Tissier** Southampton	1993–94	**25**
=	**Chris Sutton** Norwich City	1993–94	**25**
=	**Robbie Fowler** Liverpool	1994–95	**25**
=	**Les Ferdinand** Newcastle United	1995–96	**25**
=	**Alan Shearer** Newcastle United	1996–97	**25**
=	**Ruud van Nistelrooy** Manchester United	2002–03	**25**
=	**Thierry Henry** Arsenal	2004–05	**25**

Up to and including 2008–09

TOP 10 OLDEST GOALSCORERS IN THE PREMIER LEAGUE

	Player/club	Opponents	Date	Age years	days
1	**Teddy Sheringham** West Ham United	Portsmouth	26 Dec 2006	**40**	**268**
2	**Stuart Pearce** West Ham United	Southampton	25 Nov 2000	**38**	**215**
3	**Mark Hughes** Blackburn Rovers	Leicester City	30 Mar 2002	**38**	**149**
4	**Tugay Kerimoglu** Blackburn Rovers	Portsmouth	30 Nov 2008	**38**	**98**
5	**Mick Harford** Wimbledon	West Ham United	18 Mar 1997	**38**	**34**
6	**Gary Speed** Bolton Wanderers	Reading	25 Aug 2007	**37**	**351**
7	**Peter Schmeichel*** Aston Villa	Everton	20 Oct 2001	**37**	**336**
8	**Les Ferdinand** Bolton Wanderers	Manchester United	11 Sep 2004	**37**	**268**
9	**John Wark** Ipswich Town	Blackburn Rovers	28 Jan 1995	**37**	**177**
10	**Richard Gough** Everton	Southampton	21 Aug 1999	**37**	**138**

Up to and including the 2008–09 season

* Goalkeeper Peter Schmeichel's only Premier League goal

TOP 10 YOUNGEST GOALSCORERS IN THE PREMIER LEAGUE

	Player/club	Opponents	Date	Age years	days
1	**James Vaughan** Everton	Crystal Palace	10 Apr 2005	**16**	**270**
2	**James Milner** Leeds United	Sunderland	26 Dec 2002	**16**	**356**
3	**Wayne Rooney** Everton	Arsenal	19 Oct 2002	**16**	**360**
4	**Cesc Fabregas** Arsenal	Blackburn Rovers	25 Aug 2004	**17**	**113**
5	**Michael Owen** Liverpool	Wimbledon	06 May 1997	**17**	**143**
6	**Andy Turner** Tottenham Hotspur	Everton	05 Sep 1992	**17**	**166**
7	**Federico Macheda** Manchester United	Aston Villa	05 Apr 2009	**17**	**226**
8	**Mikael Forssell** Chelsea	Nottingham Forest	20 Feb 1999	**17**	**342**
9	**Danny Cadamarteri** Everton	Barnsley	20 Sep 1997	**17**	**343**
10	**Danny Welbeck** Manchester United	Stoke City	15 Nov 2008	**17**	**355**

Up to and including the 2008–09 season

Some authorities quote Darren Bent as scoring at the age of 17 years and 77 days for Ipswich Town against Middlesbrough on 24 April 2002, which is indeed when he scored his first Premier League goal. However, he was born on 6 February 1984 (not 1985, as erroneously stated in some sources), which made him 18 years and 77 days at the time.

THE 10 FIRST PLAYERS TO SCORE 100 PREMIER LEAGUE GOALS

	Player	100th goal for/against	Date
1	**Alan Shearer**	Blackburn Rovers vs. Tottenham Hotspur	**30 Dec 1995**
2	**Les Ferdinand**	Newcastle United vs. Nottingham Forest	**11 May 1997**
3	**Ian Wright**	Arsenal vs. Bolton Wanderers	**13 Sep 1997**
4	**Robbie Fowler**	Liverpool vs. Southampton	**16 Jan 1999**
5	**Andy Cole**	Manchester United vs. Arsenal	**17 Feb 1999**
6	**Dwight Yorke**	Manchester United vs. Derby County	**25 Nov 2000**
7	**Matt Le Tissier**	Southampton vs. Sunderland	**01 Apr 2001**
8	**Teddy Sheringham**	Tottenham Hotspur vs. Chelsea	**16 Sep 2001**
9	**Dion Dublin**	Aston Villa vs. West Ham United	**23 Nov 2002**
10	**Michael Owen**	Liverpool vs. West Bromwich Albion	**24 Apr 2003**

Alan Shearer's first goal in the Premier League was on the league's opening day, 15 August 1992, when he netted twice for Blackburn Rovers in a 3–3 draw at Crystal Palace. Shearer's first start in League football was for Southampton against Arsenal at The Dell on 9 April 1988 when he marked the occasion with a hat-trick, his first goals in League football. Also, at the age of 17 years 240 days, he became the youngest scorer of a hat-trick in the First Division. On 20 April 2002 he became the first and, so far, only player to achieve 200 Premier League goals when he scored against Charlton Athletic for Newcastle United at St James' Park.

TOP 10 PLAYERS WITH THE MOST HAT-TRICKS IN THE PREMIER LEAGUE

	Player	Club(s)*	Total no. of hat-tricks
1	**Alan Shearer**	Blackburn Rovers (9), Newcastle United (2)	**11**
2	**Robbie Fowler**	Liverpool (8), Leeds United (1)	9
3 =	**Thierry Henry**	Arsenal	8
=	**Michael Owen**	Liverpool (7), Newcastle United (1)	8
5 =	**Andy Cole**	Manchester United (3), Newcastle United (2)	5
=	**Ruud van Nistelrooy**	Manchester United	5
=	**Ian Wright**	Arsenal	5
8 =	**Kevin Campbell**	Arsenal (2), Nottingham Forest (1), Everton (1)	4
=	**Les Ferdinand**	Queens Park Rangers (2), Newcastle United (1), Tottenham Hotspur (1)	4
=	**Jimmy Floyd Hasselbaink**	Chelsea (3), Middlesbrough (1)	4
=	**Matt Le Tissier**	Southampton	4
=	**Teddy Sheringham**	Tottenham Hotspur (2), Portsmouth (1), Manchester United (1)	4
=	**Chris Sutton**	Blackburn Rovers (3), Norwich City (1)	4
=	**Dwight Yorke**	Manchester United (3), Aston Villa (1)	4

Up to and including the 2008–09 season

* Figures in brackets indicate the number of hat-tricks scored for each club

Alan Shearer's 11 hat-tricks were scored against: Leeds United, Ipswich Town, West Ham United (twice), Queens Park Rangers, Tottenham Hotspur, Bolton Wanderers, Nottingham Forest, Coventry City, Leicester City and Sheffield Wednesday.

TOP 10 OLDEST OUTFIELD PLAYERS IN THE PREMIER LEAGUE

	Player/club	Opponents	Date	Age years	days
1	**Teddy Sheringham** West Ham United	Manchester City	30 Dec 2006	40	272
2	**Gordon Strachan** Coventry City	Derby County	03 May 1997	40	83
3	**Bryan Robson** Middlesbrough	Arsenal	01 Jan 1997	39	356
4	**Dean Windass** Hull City	Manchester City	26 Dec 2008	39	269
5	**Ray Wilkins** Queens Park Rangers	Nottingham Forest	05 May 1996	39	234
6	**Trevor Francis** Sheffield Wednesday	Coventry City	20 Nov 1993	39	215
7	**Colin Cooper** Middlesbrough	Fulham	07 May 2006	39	68
8	**Nigel Winterburn** West Ham United	Liverpool	02 Feb 2003	39	53
9	**Stuart Pearce** West Ham United	Middlesbrough	19 May 2001	39	25
10	**Richard Gough** Everton	Bradford City	28 Apr 2001	39	23

Up to and including the 2008–09 season

The oldest player to play in the Premier League is goalkeeper John Burridge who was 43 years and 162 days when he played his final game in the top flight, in goal for Manchester City on 14 May 1995.

TOP 10 CLUBS THAT HAVE SCORED THE MOST GOALS IN THE PREMIER LEAGUE

	Club	Games played	Goals scored
1	**Manchester United**	658	**1,285**
2	**Arsenal**	658	**1,115**
3	**Liverpool**	658	**1,069**
4	**Chelsea**	658	**1,045**
5	**Newcastle United**	616	**884**
6	**Tottenham Hotspur**	658	**883**
7	**Aston Villa**	658	**836**
8	**Everton**	658	**813**
9	**Blackburn Rovers**	582	**792**
10	**Leeds United**	468	**641**

Up to and including the 2008–09 season

Source: FA Premier League

The very first Premier League goal was scored by Sheffield United (Brian Deane) on 15 August 1992 against Manchester United, who scored the first of their 1,285 goals that day through Mark Hughes.

TOP 10 CLUBS THAT HAVE SCORED THE MOST GOALS IN A PREMIER LEAGUE SEASON

	Club	Season	Goals scored
1	**Manchester United**	1999–2000	97
2 =	**Manchester United**	2001–02	87
=	**Arsenal**	2004–05	87
4	**Arsenal**	2002–03	85
5	**Manchester United**	2006–07	83
6	**Newcastle United**	1993–94	82
7 =	**Manchester United**	1993–94	80
=	**Blackburn Rovers**	1994–95	80
=	**Manchester United**	1998–99	80
=	**Manchester United**	2007–08	80

Up to and including the 2008–09 season

Manchester United's biggest wins in their record-breaking season were: 7–1 vs. West Ham United, 5–1 vs. Newcastle United and 5–1 vs. Everton. They scored four goals in a game on five more occasions, including another four past West Ham at Upton Park. United failed to score in just two matches, against Chelsea (0–5) and Newcastle United (0–3).

TOP 10 CLUBS THAT HAVE CONCEDED THE MOST GOALS IN THE PREMIER LEAGUE

	Club	Games played	Goals conceded
1	Tottenham Hotspur	658	892
2	Everton	658	845
3	Newcastle United	616	777
4	Aston Villa	658	772
5	West Ham United	540	744
6	Middlesbrough	536	741
7	Southampton	506	738
8	Blackburn Rovers	582	715
9	Liverpool	658	634
10	Manchester City	468	629

Up to and including the 2008–09 season

Source: FA Premier League

The first of Tottenham Hotspur's record 892 goals was conceded at White Hart Lane when they lost 2–0 to Coventry City on 19 August 1992.

TOP 10 CLUBS THAT HAVE KEPT THE MOST CLEAN SHEETS IN THE PREMIER LEAGUE

	Club	Games played	Clean sheets
1	**Manchester United**	658	**292**
2	**Chelsea**	658	**271**
3	**Arsenal**	658	**265**
4	**Liverpool**	658	**250**
5	**Aston Villa**	658	**207**
6	**Everton**	658	**206**
7	**Blackburn Rovers**	582	**186**
8	**Tottenham Hotspur**	658	**168**
9	**Newcastle United**	616	**165**
10	**Leeds United**	468	**157**

Up to and including the 2008–09 season

Source: FA Premier League

Manchester United did not keep their first clean sheet until their fourth Premier League game, when they won 1–0 at Southampton. It was their first Premier League win. Between 15 November 2008 and 18 February 2009 Manchester United kept a record 14 consecutive Premier League clean sheets. Chelsea kept a record 25 clean sheets in a Premier League season in 2004–05. Petr Cech was in goal on each occasion. The goalkeeper with the most clean sheets to his credit in the Premier League is David James with 167.

TOP 10 CLUBS WITH THE MOST PREMIER LEAGUE STOPPAGE-TIME GOALS 2008–09*

	Club	Stoppage-time goals
1	**Liverpool**	**9**
2	**Arsenal**	**8**
3	**Everton**	**6**
4	**Manchester United**	**5**
5 =	**Aston Villa**	**4**
=	**Newcastle United**	**4**
=	**Stoke City**	**4**
8 =	**Blackburn Rovers**	**3**
=	**Manchester City**	**3**
=	**Sunderland**	**3**
=	**Tottenham Hotspur**	**3**

* Stoppage time at the end of 90 minutes

Liverpool's nine stoppage-time goals were against: Arsenal, Blackburn Rovers, Chelsea, Fulham, Manchester City, Manchester United, Middlesbrough, Portsmouth and West Bromwich Albion.

TOP 10 PLAYERS WITH THE MOST APPEARANCES AS A SUBSTITUTE IN THE PREMIER LEAGUE

	Player	Club(s)	Appearances as a substitute
1	**Nwankwo Kanu**	Arsenal, West Bromwich Albion, Portsmouth	**101**
2	**Jermain Defoe**	West Ham United, Tottenham Hotspur, Portsmouth	**86**
3	**Ole Gunnar Solskjaer**	Manchester United	**84**
4	**Duncan Ferguson**	Everton, Newcastle United	**83**
5	**Shoala Ameobi**	Newcastle United	**81**
6	**Danny Murphy**	Liverpool, Charlton Athletic, Tottenham Hotspur, Fulham	**79**
7 =	**Luis Boa Morte**	Arsenal, Southampton, Fulham, West Ham United	**74**
=	**Paul Scholes**	Manchester United	**74**
9	**Ryan Giggs**	Manchester United	**72**
10 =	**James Beattie**	Blackburn Rovers, Southampton, Everton	**70**
=	**Andy Clarke**	Wimbledon	**70**
=	**Lomano Lua-Lua**	Newcastle United, Portsmouth	**70**

Up to and including the 2008–09 season

TOP 10 FOREIGN COUNTRIES PROVIDING THE MOST PLAYERS TO THE PREMIER LEAGUE*

	Country	Players
1	France	141
2	Netherlands	76
3 =	Norway	49
=	Sweden	49
5	Italy	46
6	Denmark	44
7 =	Australia	40
=	Spain	40
9 =	Brazil	37
=	Portugal	37

From 1992–93 to the start of the 2008–09 season
* Excluding UK countries and Republic of Ireland

THE 10 PLAYERS WITH THE MOST RED CARDS IN THE PREMIER LEAGUE

	Player	Red cards
1 =	**Richard Dunne**	**8**
=	**Duncan Ferguson**	**8**
=	**Patrick Vieira**	**8**
4 =	**Vinnie Jones**	**7**
=	**Roy Keane**	**7**
=	**Alan Smith**	**7**
7 =	**Luis Boa Morte**	**6**
=	**Nicky Butt**	**6**
=	**Eric Cantona**	**6**
=	**Andy Cole**	**6**
=	**John Hartson**	**6**
=	**Franck Queudrue**	**6**

From 1992–93 to the end of the 2008–09 season
Source: FA Premier League

THE 10 PLAYERS WHO HAVE COMMITTED THE MOST FOULS IN THE PREMIER LEAGUE

	Player	Club(s)	Fouls
1	**Kevin Davies**	Southampton, Blackburn Rovers, Bolton Wanderers	**626**
2	**Gavin McCann**	Everton, Sunderland, Aston Villa, Bolton Wanderers	**458**
3	**Gareth Barry**	Aston Villa	**456**
4	**George Boateng**	Coventry City, Aston Villa, Middlesbrough, Hull City	**455**
5	**Alan Smith**	Leeds United, Manchester United, Newcastle United	**439**
6	**Emile Heskey**	Leicester City, Liverpool, Birmingham City, Wigan Athletic, Aston Villa	**437**
7	**Luis Boa Morte**	Arsenal, Southampton, Fulham, West Ham United	**408**
8	**Robbie Savage**	Leicester City, Birmingham City, Blackburn Rovers, Derby County	**380**
9	**James Beattie**	Blackburn Rovers, Southampton, Everton, Stoke City	**361**
10	**Tim Cahill**	Everton	**340**

Up to and including the 2008–09 season
Source: FA Premier League

THE 10 CLUBS WITH THE WORST DISCIPLINARY RECORDS IN THE PREMIER LEAGUE

	Games	Matches played	Yellow cards	Red cards	Points*
1	**Everton**	658	951	64	**1,143**
2	**Chelsea**	658	982	49	**1,129**
3	**Blackburn Rovers**	582	901	66	**1,099**
4	**Arsenal**	658	931	54	**1,093**
5	**Tottenham Hotspur**	658	908	44	**1,040**
6	**West Ham United**	540	862	50	**1,012**
7	**Middlesbrough**	536	849	42	**975**
8	**Newcastle United**	616	806	53	**965**
9	**Manchester United**	658	825	43	**954**
10	**Aston Villa**	658	835	36	**943**

From 1992–93 to the end of the 2008–09 season

* Based on one point for a yellow card and three for a red card

Source: FA Premier League

Only Liverpool, out of the seven teams who have played in every season of the Premier League, do not appear on this list. They have had 754 yellow cards and 34 reds for a total of 856 points.

THE 10 WORST TRANSFER DEALS IN THE PREMIER LEAGUE*

	Player	From/to	Fee (£)	Year
1	**Juan Sebastian Veron**	Lazio to Manchester United	28,100,000	**2001**
		Manchester United to Chelsea	14,000,000	**2003**
2	**Andriy Shevchenko**	AC Milan to Chelsea	31,000,000	**2006**
3	**Thomas Brolin**	Parma to Leeds United	4,500,000	**1995**
4	**Massimo Taibi**	Venezia to Manchester United	4,400,000	**1999**
5	**Bosko Balaban**	Dinamo Zagreb to Aston Villa	5,800,000	**2001**
6	**Sergei Rebrov**	Dynamo Kiev to Tottenham Hotspur	11,000,000	**2000**
7	**Francis Jeffers**	Everton to Arsenal	8,000,000	**2001**
8	**Michael Owen**	Real Madrid to Newcastle United	16,000,000	**2005**
9	**Joey Barton**	Manchester City to Newcastle United	5,800,000	**2007**
10	**Steve Marlet**	Lyon to Fulham	11,500,000	**2001**

Source: Daily Mail *article 'The biggest transfer flops in Premier League history' 15 May 2009*

TOP 10 CLUBS WITH THE MOST TOP-FLIGHT FRENCH LEAGUE TITLES

	Club	First title	Last title	Total
1	**Saint-Etienne**	1957	1981	**10**
2 =	**Marseille***	1937	1992	**8**
=	**Nantes**	1965	2001	**8**
4 =	**AS Monaco**	1961	2000	**7**
=	**Lyon**	2002	2008	**7**
6 =	**Reims**	1949	1962	**6**
=	**Bordeaux†**	1950	2009	**6**
8	**Nice**	1951	1959	**4**
9	**Lille OSC‡**	1933	1954	**3**
10 =	**Sète**	1934	1939	**2**
=	**Sochaux**	1935	1938	**2**
=	**Paris Saint-Germain**	1986	1994	**2**

Up to and including 2008–09

* Marseille won the title in 1993 but were stripped of it for alleged match-fixing and no champions were declared in the 1992–93 season

† Formerly Girondins ASP

‡ Includes one win as Olympique Lillois

Regionalized French Leagues were held until 1932, when the first national professional league (Ligue 1) was established. Its first champions were Lille OSC.

TOP 10 GOALSCORERS IN THE FRENCH LIGUE 1

	Player	Years	Appearances	Goals
1	**Delio Onnis**	1971–86	449	**299**
2	**Bernard Lacombe**	1969–87	497	**255**
3	**Herve Revelli**	1965–78	389	**216**
4	**Thadée Cosiowski**	1947–61	286	**206**
5	**Roger Piantoni**	1950–66	394	**203**
6	**Joseph Ujlaki**	1947–64	438	**189**
7	**Fleury Di Nallo**	1960–75	425	**187**
8 =	**Gunnar Andersson**	1950–60	324	**179**
=	**Carlos Bianchi**	1973–80	220	**179**
10	**Hassan Akesbi**	1955–64	293	**173**

From 1945–46 to 2008–09

The most appearances in Ligue 1 is 602 by Jean-Luc Ettori, all for AS Monaco, between 1975–94. Roger Courtois scored 193 goals, but many of them were before 1945 and records are incomplete before this time.

TOP 10 HIGHEST-SCORING GAMES IN THE GERMAN LEAGUE*

	Winners/losers	Season	League	Score
1	**Borussia Mönchengladbach** vs. Borussia Dortmund	1977–78	Bundesliga	**12–0**
2 =	**Borussia Mönchengladbach** vs. Schalke 04	1966–67	Bundesliga	**11–0**
=	**Arminia Bielefeld** vs. Arminia Hannover	1979–80	2.Bundesliga	**11–0**
4 =	**Bayern Munich** vs. Borussia Dortmund	1971–72	Bundesliga	**11–1**
=	**Borussia Dortmund** vs. Arminia Bielefeld	1982–83	Bundesliga	**11–1**
6 =	**Borussia Mönchengladbach** vs. Borussia Neunkirchen	1967–68	Bundesliga	**10–0**
=	**Karlsruher** vs. ESV Ingolstadt	1979–80	2.Bundesliga	**10–0**
=	**Borussia Mönchengladbach** vs. Eintracht Braunschweig	1984–85	Bundesliga	**10–0**
9	**Bayern Hof** vs. BSV Schwenningen	1976–77	2.Bundesliga	**10–1**
10 =	**Freiburger** vs. Würzburger FV 04	1979–80	2.Bundesliga	**10–2**
=	**St Pauli** vs. Wolfsburg	1974–75	2.Bundesliga	**10–2**

* Based on the score of the winning team in the Bundesliga and 2.Bundesliga up to and including 2008–09

Source: Karel Stokkermans, RSSSF

Borussia Mönchengladbach's record win was on 29 April 1978, the last day of the 1977–78 season. They led 6–0 at half-time; Heynckes scored four of the 12 goals while Nielsen added a hat-trick.

TOP 10 CLUBS WITH THE MOST GERMAN BUNDESLIGA TITLES

	Club	First title	Last title	Total
1	**Bayern Munich**	1969	2008	**20**
2	**Borussia Mönchengladbach**	1970	1977	**5**
3	**Werder Bremen**	1965	2004	**4**
4 =	**Hamburger SV**	1979	1983	**3**
=	**VbF Stuttgart**	1984	2007	**3**
=	**Borussia Dortmund**	1995	2002	**3**
7 =	**Cologne**	1964	1978	**2**
=	**Kaiserslautern**	1991	1998	**2**
9 =	**1860 Munich**	1966	1966	**1**
=	**Eintracht Braunschweig**	1967	1967	**1**
=	**Nuremburg**	1968	1968	**1**
=	**Wolfsburg**	2009	2009	**1**

From 1963–64 to 2008–09

Hamburg is the only team to have played in every Fußball-Bundesliga season. The word 'Bundesliga' refers to the premier division of any sport in Germany (and Austria). Between 1902 and 1963 the German Championship was decided after play-offs involving regional champions. The first national league, the Fußball-Bundesliga, was inaugurated in 1963–64 when Cologne were the inaugural champions.

TOP 10 GOALSCORERS IN THE GERMAN BUNDESLIGA

	Player	Years	Appearances	Goals
1	**Gerd Müller**	1965–79	427	**365**
2	**Klaus Fischer**	1968–88	535	**268**
3	**Juup Heynckes**	1965–78	369	**220**
4	**Manfred Burgsmüller**	1969–90	447	**213**
5	**Ulf Kirsten**	1990–2003	350	**181**
6	**Stefan Kuntz**	1983–99	449	**179**
7 =	**Dieter Müller**	1973–85	303	**177**
=	**Klaus Allofs**	1975–93	424	**177**
9	**Johannes Löhr**	1964–77	381	**166**
10	**Karl-Heinz Rummenigge**	1974–84	310	**162**

From 1963–64 to 2008–09

All Gerd Müller's goals were scored for Bayern Munich. His first goal was in a 4–2 win over Eintracht Braunschweig on 28 August 1965.

The most appearances in the Bundesliga is 602 by Karl-Heinz Körbel of Eintracht Frankfurt between 1972 and 1991.

TOP 10 HIGHEST-SCORING GAMES IN THE ITALIAN LEAGUE*

	Winners/losers	Season	Score
1 =	**Genoa† vs. Acqui**	1914–15	**16–0**
=	**Inter Milan vs. Vicenza**	1914–15	**16–0**
3	**Inter Milan vs. AC Milanese‡**	1913–14	**15–0**
4 =	**Inter Milan† vs. Ausonia Pro Gorla**	1920–21	**14–0**
=	**Bologna† vs. Udinese**	1922–23	**14–0**
=	**Torino vs. Reggiana**	1927–28	**14–0**
7 =	**AC Milan vs. Audax Modena**	1914–15	**13–0**
=	**Pro Napoli vs. Pro Caserta**	1919–20	**13–0**
9 =	**Torino vs. US Milanese**	1909–10	**13–1**
=	**Lazio vs. Pro Roma**	1912–13	**13–1**
=	**Juventus Italia vs. Audax Modena**	1914–15	**13–1**

* Based on the score of the winning team in all Italian National Championships, from 1898 to 2008–09

† Away team

‡ Not to be confused with AC Milan

The only team to score double figures in Serie A is Torino, when they beat Alessandria 10–0 on 2 May 1948. Torino were Serie A champions that year and scored 125 goals from 40 matches.

TOP 10 CLUBS WITH THE MOST TOP-FLIGHT ITALIAN LEAGUE TITLES

	Club	First title	Last title	Total
1	**Juventus**	1905	2003	**27**
2 =	**AC Milan**	1901	2004	**17**
=	**Inter Milan***	1910	2009	**17**
4	**Genoa**	1898	1924	**9**
5 =	**Pro Vercelli**	1908	1922	**7**
=	**Bologna**	1925	1964	**7**
=	**Torino**	1928	1976	**7**
8	**AS Roma**	1942	2001	**3**
9 =	**Fiorentina**	1956	1969	**2**
=	**Napoli**	1987	1990	**2**
=	**Lazio**	1974	2000	**2**

Up to and including 2008–09

* Includes three titles as Ambrosia-Inter

The Italian League was formed in 1898, with Genoa the inaugural champions. Up to the formation of the professional Serie A, in 1929–30, the champions were decided by end-of-season play-offs involving the winners of regional leagues. Inter Milan were the first Serie A winners. Juventus won the title in 2004–05 and 2005–06 but following a scandal that involved match-fixing they were stripped of both titles. No champion was declared in 2005 but Inter Milan were awarded the title in 2006.

TOP 10 GOALSCORERS IN THE ITALIAN SERIE A

	Player	Years	Appearances	Goals
1	**Silvio Piola**	1929–54	537	**274**
2	**Gunnar Nordahl**	1948–58	291	**225**
3 =	**Giuseppe Meazza**	1929–47	367	**216**
=	**José Altafini**	1958–76	459	**216**
5	**Roberto Baggio**	1985–2004	452	**205**
6	**Kurt Hamrin**	1956–71	400	**190**
7	**Giuseppe Signori**	1991–2004	344	**188**
8	**Gabriel Batistuta**	1991–2003	318	**184**
9 =	**Giampiero Boniperti**	1946–61	444	**178**
=	**Francesco Totti**	1992–2009	419	**178**

From 1929–30 to 2008–09

Despite being the all-time Serie A top scorer, Silvio Piola only twice topped the end-of-season Serie A scoring list, in 1937 and 1943.

The most appearances in Serie A is 647 by Paolo Maldini for AC Milan between 1985 and 2009.

	Club	First title	Last title	Total
1	**Ajax Amsterdam**	1918	2004	**29**
2	**PSV Eindhoven**	1929	2008	**21**
3	**Feyenoord Rotterdam**	1924	1999	**14**
4	**HVV Den Haag**	1900	1914	**8**
5	**Sparta Rotterdam**	1909	1959	**6**
6	**Go Ahead Eagles**	1917	1933	**4**
7 =	**HBS Den Haag**	1904	1925	**3**
=	**Willem II Tilburg**	1916	1955	**3**
9 =	**RAP Amsterdam**	1898	1899	**2**
=	**Heracles Almelo**	1927	1941	**2**
=	**RCH Haarlem**	1923	1953	**2**
=	**ADO Den Haag**	1942	1943	**2**
=	**AZ'67/Alkmaar/AZ Alkmaar**	1981	2009	**2**

Up to and including 2008–09

RAP Amsterdam beat Vitesse 4–2 in the play-off final to capture the first League title in 1897–98. Until the formation of the Eredivisie (the Netherlands Premier Division) in 1956, following the introduction of professionalism, the League champions were decided by end-of-season play-offs. Between 1965 and 2008 every Netherlands League title was won by one of the country's 'Big Three' – Ajax, PSV Eindhoven and Feyenoord, with the exception of 1980–81 when AZ'67 broke the monopoly.

TOP 10 GOALSCORERS IN THE NETHERLANDS EREDIVISIE

	Player	Years	Appearances	Goals
1	**Willy van der Kuijlen**	1964–82	528	**311**
2	**Ruud Geels**	1964–84	392	**265**
3	**Johan Cruyff**	1964–84	309	**215**
4	**Kees Kist**	1972–87	411	**212**
5	**Tonny van der Linden**	1956–68	*	**204**
6	**Henk Groot**	1959–69	279	**194**
7	**Peter Houtman**	1977–91	281	**178**
8 =	**Sjaak Swart**	1957–73	461	**175**
=	**Leo van Veen**	1962–84	473	**175**
10	**Cor van der Gijp**	1956–64	199	**162**

From 1956–57 to the end of the 2008–09 season

* Appearance figures for van der Linden are unknown

TOP 10 TOP-FLIGHT PORTUGUESE CLUBS*

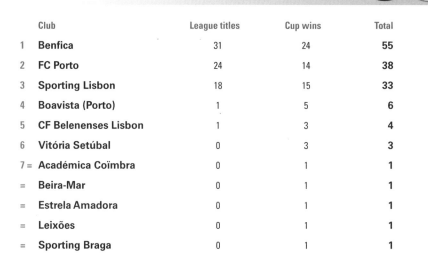

	Club	League titles	Cup wins	Total
1	**Benfica**	31	24	**55**
2	**FC Porto**	24	14	**38**
3	**Sporting Lisbon**	18	15	**33**
4	**Boavista (Porto)**	1	5	**6**
5	**CF Belenenses Lisbon**	1	3	**4**
6	**Vitória Setúbal**	0	3	**3**
7 =	**Académica Coïmbra**	0	1	**1**
=	**Beira-Mar**	0	1	**1**
=	**Estrela Amadora**	0	1	**1**
=	**Leixões**	0	1	**1**
=	**Sporting Braga**	0	1	**1**

Up to and including 2008–09

* Based on wins in the Portuguese League and Cup competitions from 1938–39 to 2008–09

Between 1921–22 and 1937–38, the Portuguese champions were the winners of a knockout cup competition. An unofficial experimental league was launched in 1934–35 and ran for four seasons. The first official Portuguese League, the Campeonato da la Divisão, was inaugurated in 1938–39. The Portuguese Cup (Taça de Portugal) was launched in 1938–39 following the inauguration of the Campeonato da la Divisão.

TOP 10 HIGHEST-SCORING GAMES IN THE SPANISH LA LIGA*

	Winners/losers	Season	Score
1	**Athletic Bilbao vs. Barcelona**	1930–31	**12–1**
2	**Sevilla vs. Barcelona**	1940–41	**11–1**
3	**Real Madrid vs. Elche**	1959–60	**11–2**
4 =	**Sevilla vs. Oviedo**	1941–42	**10–0**
=	**Athletic Bilbao vs. Celta Vigo**	1941–42	**10–0**
=	**Athletic Bilbao vs. Lleida**	1950–51	**10–0**
7 =	**Barcelona vs. Gimnàstic Tarragona**	1949–50	**10–1**
=	**Celta Vigo vs. Gimnàstic Tarragona**	1949–50	**10–1**
=	**Deportivo La Coruña vs. Lleida**	1950–51	**10–1**
=	**Athletic Bilbao vs. Real Zaragoza**	1951–52	**10–1**
=	**Real Madrid vs. Las Palmas**	1958–59	**10–1**

* Based on the score of the winning team, up to and including 2008–09

Source: Karel Stokkermans, RSSSF

Lleida conceded a staggering 134 goals from 30 games in 1950–51. It is the only instance in La Liga history that any team has conceded 100 goals or more in a season.
The highest-scoring game in terms of goals scored by both teams in La Liga was in 1932–33 when Athletic Bilbao beat Racing Santander 9–5.

The biggest away win is Barcelona's 8–0 win at Las Palmas in 1958–59.

TOP 10 CLUBS WITH THE MOST SPANISH LA LIGA TITLES

	Club	First title	Last title	Total
1	**Real Madrid**	1932	2008	**31**
2	**Barcelona**	1929	2009	**19**
3	**Athletic Bilbao**	1930	1984	**8**
4	**Atlético Madrid**	1950	1996	**7**
5	**Valencia**	1942	2004	**6**
6 =	**Atlético Aviación***	1940	1941	**2**
=	**Real Sociedad**	1981	1982	**2**
8 =	**Real Betis**	1935	1935	**1**
=	**Sevilla**	1946	1946	**1**
=	**Deportivo de La Coruña**	2000	2000	**1**

Up to and including 2008–09

* Atlético Aviación was formed as a result of a merger between Atlético Madrid and Aviación Nacional of Zaragoza in 1939 when League soccer resumed after the end of the Spanish Civil War; some sources credit their two wins to Atlético Madrid

La Liga was formed in 1928–29 and the first champions were Barcelona who beat Real Madrid to the title by two points. Prior to the formation of La Liga, League football in Spain was contested on a regional basis. Real Madrid, Barcelona and Athletic Bilbao are the only teams to have competed in every La Liga season.

TOP 10 GOALSCORERS IN THE SPANISH LA LIGA

	Player	Years	Appearances	Goals
1	**Telmo 'Zarra'**	1939–55	279	**251**
2	**Hugo Sánchez**	1981–94	347	**234**
3	**Alfredo di Stéfano**	1953–66	329	**227**
4	**'Cesar' Rodriguez**	1939–55	353	**226**
5	**'Raul' Gonzalez**	1994–2009	521	**223**
6	**Enrique Castro González 'Quini'**	1970–87	448	**219**
7	**Manuel 'Pahíño'**	1943–56	278	**210**
8	**Edmundo Suárez 'Mundo'**	1939–51	231	**195**
9	**Carlos Alonso González 'Santillana'**	1971–89	461	**186**
10	**Juan Arza**	1943–59	349	**182**

From 1928–29 to 2008–09

Name in inverted commas is that by which the player was more commonly known

All of Zarra's goals were scored for Athletic Bilbao.

The most appearances in La Liga is 622 by Andoni Zubizarreta for Athletic Bilbao, Barcelona and Valencia between 1981 and 1998.

TOP 10 CLUBS WITH THE MOST TOP-FLIGHT DOMESTIC LEAGUE TITLES IN EUROPE*

	Club	Country	Titles
1	**Rangers**	Scotland	**52**
2	**Linfield**	Northern Ireland	**48**
3	**Celtic**	Scotland	**42**
4	**Olympiakos**	Greece	**37**
5	**Rapid Vienna†**	Austria	**33**
6 =	**Benfica**	Portugal	**31**
=	**CSKA Sofia**	Bulgaria	**31**
=	**Real Madrid**	Spain	**31**
=	**Sparta Prague**	Czechoslovakia/Czech Republic	**31**
10 =	**Ajax**	Netherlands	**29**
=	**Anderlecht**	Belgium	**29**

Up to and including 2008–09

* Among UEFA affiliated countries

† Rapid Vienna's total includes one wartime German League title in 1941

The best totals for clubs from the other leading European nations are:
Italy – Juventus, 27
Germany – Bayern Munich, 20
England – Liverpool, Manchester United, 18
France – Saint-Etienne, 10.

TOP 10 CLUBS WITH THE MOST DOMESTIC CUP WINS IN EUROPE*

	Club	Country	First win	Last win	Total
1	**Linfield**	Northern Ireland	1891	2008	**39**
2	**FC Vaduz**	Liechtenstein	1952	2009	**38**
3	**Celtic**	Scotland	1892	2007	**34**
4	**Rangers**	Scotland	1894	2009	**33**
5 =	**Austria Vienna**	Austria	1921	2009	**27**
=	**Benfica**	Portugal	1930	2004	**27**
7 =	**Levski Sofia**	Bulgaria	1942	2007	**26**
=	**HB Tórshavn**	Faroe Islands	1955	2004	**26**
9	**Barcelona**	Spain	1910	2009	**25**
10 =	**Shamrock Rovers**	Ireland	1925	1987	**24**
=	**Olympiakos**	Greece	1947	2009	**24**

* Principal cup competitions in each country up to and including 2008–09

The most consecutive wins is 12 by FC Vaduz between 1998 and 2009.

TOP 10 CLUBS WITH THE LONGEST UNDEFEATED RUN IN TOP-FLIGHT FOOTBALL IN EUROPE

	Club	Country	From	To	Games unbeaten
1	**Steaua Bucharest**	Romania	17 Aug 1986	09 Sep 1989	**104**
2	**Sheriff Tiraspol**	Moldova	01 Apr 2006	12 Mar 2008	**63**
3	**Celtic**	Scotland	20 Nov 1915	21 Apr 1917	**62**
4	**Union Saint-Gilloise**	Belgium	08 Jan 1933	10 Feb 1935	**60**
5	**Pyunik Yerevan**	Armenia	20 Oct 2002	01 Nov 2004	**59**
6 =	**Olympiakos**	Greece	08 Oct 1972	21 Apr 1974	**58**
=	**AC Milan**	Italy	26 May 1991	21 Mar 1993	**58**
=	**Skonto Riga**	Latvia	17 Oct 1993	25 May 1996	**58**
9	**Benfica**	Portugal	24 Oct 1976	01 Sep 1978	**56**
10	**Shakhtar Donetsk**	Ukraine	22 Jul 2000	03 Aug 2002	**55**

Up to and including 2008–09

Celtic's run started with a 2–0 win over Kilmarnock, and ended, ironically, with a 2–0 home defeat by Kilmarnock 17 months later.

The records for other selected countries are:
Netherlands: Ajax, 52 matches, 1994–96
Wales: Barry Town, 51 matches, 1997–98
England: Arsenal, 49 matches, 2003–04
Spain: Real Sociedad, 38 matches, 1979–80
Germany: Hamburg, 36 matches, 1982–83
Northern Ireland: Linfield, 34 matches, 2006–07
France: Nantes, 32 matches, 1994–95

The longest unbeaten run in world soccer is 108 matches by ASEC Mimosas (Abidjan) of the Ivory Coast from 1989 to 1994.

TOP 10 OLDEST LEAGUES IN EUROPE

	Country	First season
1	**England**	**1888–89**
2	**Northern Ireland***	**1890–91**
3	**Scotland**	**1890–91**
4	**Belgium**	**1895–96**
5	**Sweden†**	**1896–97**
6 =	**Italy**	**1897–98**
=	**Netherlands**	**1897–98**
=	**Switzerland**	**1897–98**
9	**Hungary**	**1900–01**
10	**Germany**	**1902–03**

Pre-dates the Scottish League by one week

†*The Swedish Football Association was not formed until 1904 and the first National League not until 1925. However, between 1896 and 1925 the winners of the cup competition, Svenska Mästerskapet, were declared champions and following their formation the Swedish FA retrospectively recognized the winners from 1896–97*

Gibraltar hosted a cup competition, the Merchants' Cup, to decide the local 'champions' between 1895 and 1907, but the Gibraltar League did not come into existence until 1907–08.

TOP 10 CLUBS WITH THE MOST ARGENTINE NATIONAL TITLES

	Club	First title	Last title	Total
1	**River Plate**	1932	2008(C)*	**33**
2	**Boca Juniors**	1931	2009(A)	**23**
3	**Independiente**	1938	2002(A)	**14**
4	**San Lorenzo**	1933	2007(C)	**10**
5 =	**Racing Club**	1949	2001(A)	**7**
=	**Vélez Sarsfield**	1968	2009(C)	**7**
7	**Newell's Old Boys**	1974	2004(A)	**5**
8 =	**Rosario Central**	1973	1987	**4**
=	**Estudiantes**	1967	2006(A)	**4**
10 =	**Ferro Carril Oeste**	1982	1984	**2**
=	**Argentinos Juniors**	1984	1985	**2**

From 1931 up to and including 2009

* (A) = Apertura (C) = Clausura (see below)

An Argentine Amateur Championship existed from 1891 to 1934 and the first professional league was inaugurated in 1931. Between 1967 and 1985 there were two leagues, one for teams based in the Metropolitan Area around Buenos Aires and the other for teams from the other regions of the country. Since the 1991–92 season there have been two championships – one for the first half of the season, the Apertura (Opening) and the other for the second half, the Clausura (Closing). It is now known as the Primera División.

TOP 10 CLUBS WITH THE MOST BRAZILIAN NATIONAL TITLES*

	Club	First title	Last title	Total
1	**São Paulo**	1977	2008	6
2 =	**Flamengo**	1980	1992	4
=	**Vasco da Gama**	1974	2000	4
=	**Palmeiras**	1972	2004	4
=	**Corinthians**	1990	2005	4
6	**Internacional**	1975	1979	3
7 =	**Grêmio**	1981	1996	2
=	**Santos**	2002	2004	2
9 =	**Atlético Mineiro**	1971	1971	1
=	**Guarani**	1978	1978	1
=	**Fluminense**	1984	1984	1
=	**Coritiba**	1985	1985	1
=	**Sport Recife**	1987	1987	1
=	**Bahia**	1988	1988	1
=	**Botafogo**	1995	1995	1
=	**Atlético Paranaense**	2001	2001	1
=	**Cruzeiro**	2003	2003	1

* From 1971, when the first Brazilian national championship (Campeonato Brasileiro) was inaugurated, to 2008

Because of the size of the country, Brazil was the last major footballing nation to establish a national football championship. Previously, Brazilian football centred around two leagues, the Campeonato Paulista de Futebol, based around the São Paulo area and the Liga Metropolitana de Football, based in Rio de Janeiro. The top division of the Brazilian Championship is now known as Campeonato Brasileiro Série A.

TOP 10 HIGHEST-SCORING GAMES IN SOUTH AMERICA*

	Winners/losers	Year	Country	Score
1	**Voorwaarts vs. Bintang Merah**	1955	Suriname	**18–0**
2	**River Plate vs. Marte Atlético**	1919	Paraguay	**16–0**
3 =	**Belgrano vs. Palermo Athletic**	1897	Argentina	**14–0**
=	**Alumni vs. Reformer**	1905	Argentina	**14–0**
5 =	**Magallanes vs. Santiago National**	1934	Chile	**14–1**
=	**Unión Española vs. Morning Star**	1934	Chile	**14–1**
=	**Lota Schwager vs. Rangers**	1978	Chile	**14–1**
8 =	**Wanderers vs. French**	1908	Uruguay	**13–0**
=	**Blooming vs. Primero de Mayo**	1983	Bolivia	**13–0**
10 =	**Banfield vs. Puerto Comercial**	1974	Argentina	**13–1 †**
=	**Geldar vs. Saint-Georges**	2007	French Guyana	**13–1**

As at 5 July 2009

* Based on score of winning team in the first level of South American national championships

† A record for the professional era in Argentina

Source: Karel Stokkermans, RSSSF

The record score in the Brazilian National Championship since 1971 is Corinthians 10–1 over Tiradentes in 1983. The biggest away win in South America is Barracas Athletic's 12–0 win at Flores in the 1903 Argentinian Championship.

TOP 10 GOALSCORERS IN THE USA'S MAJOR LEAGUE SOCCER (MLS)*

	Player/country	Years	Games	Goals
1	**Jaime Moreno** Bolivia	1996–2008†	295	**122**
2	**Ante Razov** USA	1996–2008†	262	**114**
3	**Jason Kreis** USA	1996–2007	305	**108**
4	**Jeff Cunningham** Jamaica	1998–2008†	289	**104**
5	**Taylor Twellman** USA	2001–08†	172	**99**
6	**Landon Donovan** USA	2001–08†	183	**86**
7	**Roy Lassiter** USA	1996–2002	179	**88**
8 =	**Raúl Díaz Arce** El Salvador	1996–2001	150	**82**
=	**Carlos Ruíz** Guatemala	2002–08	155	**82**
10	**Predrag Radosavljevic 'Preki'** Serbia	1996–2005	242	**79**

* Regular season goals only, up to the start of the 2009 season

† Active in 2009

Source: MLS

The most appearances in MLS regular season games is 358 by Steve Ralston (USA) for Tampa Bay Mutiny and New England Revolution between 1996 and 2008. Ralston was still active in 2009.

TOP 10 HIGHEST-PAID PLAYERS IN THE USA'S MLS

	Player/country	Club	Annual salary ($)
1	**David Beckham** England	LA Galaxy	**6,500,000**
2	**Cuauhtemoc Blanco** Mexico	Chicago Fire	**2,943,702**
3	**Juan Pablo Angel** Colombia	N.Y. Red Bulls	**1,798,000**
4	**Freddie Ljungberg** Sweden	Seattle Sounders	**1,314,000**
5	**Landon Donovan** USA	LA Galaxy	**900,000**
6	**Guillermo Barros Schelleto** Argentina	Columbus Crew	**775,000**
7	**Luciano Emilio** Brazil	DC United	**758,857**
8	**Shalrie Joseph** Grenada	New England Revolution	**450,000**
9	**Dwayne DeRosario** Canada	Toronto FC	**425,750**
10	**Taylor Twellman** USA	New England Revolution	**420,000**

* As at 15 March 2009
Source: MLS Players Union

After David Beckham, the next highest-paid Englishman is the former Norwich City player Darren Huckerby, on $385,000.

TOP 10 GOALSCORERS IN LEAGUE FOOTBALL WORLDWIDE*

	Player	Countries played in	Years	Games	Goals
1	**Pelé**	Brazil, USA	1957–77	560	**541**
2	**Josef Bican**	Austria, Czechoslovakia	1931–55	358	**537**
3	**Ferenc Puskás**	Hungary, Spain	1943–66	532	**517**
4	**Romário**	Brazil, Netherlands, Spain, Australia	1985–2007	628	**502**
5	**Roberto Dinamite**	Brazil, Spain	1971–92	758	**470†**
6	**Zico**	Brazil, Italy, Japan	1971–94	681	**457**
7	**Imre Schlosser**	Hungary, Austria	1905–28	330	**417**
8	**Gyula Zsengéller**	Hungary, Italy, Colombia	1935–52	398	**416**
9	**Jimmy McGrory**	Scotland	1922–38	408	**410**
10	**Gerhard Müller**	West Germany, USA	1965–81	507	**405**

As at 5 July 2009

* Goals scored by players in the top division of a national league (or recognized leading division where regional championships applied) from the formation of the world's first league, the English Football League, in 1888

† In the Brazilian Championship and Campeonato Carioca (the Rio de Janeiro Championship)

The most goals scored by an English player is 366 from 527 games in England and Italy by Jimmy Greaves between 1957 and 1971.

Clubs	Location(s)/country
1 **Barcelona vs. Real Madrid**	Barcelona/Madrid, Spain
2 **Boca Juniors vs. River Plate**	Buenos Aires, Argentina
3 **Celtic vs. Rangers**	Glasgow, Scotland
4 **Fenerbahce vs. Galatasaray**	Istanbul, Turkey
5 **Ajax vs. Feyenoord**	Amsterdam/Rotterdam, Netherlands
6 **Lazio vs. Roma**	Rome, Italy
7 **Borussia Dortmund vs. Schalke**	Dortmund/ Gelsenkirchen, Germany
8 **Al Ahly vs. Zamalek**	Cairo, Egypt
9 **Real Betis vs. Sevilla**	Seville, Spain
10 **Partizan Belgrade vs. Red Star Belgrade**	Belgrade, Serbia

World Soccer's *'The 50 greatest derbies in world football' (July 2008)*

The Barcelona–Madrid match is known in Spain as El Clásico or El Derbi. The first League match between the two took place at the Nou Camp on 17 February 1929 when Madrid won 2–1, but Barcelona gained revenge less than three months later by winning the return fixture 1–0.

According to World Soccer, the biggest rivalry in English football is the Liverpool vs. Manchester United game; it figures at number 28 on their overall list. They feature only one other English rivalry, that between Arsenal vs. Tottenham Hotspur (at number 42).

TOP 10 PLAYERS IN THE FIFA WORLD PLAYER OF THE YEAR AWARD*

	Player/country	Wins	Runner-up	Third	Pts
1	**Zinedine Zidane** France	3	1	2	**13**
2	**Ronaldo** Brazil	3	1	1	**12**
3	**Ronaldinho** Brazil	2	0	1	**7**
4 =	**Luís Figo** Portugal	1	1	0	**5**
=	**Romário** Brazil	1	1	0	**5**
=	**George Weah** Liberia	1	1	0	**5**
7 =	**Roberto Baggio** Italy	1	0	1	**4**
=	**David Beckham** England	0	2	0	**4**
=	**Thierry Henry** France	0	2	0	**4**
=	**Lionel Messi** Argentina	0	2	0	**4**
=	**Rivaldo** Brazil	1	0	1	**4**
=	**Cristiano Ronaldo** Portugal	1	0	1	**4**
=	**Hristo Stoitchkov** Bulgaria	0	2	0	**4**

Up to and including the 2008 award

* Based on three points for winner, two points for runner-up and one point for coming third

In addition to those players on the list, the only other players to have won the award are: Lothar Matthäus, Germany (1991), Marco van Basten, Netherlands (1992), Fabio Cannavaro, Italy (2006) and Kaká, Brazil (2007). Lothar Matthäus was the first winner of the award in 1991, Jean-Pierre Papin of France second and England's Gary Lineker third.

Birgit Prinz (Germany) and Marta (Brazil) have each won the FIA Women's World Player of the Year award a record three times.

TOP 10 BIGGEST WINNING MARGINS IN THE FIFA WORLD PLAYER OF THE YEAR AWARD

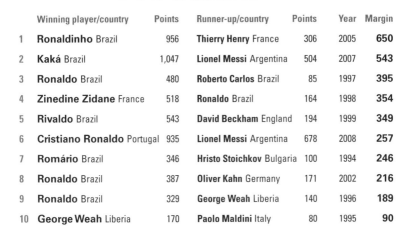

	Winning player/country	Points	Runner-up/country	Points	Year	Margin
1	**Ronaldinho** Brazil	956	**Thierry Henry** France	306	2005	**650**
2	**Kaká** Brazil	1,047	**Lionel Messi** Argentina	504	2007	**543**
3	**Ronaldo** Brazil	480	**Roberto Carlos** Brazil	85	1997	**395**
4	**Zinedine Zidane** France	518	**Ronaldo** Brazil	164	1998	**354**
5	**Rivaldo** Brazil	543	**David Beckham** England	194	1999	**349**
6	**Cristiano Ronaldo** Portugal	935	**Lionel Messi** Argentina	678	2008	**257**
7	**Romário** Brazil	346	**Hristo Stoichkov** Bulgaria	100	1994	**246**
8	**Ronaldo** Brazil	387	**Oliver Kahn** Germany	171	2002	**216**
9	**Ronaldo** Brazil	329	**George Weah** Liberia	140	1996	**189**
10	**George Weah** Liberia	170	**Paolo Maldini** Italy	80	1995	**90**

Up to and including the 2008 award

From its inception in 1991 the award was made to the player who received the most votes from national team coaches around the world. Since 2004 it has been awarded based on the votes cast by both national team coaches and captains. The closest vote was in 2001 when Luís Figo (Portugal) beat David Beckham by just 12 votes.

TOP 10 PLAYERS IN THE UEFA EUROPEAN FOOTBALLER OF THE YEAR AWARD*

	Player/country	Wins	Runner-up	Third	Pts
1 =	**Franz Beckenbauer** West Germany	2	2	1	**11**
=	**Michel Platini** France	3	0	2	**11**
3	**Johan Cruyff** Netherlands	3	0	1	**10**
4 =	**Marco van Basten** Netherlands	3	0	0	**9**
=	**Ronaldo** Brazil	2	1	1	**9**
6 =	**Kevin Keegan** England	2	1	0	**8**
=	**Karl-Heinz Rummenigge** West Germany	2	1	0	**8**
=	**Alfredo di Stéfano** Spain	2	1	0	**8**
=	**Luis Suárez** Spain	1	2	1	**8**
10 =	**Bobby Charlton** England	1	2	0	**7**
=	**Eusébio** Portugal	1	2	0	**7**
=	**Raymond Kopa** France	1	1	2	**7**
=	**Gerd Müller** West Germany	1	1	2	**7**

Up to and including the 2008 award

* Based on three points for winner, two points for runner-up and one point for coming third

Each year's winner receives Le Ballon d'Or. The award was inaugurated in 1956 by French newspaper *France Football* and today the winner is the player who polls the most votes from selected journalists from around the world. The first winner was Stanley Matthews of Blackpool who beat the Real Madrid pair of Alfredo di Stéfano and Raymond Kopa into second and third place.

Season	Player/country	Club
2008–09	**Steven Gerrard** England	Liverpool
2007–08	**Cristiano Ronaldo** Portugal	Manchester United
2006–07	**Cristiano Ronaldo** Portugal	Manchester United
2005–06	**Thierry Henry** France	Arsenal
2004–05	**Frank Lampard** England	Chelsea
2003–04	**Thierry Henry** France	Arsenal
2002–03	**Thierry Henry** France	Arsenal
2001–02	**Robert Pirès** France	Arsenal
2000–01	**Teddy Sheringham** England	Manchester United
1999–2000	**Roy Keane** Republic of Ireland	Manchester United

Steven Gerrard became the 11th Liverpool player to win the award, in 2008–09, by beating the Manchester United pair of Ryan Giggs and Wayne Rooney into second and third places. The other Liverpool winners were: Ian Callaghan (1974), Kevin Keegan (1976), Emlyn Hughes (1977), Kenny Dalglish (1979 and 1983), Terry McDermott (1980), Ian Rush (1984), John Barnes (1988 and 1990) and Steve Nicol (1989).

TOP 10 BRITISH PLAYERS WITH THE MOST MAJOR AWARDS*

	Player	First award	Last award	EFA	FWA	PFA	YPY	Total
1	**Kevin Keegan**	1976	1982	2	1	1	0	**4**
2 =	**Stanley Matthews**	1948	1963	1	2	0	0	**3**
=	**Kenny Dalglish**	1979	1983	0	2	1	0	**3**
=	**Ian Rush**	1983	1984	0	1	1	1	**3**
=	**John Barnes**	1988	1990	0	2	1	0	**3**
=	**Mark Hughes**	1985	1991	0	0	2	1	**3**
=	**Gary Lineker**	1986	1992	0	2	1	0	**3**
=	**Alan Shearer**	1994	1997	0	1	2	0	**3**
=	**Ryan Giggs**	1992	2009	0	0	1	2	**3**
=	**Steven Gerrard**	2001	2009	0	1	1	1	**3**

Up to and including the 2008–09 awards

* UEFA European Footballer of the Year (EFA); Football Writers' Association Footballer of the Year (FWA); Professional Footballers' Association Players' Player of the Year (PFA); Professional Footballers' Association Young Player of the Year (YPY)

No British player has won the FIFA World Player of the Year award.

TOP 10 CLUBS WINNING THE MOST WORLD AND EUROPEAN FOOTBALLER AND COACH AWARDS*

	Club	W	E	C	Total
1 =	**Barcelona**	6	6	1	**13**
=	**Juventus**	4	8	1	**13**
3	**AC Milan**	3	8	1	**12**
4	**Real Madrid**	4	6	1	**11**
5 =	**Bayern Munich**	0	5	1	**6**
=	**Manchester United**	1	4	1	**6**
7	**Inter Milan**	3	2	0	**5**
8 =	**Dynamo Kiev**	0	2	0	**2**
=	**Hamburg**	0	2	0	**2**
=	**Liverpool**	0	1	1	**2**
=	**Porto**	0	0	2	**2**
=	**Valencia**	0	0	2	**2**

Up to and including the 2008 awards

* In the FIFA World Player of the Year Award (W), UEFA European Footballer of the Year Award (E) and UEFA Coach of the Year Award (C)

Rivaldo and Ronaldinho are the only Barcelona players to win both the World and European awards, while Roberto Baggio and Zinedine Zidane are the only Juventus players to win both awards.

Barcelona's six World Footballer of the Year awards were won by four men, all four of whom were Brazilians: Romário, Ronaldo (twice), Rivaldo and Ronaldinho (twice). The UEFA Coach of The Year award was first made in 1998 and was won by Marcello Lippi of Juventus. The award was discontinued after 2006. José Mourinho (Porto) and Rafael Benítez (Valencia and Liverpool) are the only men to have won it twice.

TOP 10 CLUBS PROVIDING THE MOST PLAYER OF THE YEAR AWARDS IN ENGLAND*

	Club	FWA	PFA	Total
1	**Manchester United**	8	10	**18**
2	**Liverpool**	11	5	**16**
3 =	**Arsenal**	7	4	**11**
=	**Tottenham Hotspur**	8	3	**11**
5	**Leeds United**	4	1	**5**
6	**Everton**	2	2	**4**
7 =	**Aston Villa**	0	3	**3**
=	**Chelsea**	2	1	**3**
=	**Manchester City**	3	0	**3**
10 =	**Blackburn Rovers**	1	1	**2**
=	**Blackpool**	2	0	**2**
=	**Derby County**	1	1	**2**
=	**Ipswich Town**	1	1	**2**
=	**Newcastle United**	0	2	**2**
=	**Nottingham Forest**	1	1	**2**
=	**Preston North End**	2	0	**2**
=	**Stoke City**	2	0	**2**
=	**Wolverhampton Wanderers**	2	0	**2**

Up to and including the 2008–09 awards

* Football Writers' Association Footballer of the Year (FWA) and the Professional Footballers' Association Players' Player of the Year (PFA)

Sources: Football Writers' Association and Professional Footballers' Association

Football Writers' Assocation Footballer of the Year award

The first FWA award was made in the 1947–48 season and was won by Stanley Matthews. The idea for such an award came from the former player and later journalist Charles Buchan. The winning player is the one who receives the most votes each season from journalists who are members of the FWA.

Thierry Henry (Arsenal) 2003, 2004 and 2006 is the only player to have won the FWA Footballer of the Year award on three occasions. The following players have all won it twice: Tom Finney (Preston North End) 1954 and 1957; Danny Blanchflower (Tottenham Hotspur) 1958 and 1961; Stanley Matthews (Blackpool/Stoke City) 1948 and 1963; Kenny Dalglish (Liverpool) 1979 and 1983; John Barnes (Liverpool) 1988 and 1990; Gary Lineker (Everton/Tottenham Hotspur) 1986 and 1992; and Cristiano Ronaldo (Manchester United) 2007 and 2008.

Professional Footballers' Association Players' Player of the Year award

The PFA awards were inaugurated in 1973–74 when the first winner of the coveted Players' Player of the Year trophy went to Norman Hunter of Leeds United. The winner is the player who receives the most votes each season from his fellow members of the PFA.

The following have all won the award twice: Mark Hughes (Manchester United) 1989 and 1991; Alan Shearer (Blackburn Rovers/Newcastle United) 1995 and 1997; Thierry Henry (Arsenal) 2003 and 2004; and Cristiano Ronaldo (Manchester United) 2007 and 2008.

Andy Gray (Aston Villa) in 1977 and Cristano Ronaldo (Manchester United) in 2007 uniquely won the Players' Player of the Year and Young Player of the Year awards in the same season.

TOP 10 CLUBS PROVIDING THE MOST PLAYER OF THE YEAR AWARDS IN SCOTLAND*

	Club	SFWA	SPFA	Total
1	**Celtic**	16	16	**32**
2	**Rangers**	15	9	**24**
3	**Aberdeen**	4	4	**8**
4	**Dundee United**	3	2	**5**
5 =	**Heart of Midlothian**	2	0	**2**
=	**Morton**	1	1	**2**
7 =	**Airdrieonians**	0	1	**1**
=	**Hibernian**	1	0	**1**
=	**Partick Thistle**	1	0	**1**
=	**Raith Rovers**	1	0	**1**
=	**Scotland†**	1	0	**1**

Up to and including the 2008–09 awards

* Scottish Football Writers' Association Footballer of the Year (SFWA) and the Scottish Professional Footballers' Association Players' Player of the Year (SPFA)

† In 1974 the SFWA made their award to the Scotland World Cup squad

The SWFA is an association of Scottish football journalists who founded the awards in 1965. The first recipient was Billy McNeill of Celtic. The SPFA inaugurated their awards in 1977–78 when Derek Johnstone of Rangers was the first winner.

TOP 10 BIGGEST GROUNDS IN THE WORLD

	Stadium	Location	Country	Capacity
1	**Rungrado May Day Stadium**	Pyongyang	North Korea	**150,000**
2 =	**Azadi Stadium**	Tehran	Iran	**120,000**
=	**Salt Lake Stadium**	Kolkata	India	**120,000**
4	**Azteca Stadium**	Mexico City	Mexico	**114,600**
5 =	**Bukit Jalil National Stadium**	Kuala Lumpur	Malaysia	**100,000**
=	**Melbourne Cricket Ground**	Melbourne	Australia	**100,000**
7	**Camp Nou**	Barcelona	Spain	**98,772**
8	**Stade 5 Juillet 1962**	Algiers	Algeria	**96,000**
9	**Wembley Stadium**	London	England	**90,000**
10	**Maracanã***	Rio de Janeiro	Brazil	**88,992**

Based on 2009 capacity of grounds that host Association Football matches (several of these grounds also host other sports events)

* Commonly referred to as the Maracanã, its official name is the Estádio Jornalista Mário Filho

Barcelona's Camp Nou is the largest club ground in the world. The world's largest football stadium, the Rungrado May Day Stadium, opened on 1 May 1989.

TOP 10 BIGGEST CLUB GROUNDS IN EUROPE

	Stadium	Country	Home team(s)	Capacity
1	**Camp Nou**	Spain	Barcelona	**98,772**
2	**Signal Iduna Park***	Germany	Borussia Dortmund	**80,552**
3	**Bernabeu**	Spain	Real Madrid	**80,354**
4	**Stadio Giuseppe Meazza**†	Italy	AC Milan/Inter Milan	**80,074**
5	**Luzhniki Stadium**	Russia	Spartak Moscow /Torpedo Moscow	**78,360**
6	**Old Trafford**	England	Manchester United	**76,212**
7	**Atatürk Stadium**	Turkey	Belediye	**74,486**
8	**Olympiastadion**	Germany	Hertha Berlin	**74,228**
9	**Stadio Olimpico**	Italy	AS Roma/Lazio	**72,700**
10	**Olympic Stadium**	Greece	AEK Athens/Panathinaikos	**71,030**

Based on 2009 capacity

* Also known as the Westfalenstadion

† Formerly the San Siro Stadium

Dynamo Kiev play their important home games at the 83,450-capacity Olimpiysky National Sports Complex in Kiev instead of at their own ground, the Lobanovsky Dynamo Stadium. When completed in 2010, Valencia's new Mestalla Stadium will have a capacity of 75,000.

BEHIND THE RECORD
– THE CAMP NOU

Being inside the Camp Nou, or Nou Camp as it is often referred to in English, with over 90,000 Catalan football fans inside is one of the most remarkable experiences in world football.

Barcelona previously played at the Les Corts stadium but by the mid-1950s, and with the arrival of European competitions, they had outgrown the 60,000-capacity stadium and needed a new home.

Work started on the Camp Nou, then called the Nou Estadi del Futbol Club Barcelona, in 1954 and was completed in 1957. The first game at the new stadium was on 24 September 1957 when Barcelona beat Legia Warsaw of Poland 4–2, with Eulogio Martínez scoring the Camp Nou's first ever goal in the 11th minute in front of 90,000 fans.

In 2000, club members (known as socios) voted to change the name of the ground officially to the Camp Nou, which had been its nickname since its inauguration.

The stadium has hosted many European and World Cup matches and also many major rock concerts, including in 2009 U2's 360° tour.

The Nou Camp has hosted two European Cup/Champions League finals: the 1989 final which saw AC Milan beat Steaua Bucharest 4–0 and again ten years later when Manchester United scored two late goals to beat Bayern Munich 2–1 in front of 90,000 fans.

One of the most memorable matches at the Nou Camp was the 1992 Olympic football final between Spain and Poland, which the host won 3–2 with Kiko scoring a 90th-minute winner.

	Country	Club with highest average attendance	Club average	League average
1	**Germany**	Borussia Dortmund	74,830	**42,565**
2	**England**	Manchester United	75,304	**35,630**
3	**Spain**	Real Madrid	71,947	**28,276**
4	**Italy**	AC Milan	58,731	**25,045**
5	**France**	Marseille	52,276	**21,049**
6	**Netherlands**	Ajax	49,014	**19,789**
7	**England (2)***	Derby County	29,204	**17,875**
8	**Germany (2)***	Kaiserslautern	34,425	**15,730**
9	**Scotland**	Celtic	57,621	**15,537**
10	**Russia†**	Krylya Sovetov Samara	21,700	**13,334**

* All leagues are from the top level of football in each country unless indicated by (2), which indicates it is a second-level league

† The Russian season ends in November; figures are for latest completed season, 2008

Six teams from the German Bundesliga had average attendances of over 50,000 in 2008–09: Borussia Dortmund (as above), Bayern Munich (69,000), Schalke 04 (61,387), Hamburg (54,774), Hertha Berlin (52,157) and Stuttgart (51,926).

TOP 10 EUROPEAN CLUBS WITH THE HIGHEST AVERAGE ATTENDANCES IN 2008–09

	Club	Country	Average
1	**Manchester United**	England	**75,304**
2	**Borussia Dortmund**	Germany	**74,830**
3	**Real Madrid**	Spain	**71,947**
4	**Barcelona**	Spain	**71,328**
5	**Bayern Munich**	Germany	**69,000**
6	**Schalke 04**	Germany	**61,387**
7	**Arsenal**	England	**60,040**
8	**AC Milan**	Italy	**58,731**
9	**Celtic**	Scotland	**57,621**
10	**Inter Milan**	Italy	**55,345**

The best average in France was 52,276 at Marseille and in the Netherlands 49,014 at Ajax.

TOP 10 BIGGEST CLUB GROUNDS IN ENGLAND AND WALES

	Ground	Home team	Opened	Capacity
1	**Old Trafford**	Manchester United	1910	**76,212**
2	**Emirates Stadium**	Arsenal	2006	**60,355**
3	**St James' Park**	Newcastle United	1892	**52,387**
4	**Stadium of Light**	Sunderland	1997	**49,000**
5	**City of Manchester Stadium**	Manchester City	2002*	**47,726**
6	**Anfield**	Liverpool	1884	**45,362**
7	**Villa Park**	Aston Villa	1897	**42,640**
8	**Stamford Bridge**	Chelsea	1877	**42,449**
9	**Goodison Park**	Everton	1892	**40,569**
10	**Hillsborough**	Sheffield Wednesday	1899	**39,814**

Based on 2009 capacity

* The City of Manchester Stadium was first used for the Commonwealth Games in 2002 and from 2003 for Association Football

Manchester United's first game at Old Trafford was on 19 February 1910 when they lost 4–3 at home to Liverpool. The first tenants of Anfield were Everton.

All of the grounds in the list are in England. The biggest club ground in Wales is the Cardiff City Stadium, which opened in June 2009 and has a capacity of 26,828.

THE 10 SMALLEST GROUNDS IN BRITAIN*

	Ground	Home team(s)	Capacity
1	**Bayview Stadium**	East Fife	**2,000**
2	**Strathclyde Homes Stadium**	Dumbarton	**2,025**
3	**Cliftonhill Stadium**	Albion Rovers	**2,496**
4	**Recreation Park**	Alloa Athletic	**3,100**
5	**Links Park**	Montrose	**3,292**
6	**Galabank**	Annan Athletic	**3,500**
7	**Ochilview Park**	East Stirlingshire/Stenhousemuir†	**3,776**
8	**Forthbank Stadium**	Stirling Albion	**3,808**
9	**Borough Briggs**	Elgin City	**3,927**
10	**Glebe Park**	Brechin City	**3,960**

Based on 2009 capacity of Football League grounds in England and Scotland

† East Stirlingshire and Stenhousemuir currently share the Ochilview Park ground

All of the smallest grounds on the list are in Scotland. The lowest capacity Football League ground in England is Accrington Stanley's Fraser Eagle Stadium (The Crown Ground) with a capacity of 5,057. The ground with the lowest capacity in the Welsh Premier League is Prestatyn Town's Bastion Road, with a capacity of just a 1,000. The smallest ground in the Irish Football Association Premiership is Institute FC's YMCA Grounds (also known as the Riverside Stadium) at Drumahoe near Derry, with a capacity of 2,000.

TOP 10 GAMES WITH THE HIGHEST ATTENDANCES IN THE TOP FLIGHT OF ENGLISH FOOTBALL

	Winners/losers	Date	Attendance
1	**Manchester United vs. Arsenal**	17 Jan 1948	**83,260**
2	**Chelsea vs. Arsenal**	12 Oct 1935	**82,905**
3	**Manchester City vs. Arsenal**	23 Feb 1935	**79,491**
4	**Everton vs. Liverpool**	18 Sep 1948	**78,299**
5	**Chelsea vs. Blackpool**	16 Oct 1948	**77,696**
6	**Everton vs. Preston North End**	28 Aug 1954	**76,839**
7	**Manchester United vs. Blackburn Rovers**	31 Mar 2007	**76,098**
8	**Manchester United vs. Aston Villa**	13 Jan 2006	**76,073**
9	**Manchester United vs. Bolton Wanderers**	17 Mar 2007	**76,058**
10	**Manchester United vs. Watford**	31 Jan 2007	**76,032**

Up to and including the 2008–09 season

Manchester United's game against Arsenal in 1948 was at Manchester City's Maine Road ground because Old Trafford was out of action following bomb damage during the Second World War.

The record for a non-top-flight game was the 68,029 who watched Aston Villa play Coventry City at Villa Park in the old Second Division on 30 October 1937.

THE 10 LOWEST AVERAGE ATTENDANCES IN THE FOOTBALL LEAGUE SINCE THE SECOND WORLD WAR

	Club	Season	Average
1	**Workington**	1973–74	**1,173**
2	**Torquay United**	1985–86	**1,239**
3	**Rochdale**	1977–78	**1,275**
4	**Workington**	1975–76	**1,276**
5	**Halifax Town**	1986–87	**1,327**
6	**Workington**	1976–77	**1,338**
7	**Hartlepool United**	1982–83	**1,368**
8	**Halifax Town**	1984–85	**1,381**
9	**Halifax Town**	1985–86	**1,405**
10	**Halifax Town**	1983–84	**1,412**

Up to and including the 2008–09 season

All of the clubs listed were in the Fourth Division at the time. In the 1973–74 season, Workington had seven home attendances of less than 1,000, the lowest being 693 for the visit of Exeter City on 15 December 1973. Their highest attendance was 1,763 for the match against Darlington on 20 January 1974.

TOP 10 BIGGEST CLUB GROUNDS IN SCOTLAND

	Ground	Home team	Opened	Capacity
1	**Celtic Park†**	Celtic	1892	**60,832**
2	**Hampden Park**	Queen's Park	1903	**52,000**
3	**Ibrox Stadium**	Rangers	1899	**51,082**
4	**Pittodrie Stadium**	Aberdeen	1899	**22,199**
5	**Rugby Park**	Kilmarnock	1899	**18,128**
6	**Easter Road**	Hibernian	1893	**17,462**
7	**Tynecastle**	Heart of Midlothian	1886	**17,420**
8	**Tannadice Park**	Dundee United	1883	**14,223**
9	**Fir Park**	Motherwell	1895	**13,742**
10	**Firhill Stadium**	Partick Thistle	1909	**13,079**

Based on 2009 capacity

† Also known as Parkhead and 'Paradise'

Celtic Park was voted the 'Most atmospheric sports venue in the UK' in a poll conducted by the BBC in 2003.

Ibrox Stadium is one of only four UK stadiums on UEFA's list of Five-star Grounds. The others are Hampden Park, Old Trafford and Wembley Stadium. UEFA's elite list of stadiums all have capacities over 50,000 and their rating enables them to stage the finals of the European Championship, Champions League and any other UEFA tournament.

THE 10 WORST DISASTERS AT FOOTBALL STADIUMS WORLDWIDE

1 **Moscow** USSR, Date: 20 Oct 1982, No. killed: 340
   A crush in the Lenin (now Luzhniki) Stadium during a FC Spartak Moscow vs. HFC Haarlem match resulted in an official death toll of 67, but the true figure is believed to be as high as 340.

2 **Lima** Peru, Date: 24 May 1964, No. killed: 328
   A riot broke out during an Olympic qualifier between Peru and Argentina, spilling over into the streets; between 500 to 1,000 were injured.

3 **Accra** Ghana, Date: 09 May 2001, No. killed: 127
   A riot and stampede occurred during a match between Accra Hearts of Oak Sporting Club and Asante Kotoko.

4 **Sheffield** England, Date: 15 Apr 1989, No. killed: 96
   A crush during a Liverpool vs. Nottingham Forest match at Hillsborough resulted in Britain's worst football disaster, with 170 injured.

5 **Kathmandu** Nepal, Date: 12 Mar 1988, No. killed: 93
   A stampede broke out in the National Football Stadium when spectators attempted to flee a hailstorm, with over 100 injured.

6 **Guatemala City** Guatemala, Date: 16 Oct 1996, No. killed: 84
   A stampede in the Mateo Flores National Stadium during a Guatemala vs. Costa Rica World Cup qualifying match left 84 dead and 147 injured.

7 **Buenos Aires** Argentina, Date: 23 May 1968, No. killed: 73
   A riot broke out at a match between River Plate and Boca Juniors; 150 were injured.

8 **Glasgow** Scotland, Date: 2 Jan 1971, No. killed: 66
   A barrier collapsed during a Celtic vs. Rangers derby at Ibrox Park; 108 were injured.

9 **Bradford** England, Date: 11 May 1985, No. killed: 56
   Fire broke out during a Bradford City vs. Lincoln City match, with up to 200 injured.

10 **Cairo** Egypt, Date: 17 Feb 1974, No. killed: 49
   A stampede occurred when a wall collapsed at the Zamalek Stadium during a Cairo vs. Dukla Prague (Czechoslovakia) match; 47 were injured.

10 UNUSUAL GROUND FACTS

1 Griffin Park
Brentford's Griffin Park is the only ground in England to have a pub in each of the four corners of the ground: The Royal Oak, The Griffin, The Princess Royal and The New Inn.

2 Anfield Road
Anfield Road, the home of Liverpool FC, was originally Everton's home from 1884, when it was built, to 1892 when, following a disagreement with the landlord they moved to Goodison Park. Everton's first Football League title in 1891 was while they were Anfield tenants. The Anfield landlord, John Houlding, having a ground but no team, formed what is now the Liverpool club. The first League match at Anfield was on 8 September 1888, when Everton beat Accrington 2–1. Liverpool's first game at Anfield was on 1 September 1892 against Rotherham Town. Liverpool won 7–1 in front of around just 200 fans, despite the fact the stadium could hold 20,000.

3 Wembley Stadium
The first goal at the new Wembley Stadium was scored by 44-year-old former professional Mark Bright on 18 March 2007. The goalkeeper who conceded the first goal was the former England cricketer Phil Tufnell. It was during a game between the Geoff Thomas Foundation Charity XI and the Wembley Sponsors All Stars, played four days before the first FIFA-approved game between England Under-21s and Italy Under-21s. The honour of scoring the first goal in a professional match went to the Italian striker Giampaolo Pazzini, who scored after just 28 seconds. He completed a memorable Wembley debut by scoring a hat-trick, the first at the new stadium. England's first goal in a 3–3 draw was scored by David Bentley. John Terry scored the first goal for the senior England squad at the new Wembley when he netted in a 1–1 draw with Brazil on 1 June 2007. When Michael Owen scored against Israel on 8 September 2007, he became the first man to score at both the old and new Wembley for England.

4 County Ground
In 1940 the War Office commandeered Swindon Town's County Ground and turned it into a prisoner of war camp, installing huts for the prisoners on the pitch.

5 Deva Stadium
Chester's Deva Stadium is situated in two countries: the pitch is in Wales and the entrance in England.

6 Anfield Road

The first ground to be named after a sponsor was Scarborough United's Athletic Ground, which became known as the McCain Stadium after the frozen-food manufacturer, from 1988 until its closure in 2007. The ground was nicknamed the 'Theatre of Chips' and there was an unofficial club website of that name run by Chris Acklam, who died in 2001 at the young age of just 18.

7 Bramall Lane

Bramall Lane, Sheffield and The Oval in London are the only two grounds to have hosted an FA Cup final, a full England football international and an England cricket Test Match. Bramall Lane hosted the FA Cup final replay between Barnsley and West Bromwich Albion in 1912 and five England internationals were played at the ground between 1883 and 1930, with England winning three and losing two matches. The only cricket Test Match at Bramall Lane was the 1902 Test against Australia. The Oval, or Kennington Oval as it was known for many years, hosted every FA Cup final from the first final in 1872 to 1892, with the exception of 1873. It was also the home of the first ever unofficial international football match, between England and Scotland, on 5 March 1870. In total, it played host to 12 England international matches, the last being in 1889. One of the most famous cricket grounds, The Oval has been the venue for 92 Test Matches between September 1880 and August 2009.

8 Firhill Stadium

Partick Thistle's Firhill Stadium is the closest League ground to Glasgow city centre.

9 Gay Meadow

The old Shrewsbury Town ground at Gay Meadow was alongside the River Severn and on match day balls often ended up in the river. The club employed a local coracle maker, Fred Davies, known locally as 'The Coracle Man' to sit in his coracle to recover the balls and return them to the ground.

10 HSH Nordbank Arena

Over the years many football fans' last requests were to have their ashes spread across their favourite team's pitch. In 2008 SV Hamburg of Germany became the first club in the world to open a cemetery adjacent to its ground to enable fans to be buried next to their club. Built just 50 metres (164 feet) from their HSH Nordbank Arena, fans can pay up to €2,500 for a normal resting place or can acquire a family grave, known as a 'VIP Lounge' for €10,500.

10 FLOODLIGHT FACTS

1   The first game played under floodlights anywhere in the world was a match between two Sheffield representative teams at Bramall Lane, Sheffield on 14 October 1878. The power was provided by two portable generators that lit up four lights mounted on 9-metre (30-foot) high poles. They gave out the equivalent power of eight thousand candles! The match was watched by around 20,000 fans.

2   The first game in the world to be played under permanent floodlights was on 28 September 1949 at Holly Park, Garston in Liverpool, the home of South Liverpool FC, where Liverpool stars Jimmy Case and John Aldridge started their careers. Liverpool entertained a Nigerian team, the first team from that country to play in Britain. The game ended 2–2.

3   The first Football League club to install floodlights was Swindon Town in April 1951, beating Arsenal to the honour by five months.

4   The first competitive match under floodlights was at The Dell when Southampton Reserves played Tottenham Hotspur Reserves in a Football Combination match on 1 October 1951. Arsenal were the first Football League club to play under lights when they met Happoel Tel Aviv in a friendly on 19 September 1951.

5   The first FA Cup tie to be played under floodlights was on 14 September 1955 between Kidderminster Harriers and Brierley Hill Alliance. The first FA Cup tie between two Football League clubs to be played under lights was the first-round replay between Carlisle United and Darlington on 22 November 1955.

6   The first Football League game to be played under lights was between Portsmouth and Newcastle United at Fratton Park on 22 February 1956.

7   The first matches to be played under lights in Scotland were on 8 February 1956 when Hibernian played Raith Rovers and East Fife played Stenhousemuir in the Scottish Cup.

8   The first Scottish Football League game to be played under floodlights was on 7 March 1956 when Rangers beat Queen of the South 8–0.

9   The first time England played an entire game under lights at Wembley Stadium was on 20 November 1963 when they beat Northern Ireland 8–3. The lights at Wembley had first been switched on for the last 15 minutes of England's game against Spain on 30 November 1955.

10 In 1932 a London XI, made up of players from Spurs, Arsenal, Chelsea and West Ham played 'The Rest' under lights at White City. A white ball was used as an experiment. Every time it went out of play it was washed.

TOP 10 NATIONAL TEAM COACHES IN CHARGE FOR THE MOST MATCHES*

	Coach	Team	Years	Matches
1	**Sepp Herberger**	West Germany	1936–64	**167**
2	**Hugo Meisl, Bohemia**†	Austria	1912–14, 1919–37	**155**
3 =	**Walter Winterbottom**	England	1946–62	**139**
=	**Helmut Schön**‡	West Germany	1964–78	**139**
5	**John 'Bill' Pettersson**	Sweden	1921–36	**138**
6	**Lars Lagerbäck**§	Sweden	2000–09	**133**
7	**Aleksandar Tirnanić**	Yugoslavia	1946–66	**128**
8	**Guillermo Stábile**	Argentina	1939–60	**127**
9	**Bruce Arena**	USA	1998–2006	**117**
10	**Sepp Piontek, Poland**†	Denmark	1979–90	**115**

As at 1 November 2009

* As coach/manager of one country

† Coaches hailed from the country they managed unless otherwise indicated

‡ Helmut Schön was also the coach of Saar for nine matches between 1953 and 1956. Saar, at the time a protectorate state, is now part of the German state of Saarland

§ Sixty-six of Lagerbäck's matches were as joint coach with Tommy Söderberg

TOP 10 LONGEST-SERVING MANAGERS IN ENGLISH LEAGUE FOOTBALL

	Manager	Club	League	Date appointed
1	**Alex Ferguson**	Manchester United	PL*	**06 Nov 1986**
2	**Arsène Wenger**	Arsenal	PL	**28 Sep 1996**
3	**John Coleman**	Accrington Stanley	2	**10 Aug 1999**
4	**David Moyes**	Everton	PL	**15 Mar 2002**
5	**Steve Tilson†**	Southend United	1	**19 Nov 2003**
6	**John Still**	Dagenham & Redbridge	2	**17 Apr 2004**
7	**Rafael Benítez**	Liverpool	PL	**08 Jun 2004**
8	**Dave Jones**	Cardiff City	CH	**25 May 2005**
9	**Paul Trollope**	Bristol Rovers	1	**22 Sep 2005**
10	**Gary Johnson**	Bristol City	CH	**23 Sep 2005**

As at the start of the 2009–10 season

* PL = Premier League, CH = Championship, 1 = League 1, 2 = League 2

† Steve Tilson was appointed caretaker manager of Southend United in November 2003 before being offered the post permanently in 2004

Source: League Managers Association

Sir Alex Ferguson is the 17th-longest-serving manager of all-time. The longest serving manager is Fred Everiss who spent 46 seasons in charge of West Bromwich Albion from August 1902.

TOP 10 MANAGERS WITH THE MOST PREMIER LEAGUE MANAGER OF THE MONTH AWARDS

	Manager	Club(s)	First award	Last award	Total awards
1	**Alex Ferguson**	Manchester United	Aug 1993	Apr 2009	**23**
2	**Arsène Wenger**	Arsenal	Mar 1998	Dec 2007	**10**
3 =	**Bobby Robson**	Newcastle United	Feb 2000	Oct 2003	**6**
=	**Martin O'Neill**	Leicester City, Aston Villa	Sep 1997	Dec 2008	**6**
5 =	**Kevin Keegan**	Newcastle United	Nov 1993	Sep 1995	**5**
=	**Harry Redknapp**	West Ham United, Portsmouth	Nov 1998	Apr 2006	**5**
=	**David Moyes**	Everton	Nov 2002	Feb 2009	**5**
=	**Rafael Benítez**	Liverpool	Nov 2005	Mar 2009	**5**
9 =	**Joe Kinnear**	Wimbledon	Apr 1994	Sep 1996	**4**
=	**Gordon Strachan**	Coventry City, Southampton	Dec 1996	Dec 2002	**4**
=	**Sam Allardyce**	Bolton Wanderers	Aug 2001	Dec 2006	**4**

Up to and including the 2008–09 season

The award was first made in August 1993 (it was then known as the Carling Manager of the Month award) and won by the Premier League's longest-serving manager, Sir Alex Ferguson. Ferguson received a trophy, a magnum of champagne and a cheque for £750. Ferguson has won at least one award every season except 2001–02. The award is currently known as the Barclays Premier League Manager of the Month award.

Ferguson has won the Premier League Manager of the Year award on nine occasions since its inauguration in 1993–94.

TOP 10 CURRENT ENGLISH LEAGUE CLUBS WITH THE MOST MANAGERS IN THEIR HISTORY*

	Club	Managers
1	**Crystal Palace**	**48**
2	**Notts County**	**47**
3 =	**Darlington**	**45**
=	**Queens Park Rangers**	**45**
5	**Coventry City**	**44**
6 =	**Hartlepool United**	**42**
=	**Stockport County**	**42**
8 =	**Bradford City**	**41**
=	**Carlisle United**	**41**
=	**Millwall**	**41**
=	**Northampton Town**	**41**

* Including Premier League clubs, as at the start of the 2009–10 season
Source: League Managers Association

The average duration of stay of any Crystal Palace manager is 2 years 51 days.

TOP 10 CLUBS WITH THE MOST NORTHERN PREMIER LEAGUE/CONFERENCE TITLES

	Club	NPL titles	Conference titles	Total
1	**Boston United**	4	1	**5**
2	**Macclesfield Town**	3	1	**4**
3 =	**Altrincham**	1	2	**3**
=	**Barrow**	3	0	**3**
=	**Runcorn**	2	1	**3**
6 =	**Accrington Stanley**	1	1	**2**
=	**Burton Albion**	1	1	**2**
=	**Gateshead**	2	0	**2**
=	**Marine**	2	0	**2**
=	**Mossley**	2	0	**2**
=	**Stafford Rangers**	2	0	**2**
=	**Stalybridge Celtic**	2	0	**2**
=	**Wigan Athletic**	2	0	**2**

Up to and including the 2008–09 season

Altrincham were the first Football Conference winners in 1979–80. The Northern Premier League (NPL) (now known as the Unibond League Premier Division) was founded in 1968 as the northern equivalent of the Southern League and replaced the Northern League as the region's senior non-Football League competition. The first winners of the Northern Premier League were Macclesfield Town.

TOP 10 CLUBS WITH THE MOST SOUTHERN LEAGUE/CONFERENCE TITLES

	Club	Southern League titles	Conference titles	Total
1	**Southampton/Southampton St Mary's/ Southampton Reserves**	7	0	**7**
2	**Merthyr Tydfil**	6	0	**6**
3	**Yeovil Town/ Yeovil & Petters United**	4	1	**5**
4 =	**Dartford**	4	0	**4**
=	**Kettering Town**	4	0	**4**
=	**Plymouth Argyle/Plymouth Argyle Reserves**	4	0	**4**
7 =	**Bath City**	3	0	**3**
=	**Brighton & Hove Albion/Brighton & Hove Albion Reserves**	3	0	**3**
=	**Chelmsford City**	3	0	**3**
=	**Oxford United/Headington United**	3	0	**3**
=	**Wimbledon**	3	0	**3**

Up to and including the 2008–09 season

Enfield, in 1982–83, were the first southern winners of the Football Conference. The Southern League was, for many years, the most prestigious league outside the Football League. It was formed in 1894 and in 1920 all members of the Southern League First Division applied en masse to join the Football League and were duly elected into what became, originally, the Third Division, and then, the following year, the Third Division South. The Southern League Premier Division currently feeds teams into the Conference South, and occasionally Conference North. The first winners of the Southern League in 1894–95 were Millwall Athletic (Division One) and New Brompton (Division Two). From 2009–10 the Southern League became known as the Zamaretto Football League.

TOP 10 CLUBS WITH THE MOST FA TROPHY FINAL APPEARANCES

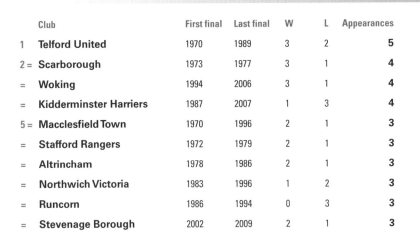

	Club	First final	Last final	W	L	Appearances
1	**Telford United**	1970	1989	3	2	5
2 =	**Scarborough**	1973	1977	3	1	4
=	**Woking**	1994	2006	3	1	4
=	**Kidderminster Harriers**	1987	2007	1	3	4
5 =	**Macclesfield Town**	1970	1996	2	1	3
=	**Stafford Rangers**	1972	1979	2	1	3
=	**Altrincham**	1978	1986	2	1	3
=	**Northwich Victoria**	1983	1996	1	2	3
=	**Runcorn**	1986	1994	0	3	3
=	**Stevenage Borough**	2002	2009	2	1	3

Up to and including the 2009 competition

The FA Trophy, or the Football Association Challenge Trophy to give it its correct title, was inaugurated in 1969 to allow semi-professional footballers outside the Football League to play in a cup competition because they were not eligible to play in the FA Amateur Cup, which was at the time the top knockout competition for non-League teams, but open to amateur teams only. Now, those teams that play in levels five–eight of the football pyramid are eligible to enter. Macclesfield Town beat Telford United 2–0 in front of 28,000 fans at Wembley Stadium to win the first final in 1970. In the first final at the new Wembley Stadium in 2007 a record 53,262 fans saw Stevenage Borough beat Kidderminster Harriers 3–2. Manager Geoff Chapple led Woking and Kingstonian to five trophies within seven years between 1994–2000.

TOP 10 ATTENDANCES AT THE FA TROPHY FINAL

	Winners/runners-up	Year	Attendance
1	**Stevenage Borough vs. Kidderminster Harriers**	2007	**53,262**
2	**Ebbsfleet United vs. Torquay United**	2008	**40,186**
3	**Wycombe Wanderers vs. Kidderminster Harriers**	1991	**34,842**
4	**Wycombe Wanderers vs. Runcorn**	1993	**32,968**
5	**Colchester United vs. Witton Albion**	1992	**32,254**
6	**Stafford Rangers vs. Kettering Town**	1979	**32,000**
7	**Telford United vs. Hillingdon Borough**	1971	**29,500**
8	**Macclesfield Town vs. Telford United**	1970	**28,000**
9	**Stevenage Borough vs. York City**	2009	**27,102**
10	**Dagenham vs. Mossley**	1980	**26,000**

Up to and including the 2009 final

All finals were played at the old Wembley Stadium between 1970 and 2000. During Wembley's rebuilding it was held at Villa Park (2001–05) and at West Ham's Upton Park ground (2006). The first final at the new Wembley Stadium attracted the record crowd of 53,262.

THE 10 FIRST CONFERENCE CLUBS PROMOTED TO THE FOOTBALL LEAGUE

	Season	Relegated from Football League	Promoted to Football League
1	1986–87	Lincoln City	**Scarborough**
2	1987–88	Newport County	**Lincoln City**
3	1988–89	Darlington	**Maidstone United**
4	1989–90	Colchester United	**Darlington**
5	1990–91	*	**Barnet**
6	1991–92	*	**Colchester United**
7	1992–93	Halifax Town	**Wycombe Wanderers**
8	1996–97	Hereford United	**Macclesfield Town**
9	1997–98	Doncaster Rovers	**Halifax Town**
10	1998–99	Scarborough	**Cheltenham Town**

* No relegation from the Football League in these seasons

From the 1986–87 season, automatic promotion between the Conference and the Football League was agreed, subject to ground conditions. Prior to 1986, promotion to the Football League was subject to election and between the start of the Conference in 1979–80 and 1986 none of its champions gained election into the League. The first team to benefit from automatic promotion was Scarborough at the expense of Lincoln City in 1987. The three successive Conference winners in 1994–96, Kidderminster Harriers, Macclesfield Town and Stevenage Borough, all missed out on automatic promotion to the Football League because their grounds did not meet League requirements. As a consequence, Northampton Town, Exeter City and Torquay United respectively were spared their League status. Barnet have twice been automatically promoted from the Conference to the League. Since 2003 two teams gain automatic promotion to the Football League.

10 UNUSUAL GROUND NAMES

	Ground name	Club	League/division
1	**Evans Bevan Field**	Baglan Red Dragon	South Wales Amateur Football League
2	**The Euronics Ground**	Barton Town Old Boys	Northern Counties East League Div. 1
3	**Perry's Crabble Stadium**	Dover Athletic	Conference South
4	**The Dripping Pan**	Lewes	Conference South
5	**Muglet Lane**	Maltby Main	Northern Counties East League Premier Div.
6	**Mackessack Park**	Rothes	Highland Football League
7	**Look Local Stadium**	Stocksbridge Park Steels	Northern Premier League Div. 1 (South)
8	**Bargain Booze Stadium***	Witton Albion	Northern Premier League Premier Div.
9	**Victor Gladwish Stadium**	Worthing/ Horsham†	Isthmian Div. 1 (South) Isthmian League Premier
10	**Kitkat Crescent**	York City	Conference National

* The name of their ground in the 2001–02 season, but still called by this name in some circles

† Ground-share with Worthing

One of the most strangely named overseas stadiums is the Middelfart Stadium, home of Middelfart G og BK who play in the Danmarksserien Group 2, the fourth level of Danish football. Athlone Town of the Football Association of Ireland 1st Division play at the quaintly named Lissywollen Ground.

10 FAMOUS PLAYERS WHO STARTED THEIR CAREERS IN NON-LEAGUE FOOTBALL

1 John Aldridge
Non-League club: South Liverpool
Professional clubs: Newport County, Oxford United, Liverpool, Real Sociedad (Spain), Tranmere Rovers

2 Garry Birtles
Non-League club: Long Eaton United
Professional clubs: Nottingham Forest, Manchester United, Notts County, Grimsby Town

3 Jimmy Bullard
Non-League club: Gravesend & Northfleet (now Ebbsfleet United)
Professional clubs: Peterborough United, Wigan Athletic, Fulham, Hull City

4 D. J. Campbell
Non-League clubs: Chesham United, Stevenage Borough, Yeading
Professional clubs: Brentford, Birmingham City, Leicester City, Blackpool

5 Stan Collymore
Non-League club: Stafford Rangers
Professional clubs: Crystal Palace, Southend United, Nottingham Forest, Liverpool, Aston Villa, Fulham, Leicester City, Bradford City, Real Oviedo (Spain)

6 Les Ferdinand
Non-League clubs: Southall, Hayes
Professional clubs: Queens Park Rangers, Brentford, Besiktas (Turkey), Newcastle United, Tottenham Hotspur, West Ham United, Leicester City, Bolton Wanderers, Reading, Watford

7 Vinnie Jones
Non-League club: Wealdstone
Professional clubs: Holmsund (Sweden), Wimbledon, Leeds United, Sheffield United, Chelsea, Queens Park Rangers

8 Kevin Phillips
Non-League club: Baldock Town
Professional clubs: Watford, Sunderland, Southampton, Aston Villa, West Bromwich Albion, Birmingham City

9 Stuart Pearce
Non-League club: Wealdstone
Professional clubs: Coventry City, Nottingham Forest, Newcastle United, West Ham United, Manchester City

10 Ian Wright
Non-League club: Greenwich Borough
Professional clubs: Crystal Palace, Arsenal, West Ham United, Nottingham Forest, Celtic, Burnley

THE 10 OLDEST ENGLISH LEAGUE CLUBS*

	Club	Year formed
1	**Notts County**	**1862**
2	**Stoke City**	**1863**
3	**Nottingham Forest**	**1865**
4	**Chesterfield**	**1866**
5	**Sheffield Wednesday**	**1867**
6	**Reading**	**1871**
7	**Wrexham**	**1873**
8 =	**Aston Villa**	**1874**
=	**Bolton Wanderers**	**1874**
10 =	**Birmingham City**	**1875**
=	**Blackburn Rovers**	**1875**

Including Premier League clubs

The first Association Football Club in England was the Sheffield Club, formed on 24 October 1857. Scotland's oldest club is Queen's Park, formed in 1867. The oldest club in Wales is Druids (now known as Cefn Druids) who were formed in 1873 and the oldest club in all Ireland is Cliftonville, founded in 1879.

THE 10 OLDEST FOOTBALL ASSOCIATIONS

	Association name	Country	Year formed
1	**Football Association**	England	**1863**
2	**Scottish Football Association**	Scotland	**1873**
3	**Football Association of Wales**	Wales	**1876**
4	**Irish Football Association**	Northern Ireland	**1880**
5 =	**Dansk Boldspil-Union**	Denmark	**1889**
=	**Koninklijke Nederlandse Voetbalbond**	Netherlands	**1889**
7	**New Zealand Football**	New Zealand	**1891**
8	**Football Association of Singapore***	Singapore	**1892**
9	**Asociación de Fútbol Argentino**	Argentina	**1893**
10 =	**Federación de Fútbol de Chile**	Chile	**1895**
=	**Schweizerischer Fussballverband**	Switzerland	**1895**
=	**Union Royale Belge des Sociétés de Football Association**	Belgium	**1895**

* Formerly the Singapore Amateur Football Association

The Football Association was founded following a meeting at the Freemasons' Tavern, Covent Garden, London, on 26 October 1863. It is disputed whether this was the present-day Freemasons Arms, Long Acre, or that it was demolished to make way for the New Connaught Rooms, Great Queen Street.

	Club	First–last final	Wins	Runners-up	Total appearances
1	**Manchester United**	1953–2007	9	4	**13**
2	**Arsenal**	1965–2009	7	1	**8**
3 =	**West Ham United**	1957–99	3	4	**7**
=	**Everton**	1961–2002	3	4	**7**
5 =	**Manchester City**	1979–2008	2	4	**6**
=	**Liverpool**	1963–2009	3	3	**6**
7 =	**Wolverhampton Wanderers**	1953–76	1	4	**5**
=	**Tottenham Hotspur**	1970–95	3	2	**5**
=	**Coventry City**	1968–2000	1	4	**5**
=	**Aston Villa**	1972–2004	3	2	**5**

Up to and including 2009

The FA Youth Cup is restricted to players under the age of 18 and was inaugurated in the 1952–53 season. Manchester United were the first winners, beating Wolverhampton Wanderers 9–3 on aggregate over two legs. The Manchester United side that won the first final included Eddie Colman, Duncan Edwards, Billy Whelan and David Pegg, who all lost their lives in the Munich air crash in 1958.

Ipswich Town have won all three finals they appeared in: 1973, 1975 and 2005.

The following teams have completed the FA Cup/FA Youth Cup double in the same season: Arsenal (1971), Everton (1984), Coventry City (1987) and Liverpool (2006).

The record attendance for an FA Youth Cup match was for the semi-final first leg between Arsenal and Manchester United at The Emirates Stadium in 2007 when 38,187 fans saw Arsenal win 1–0.

TOP 10 CLUBS WITH THE MOST MASTERS CUP TITLES

Club	Regional final wins	Grand final wins	Total wins
1 = Leicester City	6	2	8
= Liverpool	6	2	8
3 = Chelsea	5	1	6
= Rangers	5	1	6
= Wolverhampton Wanderers	5	1	6
6 = Leeds United	4	0	4
= Manchester City	3	1	4
= Middlesbrough	4	0	4
= Newcastle United	4	0	4
10 = Coventry City	3	0	3
= Nottingham Forest	2	1	3
= Tottenham Hotspur	3	0	3
= Tranmere Rovers	2	1	3

Up to and including the 2009 Masters Cup

The first Masters Cup was held in 1980. Nottingham Forest beat Rangers 3–2 in the final. Masters football is played with six-a-side on a pitch measuring 60 x 30 metres (196 feet 10 inches x 97 feet 6 inches). Play lasts for eight minutes each half and there is no offside. Players must be over the age of 35. There are eight regional competitions throughout the summer (that are concluded on a single evening), with the winner from each going through to the grand final in September. Leicester City (2005 and 2007) and Liverpool (2001 and 2002) have each won the cup a record two times.

TOP 10 CLUBS WITH THE LONGEST CONTINUAL SPELL IN TOP-FLIGHT FOOTBALL IN ENGLAND

	Club	Last season not in the top flight	Consecutive seasons
1	**Arsenal**	1914–15	**84**
2	**Everton**	1953–54	**56**
3	**Liverpool**	1961–62	**48**
4	**Manchester United**	1974–75	**35**
5	**Tottenham Hotspur**	1977–78	**32**
6	**Aston Villa**	1987–88	**22**
7	**Chelsea**	1988–89	**21**
8 =	**Blackburn Rovers**	2000–01	**9**
=	**Bolton Wanderers**	2000–01	**9**
=	**Fulham**	2000–01	**9**

Up to and including the 2009–10 season

In 1914–15, the last season before the First World War, Chelsea and Tottenham Hotspur finished in the two relegation places in the First Division. Derby County and Preston North End filled the two promotion places from the Second Division while Arsenal finished sixth (later changed to fifth) in the same division. When the Football League resumed in 1919–20, the First Division was extended from 20 to 22 teams but instead of leaving the two relegated teams in the top flight and promoting the two teams from the Second Division, the Football League relegated Tottenham Hotspur and promoted Arsenal from sixth place. The Gunners have never been out of the top flight since despite not winning promotion.

TOP 10 RICHEST FOOTBALL CLUBS*

	Club	Country	Revenue (€)
1	**Real Madrid**	Spain	**365,800,000**
2	**Manchester United**	England	**324,800,000**
3	**Barcelona**	Spain	**308,800,000**
4	**Bayern Munich**	Germany	**295,300,000**
5	**Chelsea**	England	**268,900,000**
6	**Arsenal**	England	**264,400,000**
7	**Liverpool**	England	**210,900,000**
8	**AC Milan**	Italy	**209,500,000**
9	**AS Roma**	Italy	**175,400,000**
10	**Inter Milan**	Italy	**172,900,000**

Based on total revenue figures in 2007–08

Source: Deloitte Football Money League 2009

The only newcomer on the list compared to 2006–07 figures is AS Roma who replace Tottenham Hotspur.

10 FOOTBALL MILESTONES

	Year	Milestone
1	**1863**	Football Association formed
2	**1872**	First FA Cup final
3	**1885**	Professionalism legalized
4	**1888**	Football League founded
5	**1904**	FIFA founded
6	**1930**	First World Cup
7	**1956**	First European Champion Clubs' Cup (now Champions League) final
8	**1981**	Three points for a win introduced in England
9	**1992**	FA Premier League founded
10	**1995**	The Bosman Ruling made it easy for footballers to move between European Union countries

10 FOOTBALL INNOVATIONS

	Innovation	Year adopted
1	**Laws of the game**	**1848**
2	**Corner kick**	**1872**
3	**Offside law**	**1873**
4	**Crossbar**	**1875**
5	**Floodlighting**	**1878***
6	**Shinpads**	**1880**
7	**Two-handed throw-in**	**1882**
8	**Penalty kick**	**1891**
9	**Goal nets**	**1891**
10	**Numbers on shirts**	**1928**

* Floodlighting was not officially approved for use by the Football Association until December 1950

10 FOOTBALL HOAXES

1 Imaginary player
On 12 January 2009 *The Times* ran a feature called 'Football's Top 50 Rising Stars'. At number 30 was a 16-year-old Moldovan called Masal Bugduv who they described as 'Moldova's finest'. He might have been, had he existed, but he was an imaginary player created on an Internet blog.

2 Hoax call
Graeme Souness was always a very shrewd manager and the day he got a call from the former World Footballer of the Year George Weah suggesting that he should take a look at his 30-year-old cousin Ali Dia, who was, he said, a Senegalese international and currently playing for the top French side Paris Saint-Germain, Souness signed him on a 30-day trial. But after just 20 minutes of his debut for Southampton, against Leeds United on 23 November 1996, Souness soon realized he had been duped and Dia was substituted, never to play for the team again. He wasn't a Senegalese international, he was playing as an amateur with Blyth Spartans and not Paris Saint-Germain. Furthermore, it had not been George Weah at the other end of the telephone.

3 Twelve, not eleven
When Manchester United published a team photo taken before the Champions League quarter-final with Bayern Munich in April 2001, fans were left wondering who the additional member of their team was. It was Karl Power, not a footballer but a serial prankster from Droylsden, Manchester. Nicknamed 'Fat Neck', Power hung around, dressed in full kit, awaiting the arrival of the team on to the pitch and just strolled over and joined them for the photo call.

4 Maradona to Moscow
Izvestia, the Soviet newspaper, reported in 1988 that Argentina's Diego Maradona was to join Spartak Moscow from Napoli. It turned out to be an April Fool's joke, but Associated Press accepted the story because it came from a Soviet newspaper.

5 Clough makes a substitution
When Franz Carr made his debut for Nottingham Forest in a 2–1 win at Aston Villa on 12 October 1985 he had such a good game that ATV commentator Gary Newbon wanted to interview the 19-year-old after the match. Newbon's wish was duly granted by manager Brian Clough – except Cloughie sent a lad from the youth team to do the interview instead of Carr.

6 So near, yet so far

Portugal failed to qualify for the 1998 World Cup finals in France. However, a month before the finals they were thrown a lifeline when Portuguese radio announced that Iran had been forced to pull out of the tournament because of security problems and that FIFA had pulled Portugal out of a random draw as the nation to replace them. Sadly for Portugal this was an April Fool's Day joke and they never got to France 98.

7 Interesting facts about AC Omonio

Prior to their trip to Cyprus for their UEFA Cup tie against AC Omonio in 2008–09, Manchester City fans checked up about their opponents on Wikipedia to find out that Richard Clayderman and Jean Claude van Damme were former players. Some fans may have fallen for the 'tweaking' made to the website but the *Daily Mirror* certainly did fall for it because, in their pre-match report, they also carried useful information gleaned from Wikipedia such as: the Omonio fans wore hats made from old shoes and sang a song about a 'little potato'. But surely they should have twigged when Wiki reported that the club had a new sponsor, Natasha Kaplinsky!

8 International incident – almost!

News leaked in 2003 that Coventry City goalkeeper Steve Ogrizovic had been captured by the Kazakhstan government on spying charges during his round-the-world trip to raise money for a young goalkeeper's charity. There were calls online for Prime Minister Tony Blair to intervene. However, journalists at the *Coventry Evening Telegraph* thought it strange and went along to Coventry's training ground to investigate, only to find Ogrizovic training!

9 False move

Arbroath's new signing Eddie Forrest could not resist the offer made to him by Raith Rovers' chairman Danny Smith over the telephone to join the Kirkcaldy side in 2003. He duly informed his teammates at Arbroath that he was on his way to the reigning Second Division champions, only to be more than a little disappointed when he found out that the man on the end of the phone wasn't the Raith Rovers' chairman at all but his own teammate and club captain, Paul Browne.

10 'Dream' fullback

In 1999 the *News of the World* carried the story that Liverpool manager Gerard Houllier was about to sign France Under-21 international Didier Baptise for £3.5 million. *The Times* (also owned by Rupert Murdoch) and other newspapers picked up on the *News of the World* 'exclusive', only to discover that Baptise was the fullback for Harchester United of Sky One's *Dream Team* TV programme.

10 FOOTBALL ODDITIES

1   The winning letter
The last time the winners of the top two divisions in English football started with the same letter of the alphabet was in 1990 when Liverpool won the First Division and Leeds United won the Second Division.

2   One, two, one, two
Everton opened a second club shop in the new Liverpool One shopping complex in 2009. They called it 'Everton Two', not unnaturally, because their first shop is at their Goodison Park ground. However, the postal address of the new shop is 'Everton Two, Liverpool One'.

3   Nearly 40 years of good behaviour
When Frank Saul was sent off for Tottenham Hotspur against Burnley on 4 December 1965, he was the first Spurs player since 1928 to get his marching orders in a League game.

4   Biblical reference
Scottish club Queen of the South is one of the few football clubs to be mentioned in the Bible. Matthew 12:42 says: 'The Queen of the South will rise at the judgment with this generation and condemn it; for she came from the ends of the earth to listen to Solomon's wisdom, and now one greater than Solomon is here.'

5   Hat-trick grooms
Bill Poyntz scored a hat-trick for Leeds United against Leicester City on 20 February 1922 and Southport's Billy Holmes scored a hat-trick against Carlisle United on 30 October 1954 – nothing unusual about that, except both men had got married on the morning of their respective matches.

6 Goalkeeper? Fullback?
Gordon Nisbet made his debut for West Bromwich Albion as a goalkeeper in a 3–1 defeat at Coventry City on 12 August 1969. His next match for them was as a fullback on 18 December 1971 against Arsenal, which is the position he played in for the remainder of his career.

7 Managerial hitch
When Joe Royle arrived at Boundary Park for his first day as the new Oldham Athletic manager in 1982, he turned up in a lorry after his car broke down and he hitched a lift to the ground.

8 Which way is Scotland?
South African-born John Hewie made his international debut for Scotland against England at Hampden Park on 14 April 1956. It was the first time Hewie had ever been to Scotland.

9 Five lucky grounds
Wolverhampton Wanderers are the only club to have appeared in the FA Cup final on five different grounds, playing at Kennington Oval, Fallowfield, Crystal Palace, Stamford Bridge and Wembley Stadium.

10 Eight in a half
On 4 May 1935, Exeter City played their final match of the 1934–35 season at home to Aldershot. At half-time the game was goalless but at the end of the 90 minutes Exeter had won 8–1.

TOP 10 MOST PERFORMED FOOTBALL-THEMED SONGS IN THE UK

	Song	Performer
1	**'Glory Glory Man United'**	Manchester United FC
2	**'Nessun Dorma'**	Luciano Pavarotti
3	**'Hot Stuff'**	Arsenal FC
4	**'Hey Baby'**	DJ Otzi
5	**'Blue is the Colour'**	Chelsea FC
6	**'Carnaval de Paris'**	Dario G
7	**'Three Lions'**	The Lightning Seeds featuring (David) Baddiel and (Frank) Skinner
8	**'Come On You Reds'**	Manchester United FC
9	**'Vindaloo'**	Fat Les
10	**'World in Motion'**	New Order

Source: PRS for Music

In 2009 PRS (Performing Right Society) for Music, the organization that collects royalties for songwriters and composers, analyzed millions of performances of music by broadcasters, at football grounds and in live performance to come up with this list of the UK's most popular football anthems over the past five years. Manchester United dominates the list, topping it with 'Glory Glory Man United' as well as scoring with fan favourite 'Come On You Reds'. 'Nessun Dorma' became established as a football song after being used by the BBC as the theme song for their 1990 World Cup coverage in Italy. 'Hey Baby' was the unofficial theme for the 2002 World Cup and 'Carnaval de Paris' was recorded for the 1998 World Cup in France.

TOP 10 HIGHEST-GROSSING FOOTBALL FILMS

	Film/country	Year	Worldwide box office ($)
1	**Bend It Like Beckham** (UK/Germany/USA)	2002	76,583,333
2	**She's the Man** (US/Canada)	2006	57,194,667
3	**Kicking & Screaming** (USA)	2005	56,070,433
4	**Shaolin Soccer** (Hong Kong)	2001	42,776,760
5	**Goal! The Dream Begins** (UK/USA)	2005	27,610,873
6	**The Big Green** (USA)	1995	17,736,619
7	**Ladybugs** (USA)	1992	14,796,494
8	**Escape to Victory** (USA)	1981	10,853,418
9	**Goal II: Living the Dream** (UK)	2007	7,864,905
10	**Mean Machine** (UK/USA)	2001	7,310,206

The oldest film in this list, the John Huston-directed *Escape to Victory* (distributed in the USA as *Victory*), in which Allied prisoners of war play the German team during the Second World War, was unusual in that in addition to Michael Caine, Sylvester Stallone and other actors, many of the players on both sides were world-class professional footballers including Pelé (Brazil), Bobby Moore (England), Osvaldo Ardiles (Argentina), Mike Summerbee (England), Kazimierz Deyna (Poland) and John Wark (Scotland).

10 ENGLISH LEAGUE CLUBS WITH UNIQUE NAMES*

1 **Accrington Stanley**
The original Accrington team that were founder members of the Football League in 1888, called simply 'Accrington', folded in 1893. However, another team called Stanley Villa had been formed in 1891, taking their name from the Stanley Arms where they were based. Following the demise of Accrington, Stanley Villa took the town name and became known as Accrington Stanley, abandoning the word 'Villa'. The club went out of business in 1966 and the existing Accrington Stanley was formed two years later.

2 **Aston Villa**
Named Aston Villa as they were formed in 1874 by members of the Villa Cross Wesleyan Chapel, located in the Aston area of Birmingham.

3 **Crewe Alexandra**
The club was formed in 1877 as a rival to the successful Crewe Cricket Club. They took the name 'Alexandra' from Princess Alexandra, although some authorities now believe the Princess Alexandra from which they took their name was a public house.

4 **Crystal Palace**
Crystal Palace was formed in 1905 by workers of the Crystal Palace, the famous glass building that stood at the top of Sydenham Hill in Lewisham, south-east London. The new team played on the FA Cup final ground adjacent to the Palace. The Crystal Palace was erected initially for the Great Exhibition of 1851 and was located in London's Hyde Park before its removal to Sydenham Hill. It burned down in 1936.

5 **Leyton Orient**
Originally called the Eagle Cricket Club and then, in 1888, Orient Football Club, following the suggestion from one of their players, who worked for the Orient Shipping Company (now part of P&O) at the time. They have had several name changes over the years including Clapton Orient, Leyton Orient, simply Orient and back to Leyton Orient in 1987.

6 **Nottingham Forest**
Nottingham Forest were formed in 1865 by a group of shinty (a Gaelic sport similar to hockey) players. The club got its name from its first home, The Forest Recreation Ground, which is now home of the famous annual Nottingham Goose Fair. The Recreation Ground was part of Sherwood Forest at one time.

7 Plymouth Argyle

There is speculation as to where the name 'Argyle' came from but it is likely that the club was named after the Argyle Tavern where founder members are likely to have had meetings.

8 Port Vale

Port Vale are not named after a geographical location. While an area of the Potteries called Port Vale did exist in the mid-1800s, it was not there at the time of the club's formation in 1876. They actually took their name from Port Vale House in Stoke-on-Trent where members had their first meeting. They changed their name to Burslem Port Vale when they moved to the Burslem area of the Potteries but later dropped the prefix.

9 Sheffield Wednesday

Sheffield Wednesday were born following a meeting of the Wednesday Cricket Club (so called because it was the day of the week its members took off work to play the sport) at the Adelphi public house on Arundel Street and Sycamore Street (now the home of the Crucible Theatre, snooker's best-known venue). The members decided they wanted some activity in the winter and thought members would like to play Association Football, and so the new club was created and called The Wednesday Football Club. They changed their name to Sheffield Wednesday Football Club in 1929.

10 Tottenham Hotspur

Spurs were formed in 1862 by local grammar-school boys and members of the Hotspur Cricket Club, naming their new club the Hotspur Football Club. It is believed the name 'Hotspur' came from Sir Henry Percy, known as Harry Hotspur. He lived locally and his descendants later owned land in the area. The club renamed itself as Tottenham Hotspur in 1884.

* Clubs where the second part of their names is unique (includes Premier League teams)

The only other clubs in the English Football League with unique names are: Milton Keynes Dons, Preston North End and Queens Park Rangers (Dagenham & Redbridge being excluded as a place name).

Crystal Palace is the only team in the English League whose name begins with five consonants.

	Club	Nickname
1	**Brentford**	**Bees**
2	**Brighton & Hove Albion**	**Seagulls**
3	**Crystal Palace**	**Eagles**
4	**Derby County**	**Rams**
5	**Hull City**	**Tigers**
6	**Leicester City**	**Foxes**
7	**Millwall**	**Lions**
8	**Norwich City**	**Canaries**
9	**Sheffield Wednesday**	**Owls**
10	**Sunderland**	**Black Cats**

Some people (notably Darlington supporters) refer to Hartlepool United as the 'Monkey Hangers', in reference to the townspeople who, during the Napoleonic Wars, allegedly hanged a monkey, the only survivor of a French ship wrecked off the coast of Hartlepool, believing it to be a French spy!

THE 10 LATEST WINNERS OF THE MASCOT GRAND NATIONAL

	Winning mascot	Representing	Year
1	**Stag**	Huntingdon Rugby Club	**2009**
2	**Wacky Macky Bear**	Saffron Walden	**2008**
3	**Wacky Macky Bear**	Saffron Walden	**2007**
4	**Mickey the Monkey**	Kick For Life	**2006**
5	**Scoop Six Squirrel**	*The Sun* newspaper	**2005**
6	**Graham the Gorilla**	Finedon Volta	**2004**
7	**Chaddy the Owl**	Oldham Athletic	**2003**
8	**Chaddy the Owl**	Oldham Athletic	**2002**
9	**Dazzle the Lion**	Rushden & Diamonds	**2001**
10	**Harry the Hornet**	Watford	**2000**

Now known as the John Smith's Mascot Grand National, it is held at Huntingdon racecourse each October and was the idea of the management of the course. The first race was staged in 1999 and won by Beau Brummie Bulldog representing Birmingham City. Competitors have to negotiate six fences and in 2000 there was a record field of 49 'mascoteers'. The 2004 winner, Graham the Gorrilla, was the mascot of local club Finedon Volta.

10 MORE PIECES OF FOOTBALL TRIVIA

1 **Stay optimistic**
Fulham lost 10–0 to Liverpool in the first leg of their League Cup match on 23 September 1986. However, for the return leg at Craven Cottage two weeks later, the home side printed the following notice in their programme: 'In the event of the match ending up all square at the end of 90 minutes play in the second leg...' You have to admire their optimism!

2 **The first to see red**
When outfielder Lawrie Sanchez of Reading tipped a ball over the bar in a Football League Trophy game against Oxford United on 14 August 1982, it is believed he became the first player to be red-carded for a 'professional foul'. The issuing of red cards for deliberate fouls came as a result of a foul committed by Willie Young of Arsenal in the 1980 FA Cup final, when he deliberately fouled West Ham's Paul Allen and deprived the then youngest FA Cup finalist a clear goalscoring opportunity. Referee George Courtney was powerless to do anything other than allow West Ham a free kick and issue Young with a yellow card.

3 **One time only**
Harold McNaughton played just one game for Liverpool, on 23 October 1920, when he stood in for the regular first-team goalkeeper Elisha Scott. The opponents for McNaughton's debut at Anfield were Everton. He kept a clean sheet in a 1–0 win.

4 **Heads-up**
Scotland's Joe Craig scored on his international debut before he had even kicked the ball. Against Sweden on 27 April 1977, he came on as a substitute for Kenny Burns after 75 minutes and 2 minutes later scored with his first touch of the ball – a header! He never played for Scotland again.

5 **Let's meet at Logie Green**
The only Scottish Cup final to be played outside Glasgow was in 1896 when the two Edinburgh sides Hearts and Hibernian met at Logie Green, Edinburgh, with Hearts winning 3–1 in front of 16,000 fans. Logie Green Park was the home of St Bernard's, a Scottish First Division side at the time.

6 Time to step up and shoot-out
The first match in Britain to be decided on penalties was the semi-final of the Watney Cup between Hull City and Manchester United on 5 August 1970. After the game finished 1–1, United beat Second Division Hull 4–3 on penalties. In the final United lost 4–1 to Derby County.

7 Complete collection
Scot Jimmy Delaney claimed a unique hat-trick in 1954 when he won an Irish Cup winners' medal with Derry City, adding to his collection of a Scottish Cup winners' medal with Celtic in 1937 and English Cup winners' medal with Manchester United in 1948. He also collected a runners-up medal in the Republic of Ireland with Cork Athletic in 1956.

8 He's off, you're on
Substitutes were first allowed in the Football League during the 1965–66 season and the first substitute to replace another player was Keith Peacock of Charlton Athletic who came on for Mick Rose against Bolton Wanderers on 21 August 1965. On the same day Bobby Knox of Barrow became the first substitute to score a goal. The first substitute in an FA Cup final was Dennis Clarke of West Bromwich Albion, who came on for John Kaye in the 1968 final win over Everton. Eddie Kelly of Arsenal was the first substitute to score in an FA Cup final when he netted in Arsenal's win over Liverpool in the 1971 final.

9 Importance of away goals
The first club to lose a European tie on the 'away goals' rule was Northern Irish side Glentoran who were eliminated by Portuguese giants Benfica in 1967–68 after a 1–1 draw at Glentoran's Oval ground was followed by a goalless draw in Benfica's Stadium of Light.

10 Seven and out
Spare a thought for Billy Minter of St Albans City. He once scored seven goals in a match and was on the losing side. Playing against Dulwich Hamlet in an FA Cup fourth-round qualifying game on 22 November 1922 he scored seven times, which was one less than Dulwich's total who ran out 8–7 winners.

10 FOOTBALL FANZINES

	Club	Fanzine
1	**AFC Wimbledon**	*Womble Underground Press*
2	**Brighton & Hove Albion**	*The Seagull Love Review*
3	**Burton Albion**	*Clough The Magic Dragon*
4	**Fulham**	*There's Only One 'F' In Fulham*
5	**Hartlepool United**	*Monkey Business*
6	**Manchester City**	*King Of The Kippax*
7	**Queens Park Rangers**	*A Kick Up The R's*
8	**Reading**	*Hob Nob Anyone?*
9	**Stoke City**	*The Oatcake*
10	**Wycombe Wanderers**	*Choirboys On The Net*

Britain's oldest football fanzine is *Gunflash*, the official magazine of Arsenal. It was first published on 1 September 1949.

TOP 10 HIGHEST-EARNING FOOTBALLERS IN EUROPE*

	Player	Club	Annual earnings (€)
1	**Cristiano Ronaldo**	Real Madrid	**13,000,000**
2	**Kaká**	Real Madrid	**10,000,000**
3	**Emmanuel Adebayor**	Manchester City	**9,900,000**
4	**Robinho**	Manchester City	**9,650,000**
5	**Zlatan Ibrahimović**	Inter Milan	**9,500,000**
6 =	**Frank Lampard**	Chelsea	**9,000,000**
=	**John Terry**	Chelsea	**9,000,000**
=	**Carlos Tévez**	Manchester City	**9,000,000**
9 =	**Steven Gerrard**	Liverpool	**8,400,000**
=	**Lionel Messi**	Barcelona	**8,400,000**

* Based on estimated salaries of players playing in Europe as at the start of the 2009–10 season; prices reported in sterling converted at £1.00 = €1.16

Cristiano Ronaldo's salary works out at €250,000 a week, approximately £215,000. When Ronaldo was paraded in front of his new Madrid supporters at the Bernabeu Stadium in July 2009, 80,000 fans greeted him. It was a world-record turnout for such an 'unveiling', beating the 75,000 who turned out to witness Diego Maradona's introduction to the Napoli fans in 1984.

10 SPORTSMEN WHO PLAYED FOOTBALL AND ANOTHER SPORT

1   Chris Balderstone
The former England and Yorkshire cricketer dovetailed his summer sporting activity with a professional football career that lasted 18 years from 1958, when he was signed for Huddersfield Town by Bill Shankly. Uniquely, on 15 September 1975, Balderstone played cricket for Leicestershire against Derbyshire at Chesterfield and that same night played football for Doncaster Rovers at home to Brentford.

2   Ian Botham
The former England cricket captain also played League football with Scunthorpe United. He made his debut against Bournemouth on 25 March 1980 and played nine games for the Lincolnshire side. Botham is one of three former Scunthorpe footballers to captain an England team; he captained the national cricket team, Ray Clemence and Kevin Keegan the national football team.

3   Dai Davies
Davies holds the distinction of being the only Rugby League player to win an international football cap. He played Rugby League for Salford and was the Bolton Wanderers goalkeeper in the 1904 FA Cup final. He also made his international debut for Wales that same year.

4   Reginald E. Foster
Foster is the only man to captain England at both football and cricket. He captained the England football team for the only time in his fifth and final appearance, against Wales in 1902. He then went on to captain the England cricket team in the three-match series against South Africa in 1907.

5   C. B. (Charles Burgess) Fry
C. B. Fry was one of the most versatile sportsmen Britain has ever produced. He played football for England and appeared in the 1902 FA Cup final for Southampton. He scored nearly 40,000 runs in first-class cricket and appeared in 26 Test Matches. (It is said that he attempted to persuade Hitler to have the Third Reich take up cricket.) He also played rugby for the Barbarians, held the world long jump record, stood as a Liberal party candidate and was allegedly offered the throne of Albania.

6   Geoff Hurst
When Geoff Hurst stepped out to the crease for Essex, in his only first-class cricket match, against Lancashire at Liverpool in 1962, he didn't realize he would be the subject of a sports quiz question, probably for ever! Not because he made 0 not out in the first innings and was bowled out for 0 in the second innings but because four years later he would play for England in the winning World Cup side, thus becoming the only man to play first-class cricket and win a World Cup winners' medal.

7 Kevin Moran

Kevin Moran played more than 400 League games for Manchester United, Sporting Gijon and Blackburn Rovers. He also played for the Republic of Ireland on 71 occasions. He also holds the unenviable record of being the first man to be sent off in an English FA Cup final when he received his marching orders in the 1985 final while playing for Manchester United against Everton. However, before Moran came to England he was renowned in the Republic of Ireland as a top-class Gaelic footballer and was in the Dublin side that won the All-Ireland Football Championship at Croke Park in 1976 and 1977.

8 Jimmy Scoular

The captain of Newcastle United in the 1955 FA Cup final, Scottish international Scoular played more than 600 League games for Portsmouth, Newcastle United and Bradford Park Avenue. On his retirement, Scoular concentrated on his second love, lawn bowls, and represented Hampshire many times in the national championships.

9 Jim Standen

A former West Ham United goalkeeper, Jim Standen won a unique double in 1964. He won an FA Cup winners' medal playing for West Ham and was also a member of the Worcestershire side that won cricket's County Championship for the first time. He also topped the season's bowling averages with 13.00.

10 Max Woosnam

The little-known Woosnam is one of the truly great British all-round sportsmen. He represented Cambridge University at football, golf, cricket, lawn tennis and real tennis. After university he played football for Corinthians and Chelsea before moving to Manchester City in 1919. He was still an amateur and won several amateur international caps and one full cap against Wales in March 1922. Woosnam was selected to captain the British football team at the 1920 Olympic Games but refused because of his tennis commitments in the Games, where he won gold in the men's doubles and silver in the mixed doubles. He went on to win the Wimbledon men's doubles title in 1921 and also captained the Great Britain Davis Cup team.

	Goalkeeper	Country	Career span
1	**Lev Yashin**	USSR	**1949–71**
2	**Gordon Banks**	England	**1955–78**
3	**Dino Zoff**	Italy	**1961–83**
4	**Sepp Maier**	Germany	**1965–80**
5	**Ricardo Zamora**	Spain	**1916–38**
6	**José Luis Chilavert**	Paraguay	**1982–2004**
7	**Peter Schmeichel**	Denmark	**1981–2003**
8	**Peter Shilton**	England	**1966–97**
9	**Frantisek Plánicka**	Czechoslovakia	**1923–39**
10	**Amadeo Carrizo**	Argentina	**1945–71**

As voted by the International Federation of Football History & Statistics (IFFHS)

Despite enjoying a 22-year career with Dynamo Moscow and the Soviet national team, Lev Yashin did not receive as many domestic or international honours as his great goalkeeping skills deserved. He was a member of the Dynamo team that won five Soviet titles and three Soviet Cups but at international level his only major honours were in winning a gold medal at the 1956 Olympics and the 1960 European Championship. Personal honours saw him win the European Footballer of the Year in 1963 and the FIFA World Goalkeeper of the Century award in 2000.

10 FAMOUS FOOTBALL CLUB DIRECTORS, CHAIRMEN AND PRESIDENTS

Person/title	Club	Occupation
1 **Mohamed Al-Fayed** Chairman	Fulham	**Harrods owner**
2 **Richard Attenborough** Life President	Chelsea	**Film actor, director and producer**
3 **Greg Dyke** Chairman	Brentford	**Ex-BBC Director-General**
4 **Uri Geller*** Co-chairman	Exeter City	**Psychic, spoon-bender**
5 **Barry Hearn** Chairman	Leyton Orient	**Sports management**
6 **Elton John** Life President	Watford	**Singer/songwriter**
7 **Bill Kenwright** Chairman	Everton	**Ex-Coronation Street actor, theatrical producer**
8 **John Reid** Chairman	Celtic	**Ex-Home Secretary**
9 **Delia Smith** Director†	Norwich City	**Chef, author, TV personality**
10 **David Sullivan** Chairman	Birmingham City	**Adult magazine publisher, newspaper proprietor**

* Former director or chairman

† Delia Smith's official title is Joint majority shareholder

1 **Brian and Nigel Clough**
Following in the footsteps of one of the great football managers is never easy, but Brian Clough's son Nigel has already shown that some of the 'Clough magic' has rubbed off on him. Now manager of Derby County, one of his father's old clubs, he was also responsible for guiding Burton Albion on to the road to the Football League, which they reached in 2008–09.

2 **Johan and Jordi Cruyff**
Jordi Cruyff, the son of Ajax, Barcelona and Dutch international Johan, failed to live up to his father's legendary name. After a spell at Barcelona he had an unsuccessful stint at Manchester United before returning to Spain to play for Celta Vigo, Alavés and Españyol.

3 **George Eastham Senior and George Eastham Junior**
The Easthams played together for Ards in the Irish league in the 1954–55 season. George Senior played for Bolton, Brentford, Blackpool and Swansea and was also an England international like his son, who found fame with Newcastle, Arsenal and Stoke City. George Junior was involved in a court case in the early 1960s that led to players being given greater freedom to move between clubs.

4 **Alex and Darren Ferguson**
Emulating Alex Ferguson is a difficult job for any football manager but when you are Ferguson's son the pressure to do so becomes even greater. But Darren Ferguson has already shown, in his brief spell in management at Peterborough United, that he has his father's qualities and will one day be a top manager.

5 **Alec and David Herd**
Not only did Alec and David Herd both play professional football but on Saturday 5 May 1951 they made history when they appeared together in the same Football League game, turning out for Stockport County against Hartlepools United. Both men won League and FA Cup winners' medals, Alec with Manchester City and David with Manchester United.

6   Frank Lampard Senior and Frank Lampard Junior
Like his father before him, Frank Junior started his career with West Ham United but played nowhere near the 500 games Frank Senior had for the Hammers. However, he is now approaching 450 League games in total for West Ham and his current club, Chelsea. Both men have played for England and each won two FA Cup winners' medals while Frank Junior has also won two Premier League titles and two League Cup winners' medals.

7   Cesare and Paolo Maldini
The Maldinis are one of the best-known footballing families in Italy. Cesare played over 300 games for AC Milan and played in two World Cups. He later coached the national team and guided them to the 1998 World Cup quarter-finals, the team being skippered by his son Paolo. A third generation of Maldinis is on the horizon as Paolo's son Christian is a member of the Milan youth team.

8   Harry and Jamie Redknapp
After finishing their playing days, the two men have stayed in football but in different spheres. Harry, a former player with West Ham United and Bournemouth, has become a successful manager with Bournemouth, West Ham, Portsmouth and now Spurs, while Jamie, who had a distinguished career with Liverpool and England, is now a much-respected and knowledgeable broadcaster and writer.

9   Miguel and José Reina
Miguel Reina was in goal for Atlético Madrid when they lost to Bayern Munich in the 1974 European Cup final. Thirty-three years later his son José, better known as Pepe, was a member of the Liverpool side beaten in the Champions League final by AC Milan.

10   Peter and Kasper Schmeichel
Kasper followed his Danish international father between the sticks and also to Maine Road but he has not been able to live up to his father's high standard as the former Manchester United hero's son has spent much of the past three seasons out on loan.

1 Ivor and Len Allchurch
They played together for their hometown team, Swansea Town for seven seasons before Ivor moved to Newcastle United and Len to Sheffield United. In 1955, along with the Charles brothers, they played for Wales against Northern Ireland.

2 John and Mel Charles
John had a career with Leeds, Juventus and Roma before teaming up with brother Mel at Cardiff City in 1963. They played together for Wales many times.

3 Jack and Bobby Charlton
They played over 1,400 League games between them and won more than 140 international caps, including the 1966 World Cup final.

4 Denis and Leslie Compton
Both men played football and cricket internationally, both men winning FA Cup winners' medals in 1950 when Arsenal beat Liverpool 2–0 at Wembley Stadium.

5 Frank and Ronald de Boer
Twins, these Dutch internationals' careers followed similar paths with both playing for Ajax, Barcelona and Rangers. Both scored 13 goals for their national side.

6 Rio and Anton Ferdinand
Anton Ferdinand started his career at West Ham United and moved to Sunderland. Rio went from the Hammers to Leeds United and then to Manchester United.

7 Ron and Paul Futcher
Chester-born twins Ron and Paul Futcher started their careers with their hometown team. They also played together at Luton Town and Manchester City before going separate ways. Paul's son Ben played for Bury in 2008–09.

8 Jimmy and Brian Greenhoff
While Jimmy Greenhoff spent most of his career at Stoke City, he teamed up with brother Brian at Manchester United in 1976. The pair of them played together for Rochdale at the end of their careers.

9 Ian and Roger Morgan
Twins Ian and Roger Morgan started their careers with Queens Park Rangers in 1964 and were in the League Cup-winning side when, as a Third Division side, they beat West Bromwich Albion 3–2 at Wembley Stadium in 1967. Roger moved on to Spurs in 1969.

10 Gary and Phil Neville
The two Neville brothers came through the Manchester United youth system and went on to become established England internationals and regular Manchester United fullbacks. Phil has played for Everton since a £3.5 million move in 2005.

10 FOOTBALLERS WHO ACHIEVED FAME IN OTHER FIELDS

1 Derek Acorah
A member of the Liverpool playing staff in Bill Shankly's days (as Derek Johnson), Acorah is well known as a medium and presenter of the *Most Haunted* TV series.

2 Mick Channon
Mick Channon scored 232 League goals in his 20-year career, as well as 21 in 46 games for England. After retiring, he became one of Britain's foremost racehorse trainers, with winners of several Group One races to his credit.

3 David Ginola
After a career in France and England, he moved into films briefly and then became well known for advertising L'Oréal hair products.

4 Vinnie Jones
During his playing days Vinnie Jones was one of football's 'hard men' and he carried that image to the screen, playing the part of Big Chris in *Lock, Stock and Two Smoking Barrels*. He has now appeared in more than 35 films.

5 Francis Lee
After a 17-year career, Francis Lee retired in 1976. He then turned his attention to paper recycling, his firm F.H. Lee Limited becoming a multi-million pound business. He also had a short spell as a racehorse trainer.

6 Gary Lineker
After finishing his playing career, one of Britain's best-loved footballers became one of Britain's best-loved broadcasters and is the host of *Match of the Day* and major golfing events for the BBC. He also features in Walkers Crisps adverts.

7 Terry Venables
After hanging up his boots, Terry Venables went into management and has been involved in football for over 40 years. In the 1970s he co-created the detective Hazell, played on TV by Nicholas Ball, which ran for 22 episodes (1978–80).

8 Dave Whelan
Whelan broke a leg in the 1960 FA Cup final defeat playing for Blackburn Rovers against Wolverhampton Wanderers. In 1977 he established sports goods retailers, JJB Sports and is now the chairman of Wigan Athletic.

9 Charlie Williams
Williams played for Doncaster from 1948 to 1959. After retiring he sang in local clubs and appeared on the TV show *The Comedians*.

10 Karol Józef Wojtyla
During his time at school and at university in the 1930s, Karol Józef Wojtyla regularly played in goal for his college team. He later became Pope John Paul II.

1 **Chiqui Arce** (1972–)
'Chiqui' was the nickname of Paraguayan footballer Francisco Arce. He celebrated his nickname by displaying it on his shirt.

2 **Andrei Arshavin** (1981–)
Russian footballer, formerly of FC Zenit Saint Petersburg, now Arsenal.

3 **Segar Bastard** (1854–1921)
UK footballer (Upton Park 1873–87) and referee of the 1879 FA Cup final and the first ever England vs. Wales match in 1879 (thereby confirming most spectators' view that all referees are bastards). He played for England vs. Scotland on 13 March 1880; England lost 5–4.

4 **Paul Dickov** (1972–)
Scottish footballer who is on Leicester City's books.

5 **David Goodwillie** (1989–)
Goodwillie became the youngest scorer in the Scottish Premier League when he scored for Dundee United against Hibs in 2006.

6 **Andreas Ivanschitz** (1983–)
Austrian footballer with Panathinaikos since 2006.

7 **Stefan Kuntz** (1962–)
German footballer.

8 **Quim** (1975–)
The Portuguese goalkeeper's full name is Joaquim Manuel Sampaio da Silva, but he plays under his nickname, Quim.

9 **Danny Shittu** (1980–)
Nigerian footballer who plays for Bolton Wanderers.

10 **Roberto López Ufarte** (1958–)
Spanish footballer.

THE 10 LATEST PROFESSIONAL FOOTBALLERS TO RECEIVE KNIGHTHOODS

	Player	Club(s)*	Knighted
1	**Trevor Brooking**	West Ham United	**2004**
2	**Bobby Robson**	Fulham, West Bromwich Albion	**2002**
3	**Alex Ferguson**	Queen's Park, St Johnstone, Dunfermline Athletic, Rangers, Falkirk, Ayr United	**1999**
4	**Geoff Hurst**	West Ham United, Stoke City, West Bromwich Albion	**1998**
5	**Tom Finney**	Preston North End	**1998**
6	**Bobby Charlton**	Manchester United, Preston North End	**1994**
7	**Walter Winterbottom**	Manchester United	**1978**
8	**Matt Busby**	Manchester City, Liverpool	**1969**
9	**Alf Ramsey**	Southampton, Tottenham Hotspur	**1967**
10	**Stanley Matthews**	Stoke City, Blackpool	**1965**

As at 1 November 2009

* English/Scottish League clubs played for

Charles Clegg, a former chairman and president of the FA, is thought to be the first man knighted for services to football (1927). He was a former England international but he played in the days before professionalism. Stanley Matthews is the only player to receive a knighthood while still playing. Bert Millichip, the former chairman of the FA was knighted in 1991. As a youngster he was on the books of West Bromwich Albion but only played for their third team.

10 FAMOUS FOOTBALLERS' WIVES

1 Victoria Adams
Better known as Posh Spice of the Spice Girls, Victoria married David Beckham in 1999. They are now one of the best-known celebrity couples in the world.

2 Leslie Ash
The star of popular television programmes like *Men Behaving Badly* and *C.A.T.S. Eyes*, Leslie Ash has been the wife of the former Stoke City, Sheffield Wednesday and Leeds United footballer Lee Chapman since 1988.

3 Joy Beverley
A member of the top 1950s singing group the Beverley Sisters, Joy Beverley married England captain Billy Wright in 1958. It was the first high-profile football/show business marriage.

4 Alex Curran
Former model Alex Curran has been Liverpool captain Steven Gerrard's wife since 2007. She has her own fragrance called Alex.

5 Milene Domingues
The wife of Brazilian footballer Ronaldo from 1999 to 2003, Milene was also a Brazilian footballer and was one of the best female players in the world. She once commanded a world record transfer fee of more than £200,000.

6 Coleen McLoughlin
Shortly after leaving school Coleen McLoughlin landed a small part in the TV programme *Hollyoaks*. She is now a TV presenter and magazine columnist, and has been Wayne Rooney's wife since their elaborate wedding in Portofino, Italy, in 2008.

7 Sheree Murphy
Best known for playing Tricia Dingle in the ITV soap opera *Emmerdale*, Sheree Murphy is married to the former Leeds United and Liverpool player Harry Kewell.

8 Louise Nurding
The former Eternal singer, Louise married the former Liverpool, Spurs and England footballer Jamie Redknapp in 1998.

9 Alex Pursey
A former model, contestant on *I'm a Celebrity, Get Me Out of Here!* and the winner of the 2004 Rear of the Year award, she was George Best's second wife. They married in 1995.

10 Cheryl Tweedy
A member of Girls Aloud and an *X Factor* judge, she married Chelsea and England fullback Ashley Cole in 2006.

10 FOOTBALLING 'TRAITORS'

	Player	Moved from	To
1	**Sol Campbell**	Tottenham Hotspur	Arsenal
2	**Luis Figo**	Barcelona	Real Madrid
3	**Mo Johnston**	Nantes	Rangers
4	**Harry Redknapp***	Portsmouth	Southampton
5	**Jermain Defoe**	West Ham United	Tottenham Hotspur
6	**Nick Barmby**	Everton	Liverpool
7	**Paul Ince**	West Ham United	Manchester United
8	**Alan Smith**	Leeds United	Manchester United
9	**Wayne Rooney**	Everton	Manchester United
10	**Ashley Cole**	Arsenal	Chelsea

Manager

Source: Daily Mail

'Traitors' are generally regarded as players, or managers, who switch clubs to play for a bitter rival, which is the case with the majority on this list, although there are some exceptions (although often the rivalry is in the chain of moves somewhere).

Mo Johnston played 140 games for Celtic before joining French club Nantes in 1987. Two years later he returned to Scotland, but to join Celtic's arch rivals Rangers.

Jermaine Defoe handed in his transfer request within 24 hours of West Ham's relegation in 2003.

Prior to his 1989 move to Manchester United, Paul Ince was seen wearing a United shirt while still a West Ham player, much to the annoyance of the West Ham fans.

When Leeds United were relegated at the end of the 2003–04 season, Alan Smith was seen kissing the Leeds badge and was crying at the end of the last match of the season. His loyalty didn't last long. He put in a transfer request and started the next season as a Manchester United player.

Young Everton starlet Wayne Rooney proudly pronounced himself as: 'Once a Blue always a Blue', which he was for 67 Premier League games. And then it became: 'Once a Blue always a Manc', as Liverpool fans joked, after he joined Manchester United in a multi-million pound deal.

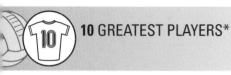

10 GREATEST PLAYERS*

1 Franz Beckenbauer Germany
Beckenbauer was a majestic midfielder with Bayern Munich and the German national side, for whom he played 103 times. He won the Bundesliga four times with Munich and once with Hamburg. He was also on three European Cup-winning teams. He played for the 1974 West German World Cup-winning team and was the coach when they won in 1990.

2 Bobby Charlton England
A survivor of the Munich air crash in 1958, a large part of Manchester United's rebuilding lay on the shoulders of the 20-year-old Charlton. He played his part in helping United to two more League titles, one FA Cup and the European Cup in 1968. On the international arena, Charlton played for England 106 times, scoring a record 49 goals, and he was a member of the 1966 World Cup-winning team.

3 Johan Cruyff Netherlands
Johan Cruyff was a complete footballer and an instinctive goalscorer. He scored 190 goals in 240 games for Ajax in his first spell with the club before moving to Barcelona in 1973, where he became a great favourite with the Catalan fans. He played in three successive European Cup-winning teams for Ajax and was the manager of Barcelona when they won the trophy in 1992. Cruyff was three times voted the European Footballer of the Year.

4 Eusébio Portugal
'The Black Panther', as he was known, was the star of the 1966 World Cup in England where he was the leading scorer with nine goals as Portugal finished third. For his club side Benfica, he scored 317 goals in 301 League games and won the European Cup with them in 1962 as a 20-year-old. He was also a member of the Benfica team that won the Portuguese title 11 times between 1961 and 1975.

5 Diego Maradona Argentina
Forget Maradona's moment of madness in scoring the first goal against England in the 1986 World Cup because his second goal was sheer brilliance and is how we best remember this footballing genius. In Europe he played for Barcelona, Napoli and Sevilla. His biggest achievement as a club player was in winning the UEFA Cup with Napoli in 1989. He captained the side that won the World Cup in 1986. He was appointed the Argentina national coach in November 2008.

6 Gerd Müller Germany
One of the most prolific goalscorers in German football, Gerd Müller scored nearly 400 League goals for Bayern Munich between 1964 and 1979. He is also (West) Germany's leading goalscorer with 68 goals from 62 appearances. His 14 World Cup goals was also a record until surpassed by Ronaldo. He was a member of the Bayern team that won the European Cup in 1974, 1975 and 1976 and he won the World Cup with Germany in 1974.

7 **Pelé** Brazil

He was simply the greatest ever footballer. He was first seen on the world stage as a 17-year-old at the 1958 World Cup in Sweden where he scored two goals in the final to help Brazil win the trophy for the first time. Pelé went on to score over 1,000 senior goals, including 77 for Brazil in 92 appearances. He played in two World Cup finals and was on the winning side three times. It might have been four had he not been kicked 'off the park' first by the Bulgarians and then the Portuguese in 1966.

8 **Michel Platini** France

His nine goals in helping France to win the 1984 European Championship remains an all-time record for the competition. He appeared in three World Cups and is one of only three men (along with Johan Cruyff and Marco van Basten) to win the European Footballer of the Year award three times. At club level he won the European Cup with Juventus in 1985 when he scored the only goal of the ill-fated match at Heysel. Coach to the French national side from 1988 to 1992, he became president of UEFA in 2007.

9 **Ferenc Puskás** Hungary

He was a member of the 'Magnificent' Magyars in the 1950s and at Wembley Stadium in November 1953 British fans got to see his goalscoring skills as he scored twice in Hungary's 6–3 demolition of England. A prolific goalscorer, he scored 514 goals in 529 League games in Hungary and Spain, where he was a star of the Real Madrid side of the late 1950s and early 1960s. He appeared in three of Real Madrid's European Cup-winning teams. For Hungary he netted 84 times in 85 games, including four in the 1954 World Cup when Hungary finished runners-up.

10 **Dino Zoff** Italy

The only goalkeeper on the list, he played over 600 League games, all in Italy. He spent most of his career at Juventus (1972–83). The only European title he won at Juventus was the 1977 UEFA Cup. He played for Italy 112 times and captained them to victory in the 1982 World Cup when, at the age of 40, he became the oldest World Cup winner. He once went over 19 hours without conceding a goal for Italy. As a manager he was coach to Juventus, winning the 1990 UEFA Cup and he became coach to the national squad in 1998 but resigned a few days after defeat in extra time by France in the Euro 2000 final.

* In alphabetical order

This list, like any such similar list, is inevitably wide open to debate but there must be seven players on it that would appear on everybody's list of the ten greatest footballers.

10 FORMER INTERNATIONAL FOOTBALLERS WHO BECAME TV PUNDITS

	Pundit	Club most League appearances for	Country played for
1	**Gerry Armstrong**	Tottenham Hotspur	Northern Ireland
2	**Andy Gray**	Wolverhampton Wanderers	Scotland
3	**Jimmy Greaves**	Tottenham Hotspur	England
4	**Alan Hansen**	Liverpool	Scotland
5	**Mark Lawrenson**	Liverpool	Republic of of Ireland
6	**Gary Lineker**	Leicester City	England
7	**Charlie Nicholas**	Celtic	Scotland
8	**Jamie Redknapp**	Liverpool	England
9	**Ian St John**	Liverpool	Scotland
10	**Andy Townsend**	Aston Villa	Republic of of Ireland

One of the first ex-footballers to become a TV pundit was Jimmy Hill, who moved into broadcasting after ending his managerial career with Coventry City in 1967. He was Head of Sport at London Weekend Television until 1972. He has fronted many programmes since then, including *Match of the Day* from 1973 to 1988.

Ian St John might have got into commentating earlier than he did if it had not been for Alf Ramsey. The BBC ran a competition to find an extra commentator for the 1970 World Cup. Six entrants took part and it was a tie for first place between St John and Welshman Idwal Robling, the casting vote going to the England manager who chose Robling. As a consolation, St John was hired as a pundit for the competition.

10 UNUSUAL FOOTBALL INJURIES

1   Playing for FC Servette in Switzerland during the 2004–05 season, midfielder Paulo Diogo lost part of a finger during a goal celebration. He jumped over a perimeter fence and caught his wedding ring on the fence, tearing off part of his finger, which could not be reattached. The referee booked Diogo for excessive celebration.

2   Brentford goalkeeper Chic Brodie's career was ended following a collision with a dog that ran on to the pitch during a game with Colchester United in November 1970. The collision left Brodie with a shattered knee bone and he never played full-time professional football again.

3   Former England goalkeeper David Beasant was once sidelined with a foot injury caused by a jar of salad cream! During his time at Southampton, he was carrying a plate of food when the salad cream fell and he put out a foot to break its fall, rupturing ankle ligaments in the process.

4   After scoring the winning goal for Arsenal against Sheffield Wednesday in the 1993 League Cup final, Northern Ireland international Steve Morrow was hoisted into the air by skipper Tony Adams in the post-match celebrations only to be dropped by Adams, breaking his arm. Morrow was rushed to hospital and missed the medal presentation and the rest of the season, including the FA Cup final, also against Wednesday. He was presented with his League Cup winners' medal before the start of the FA Cup final.

5   Norwegian international defender Svein Grøndalen once had to withdraw from the national squad because of an accident he had while out jogging – he collided with a moose!

6   Barnsley's Welsh international Darren Barnard missed five months of 1999 due to knee ligament damage suffered when he slipped in a puddle of urine left on the kitchen floor by his new puppy Zak.

7   David Batty's return from an Achilles tendon injury was put back after his toddler ran over his leg on his tricycle.

8   While warming up for an FA Cup tie against Chelsea at Goodison Park in January 2006, the Everton goalkeeper Richard Wright was ruled out of the match after falling over a wooden sign on the pitch and twisting an ankle. The sign read: 'Do not practise here'.

9   In August 1975, in a game against Birmingham City, Manchester United goalkeeper Alex Stepney dislocated his jaw while shouting at his defenders.

10 Arsenal's Perry Groves once knocked himself unconscious when he jumped up to celebrate an Arsenal goal while he was on the substitutes' bench, having forgotten that the dugout had a roof.

1   'It's a lot harder to play football when you haven't got the ball.'
    Andy Gray

2   'Barnsley have started off the way they mean to begin.'
    Chris Kamara

3   'He reminds me of a completely different version of Robbie Earle.'
    Mark Lawrenson

4   'We [England] haven't been scoring goals, but football's not just about scoring goals.
    It's about winning.'
    Alan Shearer

5   'It's nice for us to have a fresh face in the camp to bounce things off.'
    Lawrie Snachez

6   'We deserved to win this game after hammering them 0–0 in the first half.'
    Kevin Keegan

7   'Hodge scored for Forest after 22 seconds – totally against the run of play.'
    Peter Lorenzo

8   'No regrets, none at all. My only regret is that we went out on penalties. That's my
    only regret but no, no regrets.'
    Mick McCarthy

9   'If you were in the Brondby dressing room right now, which of the Liverpool players
    would you be looking at?'
    Ray Stubbs

10 'Batistuta gets most of his goals with the ball.'
    Ian St John

The term 'Colemanballs' was coined by *Private Eye* magazine to highlight gaffes made by broadcasters, notably sports broadcasters, live on air and is named after the renowned BBC commentator David Coleman. The first *Private Eye Colemanballs* book was published in 1982.

10 CELEBRITIES WHO PLAYED FOR OR HAD TRIALS WITH PROFESSIONAL CLUBS

	Celebrity	Profession	Club(s)
1	**Angus Deayton**	Comedian/broadcaster	Crystal Palace
2	**Sir David Frost**	Broadcaster	Nottingham Forest
3	**Perry Fenwick**	Actor	Leyton Orient
4	**Audley Harrison**	Boxer	Watford
5	**Mick Miller**	Comedian	Port Vale
6	**Des O'Connor**	Singer/TV personality	Northampton Town
7	**Mark Owen**	Take That member	Manchester United, Huddersfield Town, Rochdale
8	**Rod Stewart**	Rock legend	Brentford
9	**Bradley Walsh**	Actor/ TV personality	Brentford
10	**Duke of Westminster**	Billionaire landowner	Fulham

Actor Ralf Little, best known for playing the part of Jonny in *Two Pints of Lager and a Packet of Crisps*, has played non-league football at a high level alongside his acting career, for Maidstone United, Edgware Town and Chertsey Town.

Ian Morrison, co-author of this book, had a trial with Stoke City.

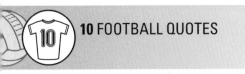

1 'This is a terrible day … for Leeds United.'
Brian Clough, upon being sacked after only 44 days as manager of the club.

2 'I met Mick Jagger when I was playing for Oxford United and the Rolling Stones played a concert there. Little did I know that one day he'd be almost as famous as me.'
Ron Atkinson, in 1993.

3 'The ideal board of directors should be made up of three men – two dead and the other dying.'
Tommy Docherty's views on football club directors.

4 'It's a bit ironic that when nobody will let me have a passport, it's left to me to save the England team.'
Mohamed Al-Fayed commenting on the constant refusal of the government to allow him UK citizenship while he allowed Kevin Keegan to leave the manager's job at Fayed's club, Fulham, in 1999, to take over as England manager.

5 'Football is a simple game. The hard part is making it look simple.'
Former England manager Ron Greenwood.

6 'The FA have given me a pat on the back. I've taken football violence off the terracing and on to the pitch.'
Vinnie Jones, speaking to the Oxford Union in 1995.

7 'Some people think football is a matter of life and death, I don't like that attitude. I can assure them it is much more serious than that.'
Bill Shankly, in 1973.

8 'Of course I didn't take my wife to see Rochdale as an anniversary present – it was her birthday. Would I have got married during the football season? And anyway, it wasn't Rochdale, it was Rochdale Reserves.'
Bill Shankly.

9 'I'm not a defender of old or new football managers. I believe in good ones and bad ones, those that achieve success and those that don't. Please don't call me arrogant, but I'm European champion and I think I'm a special one.'
José Mourinho, introducing himself at Chelsea when he arrived in June 2004. After this press conference he was constantly dubbed 'The Special One'.

10 'If Roman Abramovich helped me out in training we would be bottom of the league, and if I had to work in his world of big business, we would be bankrupt!'
José Mourinho, about his boss.

10 FAMOUS – OR INFAMOUS – FOOTBALL FANS

Fan(s)	Occupation	Club
1 **Chuckle Brothers**	Funnymen	Rotherham United
2 **Gordon Brown**	Prime minister	Raith Rovers
3 **Adolf Hitler**	Dictator	Schalke 04
4 **Heather Mills**	Millionairess	Sunderland
5 **Michael Parkinson**	Interviewer	Barnsley
6 **Harold Shipman**	Serial killer	Notts County
7 **Sylvester Stallone**	Actor	Everton
8 **Prince William**	Heir to the throne	Aston Villa
9 **Robbie Williams**	Singer	Port Vale
10 **Catherine Zeta Jones**	Actress	Swansea City

There is no evidence that Adolf Hitler ever went to watch Schalke 04 play, but he certainly was a fan in as much that he jumped on the Schalke bandwagon as they were German champions six times between 1934 and 1942. The Führer used his support of the team as yet another propoganda stunt.

TOP 10 TRANSFERS WORLDWIDE

	Player/country	From	To	Year	Fee (£)
1	**Cristiano Ronaldo** Portugal	Manchester United	Real Madrid	2009	**80,000,000**
2	**Zlatan Ibrahimović** Sweden	Inter Milan	Barcelona	2009	**60,500,000**
3	**Kaká** Brazil	AC Milan	Real Madrid	2009	**56,000,000**
4	**Zinedine Zidane** France	Juventus	Real Madrid	2001	**47,700,000**
5	**Luís Figo** Portugal	Barcelona	Real Madrid	2000	**37,400,000**
6	**Hernan Crespo** Argentina	Parma	Lazio	2000	**35,700,000**
7	**Gianluigi Buffon** Italy	Parma	Juventus	2001	**33,000,000**
8	**Robinho** Brazil	Real Madrid	Manchester City	2008	**32,500,000**
9	**Christian Vieri** Italy	Lazio	Inter Milan	1999	**31,000,000**
10	**Dimitar Berbatov** Bulgaria	Tottenham Hotspur	Manchester United	2008	**30,750,000**

As at 1 November 2009

The world's first £1,000,000 footballer was Giuseppe Savoldi, when he moved from Bologna to Napoli in 1975 for £1.2 million.

In June 2009, Kaká held the world transfer record for just over two weeks, before it was beaten by Ronaldo's move to the same team, Real Madrid.

The record transfer fee paid for a goalkeeper is the £33,000,000 paid by Juventus for Gianluigi Buffon.

TOP 10 TRANSFERS BETWEEN BRITISH CLUBS

	Player	From	To	Year	Fee (£)
1	**Dimitar Berbatov**	Tottenham Hotspur	Manchester United	2008	**30,750,000**
2	**Rio Ferdinand**	Leeds United	Manchester United	2002	**29,100,000**
3	**Emmanuel Adebayor**	Arsenal	Manchester City	2009	**25,000,000**
4	**Joleon Lescott**	Everton	Manchester City	2009	**22,000,000**
5	**Shaun Wright-Phillips**	Manchester City	Chelsea	2005	**21,000,000**
6	**Wayne Rooney**	Everton	Manchester United	2004	**20,000,000***
7	**Robbie Keane**	Tottenham Hotspur	Liverpool	2008	**19,000,000**
8	**Rio Ferdinand**	West Ham United	Leeds United	2000	**18,000,000**
9 =	**Damien Duff**	Blackburn Rovers	Chelsea	2003	**17,000,000**
=	**Roque Santa Cruz**	Blackburn Rovers	Manchester City	2009	**17,000,000**

As at the end of the summer 2009 transfer window

* Manchester United initially paid a fee of £20,000,000 for Rooney, with this possibly rising by 5 or 6 million more, depending on future performances

Carlos Tévez joined Manchester City for £25 million in July 2009 but while his last club was Manchester United, they did not hold his contract, which was sold to City by his economic advisers Media Sports Investments.

The record for a deal between two Scottish clubs is £4,400,000 paid by Celtic for Hibernian's Scott Brown in July 2007. This beat the record of £4 million set in 1993 when Rangers bought Duncan Ferguson from Dundee United – also a British record at the time.

THE 10 LATEST OCCASIONS THAT THE BRITISH TRANSFER RECORD WAS BROKEN

	Player	From	To	Year	Fee (£)
1	**Cristiano Ronaldo**	Manchester United	Real Madrid	2009	**80,000,000**
2	**Robinho**	Real Madrid	Manchester City	2008	**32,500,000**
3	**Andriy Shevchenko**	AC Milan	Chelsea	2006	**30,800,000**
4	**Rio Ferdinand**	Leeds United	Manchester United	2002	**29,100,000**
5	**Juan Sebastián Verón**	Lazio	Manchester United	2001	**28,100,000**
6	**Nicolas Anelka**	Arsenal	Real Madrid	1999	**22,500,000**
7	**Alan Shearer**	Blackburn Rovers	Newcastle United	1996	**15,000,000**
8	**Stan Collymore**	Nottingham Forest	Liverpool	1995	**8,500,000**
9	**Dennis Bergkamp**	Inter Milan	Arsenal	1995	**7,500,000**
10	**Andy Cole**	Newcastle United	Manchester United	1995	**7,000,000**

As at 1 November 2009

BRITISH TRANSFER MILESTONES

Transfer firsts	Player	Transfer from/to	Year
£100	**Willie Groves** Aston Villa	West Bromwich Albion to	**1892**
£500	**Alf Common**	Sheffield United to Sunderland	**1902**
£1,000	**Alf Common**	Sunderland to Middlesbrough	**1905**
£5,000	**Syd Puddefoot**	West Ham United to Falkirk	**1922**
£10,000	**David Jack** (£10,890)	Bolton Wanderers to Arsenal	**1929**
£20,000	**Tommy Lawton**	Chelsea to Notts County	**1947**
£50,000	**Denis Law** (£55,000)	Huddersfield Town to Manchester City	**1960**
£100,000	**Denis Law** (£110,000)	Manchester City to Torino	**1962**
£500,000	**David Mills**	Middlesbrough to West Bromwich Albion	**1979**
£1 million	**Trevor Francis** (£1,180,000)	Birmingham City to Nottingham Forest	**1979**
£5 million	**David Platt** (£5,500,000)	Aston Villa to Bari	**1991**
£10/15 million	**Alan Shearer** (£15,000,000)	Blackburn Rovers to Newcastle United	**1996**
£20 million	**Nicolas Anelka** (£22,500,000)	Arsenal to Real Madrid	**1999**
£25 million	**Juan Sebastián Verón** (£28,100,000)	Lazio to Manchester United	**2001**
£30 million	**Andriy Shevchenko** (£30,800,000)	AC Milan to Chelsea	**2006**
£40/80 million	**Cristiano Ronaldo** (£80,000,000)	Manchester United to Real Madrid	**2009**

Figures in brackets refer to exact transfer fee

10 BEST BRITISH TRANSFER DEALS*

	Player	From	To	Year	Fee (£)
1	**Eric Cantona**	Leeds United	Manchester United	1992	**1,200,000**
2	**Ian Rush**	Chester	Liverpool	1980	**300,000**
3	**Thierry Henry**	Juventus	Arsenal	1999	**10,500,000**
4	**Nicolas Anelka**	Paris Saint-Germain	Arsenal	1997	**500,000**
5	**Kevin Keegan**	Scunthorpe United	Liverpool	1971	**35,000**
6	**Ian Wright**	Greenwich Borough	Crystal Palace	1985	**Free**
7	**Patrick Vieira**	AC Milan	Arsenal	1996	**3,500,000**
8	**Roy Keane**	Cobh Ramblers	Nottingham Forest	1990	**47,000**
9	**Alan Shearer**	Southampton	Blackburn Rovers	1992	**3,300,000**
10	**Peter Schmeichel**	Brondby	Manchester United	1991	**500,000**

* Representing value for money

Source: Daily Mail

Eric Cantona remains one of Alex Ferguson's best signings, despite being a surprise to many at the time. But Cantona went on to become a United legend and played in four Premier League-winning teams and was a member of the United side that completed the Premier League and FA Cup double in 1994 and 1996.

TOP 10 WINNERS OF THE FA WOMEN'S CUP

	Club	First win	Last win	Total
1	**Arsenal**	1993	2009	**10**
2	**Southampton**	1971	1981	**8**
3	**Doncaster Belles**	1983	1994	**6**
4 =	**Millwall Lionesses**	1991	1997	**2**
=	**Croydon**	1996	2000	**2**
=	**Fulham**	2002	2003	**2**
7 =	**Foxdens**	1974	1974	**1**
=	**Queens Park Rangers**	1977	1977	**1**
=	**St Helens**	1980	1980	**1**
=	**Lowestoft**	1982	1982	**1**
=	**Howbury Grange**	1984	1984	**1**
=	**Friends of Fulham**	1985	1985	**1**
=	**Norwich**	1986	1986	**1**
=	**Leasowe Pacific**	1989	1989	**1**
=	**Charlton Athletic**	2005	2005	**1**

Source: The Football Association

The first women's cup competition was held in the 1970–71 season and was called the Women's Football Association Mitre Challenge Trophy. The 71 entrants included teams from Wales and Scotland and in the final Southampton beat the Scottish team Stewarton and Thistle at London's Crystal Palace sports stadium. The Football Association's competitions department took over the running of the cup in the 1993–94 season and the event was renamed the FA Women's Challenge Cup. Doncaster Belles have competed in a record 13 finals.

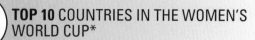
	Country	Pl	W	D	L	F	A	Pts
1	**USA**	30	24	3	3	85	24	**75**
2	**Germany**	28	20	3	5	84	27	**63**
3	**Norway**	28	19	2	7	75	36	**59**
4	**China**	24	13	5	6	48	25	**44**
5	**Sweden**	23	13	2	8	44	28	**41**
6	**Brazil**	22	12	3	7	46	32	**39**
7	**Canada**	15	4	3	8	24	39	**15**
8	**Russia**	8	4	0	4	16	14	**12**
9 =	**England**	8	3	2	3	14	15	**11**
=	**Japan**	16	3	2	11	13	40	**11**

* Based on three points for a win and one point for a draw

Kristine Lilly (USA) is the only player to have appeared in all five Women's World Cups in 1991, 1995, 1999, 2003 and 2007. Bente Nordby (Norway) has been to all five tournaments as a player but did not play in 1991.

HISTORY OF THE WOMEN'S WORLD CUP

The first Women's World Cup, the idea of the then FIFA President João Havelange, was held in China in 1991. Twelve nations competed in the first competition. By the time the competition reached the USA in 1999, the women's branch of the sport was starting to receive global recognition and the World Cup was attended by more than half a million spectators with billions more watching on television. The final between the USA and China drew 90,185 to the Pasadena Rose Bowl, a world-record attendance for a women's football match.

Because of the outbreak of the SARS virus in China, the 2003 World Cup could not be played there and the USA played host again, but China were awarded the competition in 2007. The next World Cup will be in Germany in 2011.

Women's World Cup final results

Year	Host	Winner	Runner-up	Score	Attendance	Third place
1991	China	**USA**	Norway	2–1	63,000	Sweden
1995	Sweden	**Norway**	Germany	2–0	17,158	USA
1999	USA	**USA**	China	0–0*	90,185	Brazil
2003	USA	**Germany**	Sweden	2–1	26,137	USA
2007	China	**Germany**	Brazil	2–0	31,000	USA

USA won 5–4 on penalties

TOP 10 GOALSCORERS IN THE WOMEN'S WORLD CUP

	Player	Country	Goals
1	**Birgit Prinz**	Germany	**14**
2	**Michelle Akers**	USA	**12**
3 =	**Sun Wen**	China	**11**
=	**Bettina Wiegmann**	Germany	**11**
5 =	**Ann Kristin Aarønes**	Norway	**10**
=	**Marta**	Brazil	**10**
=	**Heidi Mohr**	Germany	**10**
8 =	**Linda Medalen**	Norway	**9**
=	**Hege Riise**	Norway	**9**
=	**Abby Wambach**	USA	**9**

Up to and including the 2007 World Cup

BEHIND THE RECORD
– BIRGIT PRINZ'S RECORD WORLD CUP HAUL

Birgit Prinz hails from Frankfurt in Germany and was voted the Women's World Player of the Year in 2003, 2004 and 2005. She has played for the German national team since 1994 and has scored over 100 goals from nearly 200 appearances. She was a member of the German team that took the bronze medal at three consecutive Olympics – 2000, 2004 and 2008. She first appeared in the World Cup in 1995 when Germany were runners-up. She played again in 1999, and also in 2003 and 2007 when they won the trophy on each occasion. Her record haul of 14 goals was as follows:

1995 World Cup – Sweden

Date	Stage	Opponents	Venue	Result	Goals
09 Jun	Group	**Brazil**	Karlstad	won 6–1	**1**

1999 World Cup – United States

Date	Stage	Opponents	Venue	Result	Goals
27 Jun	Group	**Brazil**	Landover	drew 3–3	**1**

2003 World Cup – United States

Date	Stage	Opponents	Venue	Result	Goals
20 Sep	Group	**Canada**	Columbus	won 4–1	**1**
24 Sep	Group	**Japan**	Columbus	won 4–0	**2**
27 Sep	Group	**Argentina**	Washington	won 6–1	**1**
02 Oct	Quarter-final	**Russia**	Portland	won 7–1	**2**
05 Oct	Semi-final	**USA**	Portland	won 3–0	**1**

2007 World Cup – China

Date	Stage	Opponents	Venue	Result	Goals
10 Sep	Group	**Argentina**	Shanghai	won 11–0	**3**
17 Sep	Group	**Japan**	Hangzhou	won 2–0	**1**
30 Sep	Final	**Brazil**	Shanghai	won 2–0	**1**

ACKNOWLEDGEMENTS

Mark Bennett
Jim Bryceland
David Ross (www.scottishleague.net/author.htm)
Karel Stokkermans (RSSSF)

BBC
Daily Mail
Deloitte Football Money League 2009
www.englandstats.com
FA Premier League
FIFA
The Football Association
Football Association of Wales
The Football League
IFFHS (International Federation of Football History & Statistics)
Irish Football Association (Northern Ireland)
Football Association of Ireland (Republic of Ireland)
Football Writers' Association
League Managers Association
MLS
MLS Players Union
Private Eye
Professional Footballers' Association
PRS for Music
RSSSF (Rec.Sport.Soccer Statistics Foundation)
The Scottish Football Association
The Scottish Football Historical Archive (scottish-football-historical-archive.com)
UEFA
The Welsh Football League
Welsh Premier League
World Soccer

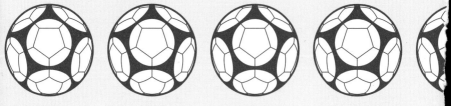

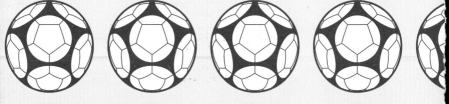